JEEP 2007 PRESENT WRANGLER JK

Don Alexander and Quinn Thomas

CarTech®

CarTech®

CarTech®, Inc.
838 Lake Street South
Forest Lake, MN 55025
Phone: 651-277-1200 or 800-551-4754
Fax: 651-277-1203
www.cartechbooks.com

Edit by Paul Johnson
Layout by Monica Seiberlich

ISBN 978-1-61325-359-5
Item No. SA405

Library of Congress Cataloging-in-Publication Data

Names: Alexander, Don, author. | Thomas, Quinn, author.
Title: Jeep Wrangler JK 2007-present : advanced performance modifications / Don Alexander, Quinn Thomas.
Description: Forest Lake, MN : CarTech, [2018]
Identifiers: LCCN 2017034024 | ISBN 9781613253595
Subjects: LCSH: Wrangler sport utility vehicle–Performance–Handbooks, manuals, etc. | Wrangler sport utility vehicle–Motors–Handbooks, manuals, etc. | Jeep automobile–Maintenance and repair–Handbooks, manuals, etc.
Classification: LCC TL215.W73 A54 2018 | DDC 629.28/722–dc23
LC record available at https://lccn.loc.gov/2017034024

Written, edited, and designed in the U.S.A.
Printed in China
10 9 8 7 6 5 4 3 2 1

Title Page: *The* Terremoto *climbing scales slick rock ledges with precision at Moab. Bulletproof components, lightweight aluminum accessories, V-8 power and great traction make rock crawling and hill climbing easy for the* Terremoto. *(Photo Courtesy GenRight)*

Back Cover Photos

Top: *The MetalCloak JK Wrangler Game-Changer Mid Arm Suspension System allows travel found only in long-arm kits. This system features the 6Pak long travel shocks, MetalCloak True Dual Rate coil springs, Duroflex control arms with the patented Duroflex joint, and front and rear solid chrome-moly track bars. This system bolts onto stock mounts and has 14 inches of shock travel. (Photo Courtesy MetalCloak)*

Upper Middle: *When JKs are lifted and 31-inch or larger tires are installed, many owners desire more torque and horsepower than the stock V-6 delivers. Prodigy Performance makes turbocharger kits for both the 3.8-liter V-6 and the 3.6-liter Pentastar V-6. The Prodigy kits are available at two levels of tune. The system features either a Precision or a Garret turbo, a large intercooler, and all the hardware and wiring necessary for the installation.*

Lower Middle: *A Wrangler JK needs heavy-duty axles and suspension for rock crawling and other off-road service. This JK has a Currie F9 9-inch rear axle housing with Currie 35-spline axles and an ARB air locker with a 4.56 ratio. Rear shocks are 2-inch King bypass. Currie Antirock sway bars control body roll.*

Bottom: *Mounted on a 17-inch wheel, the Falken WildPeak A/T 3W features a very tough E-rated sidewall that's resistant to cuts and punctures. Aired-down this tire does a great job conforming to rocks for improved traction. Traction climbing up steep rock faces determines the capability of any off-road tire. The WildPeak A/T 3W has plenty of grip to climb steep rocks.*

DISTRIBUTION BY:

Europe
PGUK
63 Hatton Garden
London EC1N 8IE, England
Phone: 020 7061 1980 • Fax: 020 7242 3725
www.pguk.co.uk

Australia
Renniks Publications Ltd.
3/37-39 Green Street
Banksmeadow, NSW 2109, Australia
Phone: 2 9695 7055 • Fax: 2 9695 7355
www.renniks.com

Canada
Login Canada
300 Saulteaux Crescent
Winnipeg, MB, R3J 3T2 Canada
Phone: 800 665 1148 • Fax: 800 665 0103
www.lb.ca

CONTENTS

Acknowledgments 4
About the Authors 5
Introduction 7

Chapter 1: Wheels and Tires..........9
All-Terrain Versus
    Mud-Terrain 9
Off-Road Tire Performance......11
Tire Size, Diameters, and
    Ground Clearance.................12
Off-Road Tests 13
On-Road Tests..........................14
Wheels and Tires 20

**Chapter 2: Suspension, Lifts,
    and Steering..........................25**
Lifting for Off-Road Clearance .25
Suspension Springs...................27
Suspension Control Arms 29
Track Bars 31
Shock Absorbers 31
Anti-Roll Bars and Articulation.. 35
Steering System........................38
Suspension and Steering
    Alignment 42
Jeep JK Profile: Fabtech
    Motorsports's 2014 Wrangler
    JK Unlimited Rubicon 43

Chapter 3: Brake Upgrades 46
Increase Brake Performance......46
Brake Rotors............................47
Brake Calipers 49
Brake Master Cylinders...........51
Brake Pads...............................51
Brake Kits 52
Brake Flex Lines 52
Brake Fluid 53
Jeep JK Profile: Heather and
    Quinn Thomas's All J Products
    2007 JK Unlimited Hemi 54

**Chapter 4: Bumpers, Armor,
    and Protection.....................57**
Skidplates 57

Rock Sliders 61
Body Armor 62
Door Options 63
Fenders 63
Tire Size...................................63
Modifying Stock Fenders
    for Clearance 63
Front Bumpers 64
Rear Bumpers 66
Jeep JK Profile: John and Cinde
    Angelastro's sPOD JK.........67

**Chapter 5: Drivelines, Axles,
    and Lockers..........................70**
Tire Size versus Ratio...............72
Ring and Pinion Gear Upgrades.. 73
Axle Upgrades 73
Axle Housing Reinforcements..78
Full Axle Assembly Swaps 79
Axle Lockers 81
Limited-Slip and Detroit
    Lockers 82
Driveshafts, Yokes,
    CV Joints, and U-joints........82
Jeep JK Profile: John Currie's
    2015 Jeep Wrangler JK
    Unlimited..............................83

**Chapter 6: Engines, Engine Swaps
    and Transmissions 86**
Cold-Air Intakes 86
Performance Exhausts 87
Engine Tuners 88
Superchargers...........................89
Turbochargers...........................90
Air-Intake Snorkels 91
Engine Swaps 91
Transmission and
    Cooling Systems 98
Heavy-Duty Clutch Kits..........99
Automatic Transmissions 100
Cooling Systems......................100
Jeep JK Profile: Norbert "Nobby"
    and Deanna Schnabel.........101

**Chapter 7: Styling and
    Storage Upgrades 104**
Aftermarket Tops 104
Sun Shades..............................106
Tube Doors 106
Half Doors 107
MOLLE System Soft-Bag
    Storage................................107
Metal Storage Boxes................107
Interior Storage.......................108
Fluid Storage 109
Door Hinges and Stops 109
Mirrors 110
Roof Racks 110
Mud Flaps 110
Jeep JK Profile: GenRight
    Terremoto Jeep JK...............111

Chapter 8: Electrical and Lights.. 114
Battery Upgrades 114
Battery Cables and Terminals .115
Auxiliary Lighting...................116
Jeep JK Profile: Ray Currie's
    2007 JK Unlimited 119

**Chapter 9: Winches, Vehicle Recovery
    Gear, and Trail Tools 122**
Selecting a Winch 123
Winch Accessories...................125
Ground Anchor for Winching. 133
Extraction Boards, Sand Ladders,
    and Bridging Ladders 133
Trail Tools and Spare Parts......135
Fluid Storage...........................135
Tire Repair Kit........................136
Spare Parts...............................136
GPS Systems 137
Jeep JK Profile: Don Alexander's
    Jeep 4x4 School 2013 JKU
    Grizzlycon 138

Source Guide 142

ACKNOWLEDGMENTS

Writing a book such as this requires support from the home front, the off-road industry, and many other individuals. We want to thank the following people for their indispensable support during the creation of this book. Our wives, Christie Helm and Heather Thomas, provided support and editing expertise. Paul Johnson, editor at CarTech Books, offered sage guidance. We would be remiss if we didn't recognize the contributions of the All J Products crew, Corey, Loren, and Casey; Our Fellow Bear Valley 4x4 club members for help with testing; Tom Krost, Steve Snyder, Steve Blanchard, Nobby Schnabel, Deanna Schnabel; Greg Hoffman at the U.S. Forest Service; Doug Walton with Big Bear Off Road Adventures; and Desi Hauer of Big Bear Jeep Experience. And, of course, we extend our thanks to All J Products and Jeep 4x4 School customers Peter Wade, Phillip Beidelman, and Jan Horst.

We also acknowledge the support and contributions from our friends and associates across the awesome Jeep aftermarket: Ray Currie, John Currie, Garrett Akeney, Brian Shepard of Currie Enterprises; Casey Currie with Casey Currie Racing; Richard Smallwood with Sumitomo Rubber USA; Mark Richter, Rick Brennen, Drew Howlett, Angel LaMarca of Falken Tire; Brian Cole of 4 Wheel Parts; Steve Sasaki and Bob Mastro of Power Tank; John and Cinde Angelastro of sPOD; Chris Nissley with Off Road Warehouse; Doug Pettis and Matt Glass of ARB USA; Blaine Johnson with Black Magic Brakes; Don Sneddon and Willy Woo with Mickey Thompson Tires; Greg Mulkey of Raceline Wheels; Camee Edelbrock and Eric Blakely of Edelbrock; Tony and Jamie Pellegrino of GenRight Off Road; James Barth with Rock Hard 4x4; Michael Costa, and Justin Andrews with Factor 55; Dave Luman, Phillip MacKay, Lynn Hendrixon of Rock-Slide Engineering; Brad McCarthy with MaxTrax; Scott Porter with Warn Winches; Tony Fileccia of Fabtech; Shari McCullough Arfons at McCullough PR; Jason Buckles Strattec (Bolt Locks); Wilfred Eibach, Julian Gill, Greg Cooley, Christian Sebralla, Mark Krumme of Eibach Springs; David Borla and Ed Taylor of Borla Exhaust; Tim Pellegrino and Chris Plaisance of SpiderWebShade; and Jim Reel of JE Reel Drivelines.

Others provided essential assistance and product information, including Greg Cotrell, Mike Ruzicka with Rugged Radios; Dan Eckardt of Baja Designs; Bryan Wilson with Centerforce Clutches; Doug Burke at Wilwood Brakes; Matson Breakey and Scott Becker of MetalCloak; Brennen Riddle at Red Peak Off Road (Rubicam); Darlene Oleksik with Eaton; Don McMillan of Daystar; Erica Kelt from Global Star (Spot Satellite Tracker); George and Tamara Carousos with Extreme Outback; Gerald Lee of Savvy Off Road; Dale Dotson at B&M Racing; Jacquie Parral of Off Road Expo; Steve von Seggern from Magellan GPS; Loren Campbell with Redlands Jeep; Maria Orlando-Krick at Enersys (Odyssey Batteries); Mike Bishop of ACORA; Scott Brown of FCA Jeep PR; Terry Shofron with Wild Boar Off Road; Steve Marronne and Henry Valesquez of Dynatrac; Ross Berlanga with K&N Filters; and Dan Marra of Prodigy Performance.

For all who have provided invaluable assistance and support for this project, we are grateful.

ABOUT THE AUTHORS

Don Alexander

With a racing and automotive journalism career spanning nearly six decades, Don Alexander is one of the nation's most noted and respected off roaders, race driving experts, writers, test drivers and racers. Don has been involved in off roading for more than 25 years and raced competitively in oval track and road racing for 50 years. But he is best known as a driver for setting land-speed records. In 2002, Don set five International and National land-speed records at Bonneville driving the Banks Sidewinder to a top speed of 222.139 mph, making it the world's fastest pickup truck of any type. The Sidewinder is a Dodge Dakota pickup with 5.9-liter Cummins Turbo Diesel engine producing 735 hp and 1,300 ft-lbs of torque.

Alexander has more than 50 years of auto racing experience as a driver, racing instructor, and author. Don has taught more than 5,000 individuals the skills needed to drive race cars, defensive driving, high-performance driving, and off roading. Don has instructed at the Bob Bondurant School of High Performance Driving, the Fastlane School, and Drivetech where he was the chief instructor. He currently operates the Jeep 4x4 School, teaching off-road driving skills to new Jeep owners.

Don has reached thousands of others with his 15 books and hundreds of magazine articles. Two of his books are race driving technique books including *Think To Win* and *Stock Car Driving Techniques*. *Formula Car Technology* earned the 1980 Auto Racing Writers and Broadcasters Association Book of the Year. He has also written several suspension and handling books.

Don was the editor of *Circle Track* magazine. His *Learn to Race & Win* and *Race Car Setup* article series were the most popular in the magazine's history. Don has written for many magazines including *Motor Trend, Mustang Illustrated, Turbo, All Chevy,* and *Grassroots Motorsports*. His concise, understandable writing style has made his work very popular.

In 1995, Don conducted a national seminar series called Think to Win Seminars with the legendary Smokey Yunick. The series was popular, reaching racers in nine cities. Alexander also conducted a national seminar series in 1988–1989 covering road racing chassis setup and tuning. Don has appeared at many club meetings and conventions, including SEMA, PRI, and the International Auto Salon as a guest speaker, talking about a variety of racing and automotive topics.

Alexander's racing career spans five decades and a wide variety of racing machines. He began racing in 1959 in Go Karts. This was followed by a stint of bracket racing at Southern California drag strips. Don began SCCA racing in 1969, racing an Alfa in the production category. During his road-racing career, Alexander has driven in Formula Vee, Formula Ford, Formula Atlantic, Formula 5000, Trans Am, Improved Touring, Showroom Stock, Spec Racer, Firestone Firehawk, and several classes with NASA. He has won several road racing and endurance racing championships and set several track records. Don began short track racing in 1976 at Speedway 605 and has driven many types of cars including modifieds, late-model stock cars, Southwest Tour, ASA, sprint cars, and others on both dirt and asphalt tracks.

In 2000, Alexander was invited to compete in the Beetle Cup All Star Race at Road Atlanta. Alexander was representing *Motor Trend* magazine in the event. Don finished 9th racing against some of the best road racers in the world: Hans Stuck, Danny Sullivan, Tommy Kendall, Jack Baldwin, Price Cobb, Brian Redman, Scott Sharp, Scott Goodyear, Bill Adam, and others.

As a test driver, Don has worked for several suspension and tire companies. He was the test driver for *Motor Trend* magazine and has proved track testing for several other magazines, including *Hot Rod*. In addition to operating the off-road training program, Don produces videos and also tests off-road tires for several companies in the Big Bear Lake, California, area.

Quinn Thomas

I have always been a gear-head and into anything with an engine. I started four wheeling when I was 17; however, I didn't get my first Jeep until I was 20. What got me into this crazy Jeep world? My stepdad, Steve, was my mentor and taught me a lot of what I know about mechanics and Jeeps. Steve 'wheeled all the way back in the 1960s! He got me hooked on four wheeling and that has been a huge part of my life ever since! In 1996, I married Heather. A short time later, Steve and I started All J Products. Our vision was to build awesome Jeep parts and help people get on the trail with confidence in their Jeeps.

Through the years the shop grew, and we moved to Big Bear Lake more than a decade ago. All J took on a new life as Big Bear's Jeep Shop and 4x4. Heather and I own and run the shop together; she runs the office, I run the shop. As you may have guessed, we specialize in Jeeps. Our kids have grown up knowing Jeeps and off roading. Our son, Mitchel, got a 1993 ZJ Grand Cherokee as his first vehicle. He still drives that heavily-modified ZJ. Our daughter,

Miranda, got a 2004 TJ Wrangler Sahara as her first vehicle. It was bone-stock when we got it for her. We worked on it together and built it for off roading. She drove that Jeep all through high school.

I have owned more than 15 Jeeps in my life, 11 of them at the same time (until Heather put her foot down and made me thin the herd). Today's JK owners are the luckiest around. You can build just about any kind of JK with the aftermarket parts readily available. However, back in the early days we had to adapt and build parts to modify our Jeeps. We spent hours in the junkyards looking for parts that we could use to add power steering to our manual steering Jeeps, swap engines for bigger and better running versions, and everything else we wanted to do. It is so much easier now!

Early in my wheeling career I traveled all over the Southwest in a 1964 CJ5 (M38A1 mixed in with it; I remember the junk yard parts searching). When I met Heather, my CJ5 needed an engine, and after dating awhile, she said, "I'll buy that engine for you." Then the next time out on the trail, she drove it and took it over

until 1996 when we got married. We then bought the new 1997 TJ Wrangler. I got my CJ5 back. The new 1997 TJ was the new family Jeep. It was actually the reason we started the shop. We started building cool parts for our then brand-new TJ and people wanted them for their TJs too.

Later, when we bought the new 2007 JK, it took over the job as our new family wagon, a duty it still fulfills. Through the years I have been a part of many Jeep clubs. I *love* being out Jeepin', traveling, and camping all over. I am happiest away from the rat race and being in the backcountry. I have met some of the greatest people and my best friends through the years in my Jeep and four-wheeling travels, Don Alexander being one of them.

One of the things I really love to do is teach people to go out and four wheel. I get to teach people about 'wheeling and Jeeps every day at our shop. What could be better in life? Getting to do what I love, working with my wife, and sharing it all with others! I am also a proud member of our local adopt-a-trail program, which helps keep trails maintained and open for use by all.

INTRODUCTION

After 50 years of competitive racing, my wife, Christie, is always kidding me about "Mr. Speed Demon" having fun in the forest driving at 5 mph. I raced sports cars, open-wheel cars, stock cars, and sprint cars. I also hold the FIA Land Speed Record for diesel pickup trucks driving the Banks Sidewinder at Bonneville at more than 222 mph. Speed demon, indeed!

Although setting lap records, winning races, and nailing down a land-speed record offered incredible challenges, none were more challenging than tackling rock crawling trails in a Jeep at 5 mph. The unique characteristics of off roading require a high level of focus and great deal of skill. I have taught thousands of students racing and high-performance driving through the years, and I have been fortunate to have a great mentor help me learn the often counterintuitive techniques of off roading.

Quinn Thomas, my coauthor and a lifelong off roader, is a highly skilled driver. But more important to this project, Quinn knows more about Jeeps in general and the JK specifically than anyone I have encountered. Quinn and his wife, Heather, make their living building, modifying, and repairing Jeeps at the shop, All J Products, in Big Bear Lake, California. Quinn's product knowledge is key to making this book an essential resource for new, prospective,

and current owners of Jeep Wrangler JKs. Why?

It's complicated. The Jeep Wrangler JK is the most modified vehicle in the history of the automotive aftermarket. And there are more parts and options available for the JK than for any vehicle ever. In fact, so many types of products are available for the JK we cannot cover them all, let alone every product and brand available. We would need 1,000 pages. The biggest issue facing us when compiling this book was choosing product categories and then specific products as examples.

The selection process is important to understand. Based upon the criteria I've established as a writer and magazine editor over many years, we try to choose products that meet specific goals for a build or mild modifications. Then we choose specific products that we have experience with and that we know have the quality and high-level of durability we desire. Although the products we showcase here fit the needs of most Jeep Wrangler JK owners, new products are being introduced almost daily. Within a product category, we only feature products that we know are good; that does not mean there are not other products from other companies that are high quality. On the other hand, we do not promote products that are substandard. We tell you if a product is dangerous, but we have not encountered any

products known to be hazardous or dangerous. A suspension bushing may wear prematurely or a light bar may fail early on, and, while annoying, these issues are not dangerous. Where good products may be dangerous to use, such as recovery gear including jacks and winches, we try to offer sound safety guidelines.

Most JK modifications have consequences, often not obvious. Here's an example: When a JK owner upgrades to 37-inch tires, most owners realize that a gear ratio change in the axle housings is needed. But what about ball joints or power steering? A suspension lift on a JK often means that the front driveshaft may rub the exhaust pipe at extreme travel. We have attempted to provide sound information about the consequences of upgrading in one area and the effect in other areas.

The information in this book will help you regardless of the type of four wheeling you plan to enjoy, except maybe for "mall crawling." Before you begin the process of modifying a JK, it is important to know how you plan to use your Wrangler. Keep in mind that all Jeep Wrangler JKs are capable off-road vehicles. A stock Wrangler JK Rubicon can handle about 90 percent of all trails in the United States in good weather. If you want to partake of some mild rock crawling, then some modifications are called for. If you plan more extreme rock crawling and hill climbing, such as the slick rock in Moab, more upgrades will be necessary. If you plan expedition-style overlanding, a different set of modifications will be required. Whatever style of off roading you prefer, you need specific equipment and gear, such as a jack, tow strap, and possibly a winch. The better idea you have concerning your desired use of your JK, the easier it is to formulate a plan.

A budget is just as important. An average off-road JK build costs about $10,000. However, it's not unusual for JK builds to exceed $40,000, and Quinn has built several JKs at this price level. I have students who have spent more than $100,000, not counting the initial cost of the JK. The joke about what JEEP stands for is no surprise: Just Empty Every Pocket! And the reality is that a Jeep build is never really finished. Jeep Wrangler JKs and the associated builds are not cheap, but the adventures and family fun are worth the cost.

When planning a JK build, keep in mind that not everything needs to be done at once. You can use this book to develop a plan, prioritize modifications and product installs, and then build your JK. In addition, you can use a shop that can guide you in the right direction. A JK build can be done in stages, but it is important, as previously mentioned, that all parts needed for a stage of a build be done at the same time; for example, going to taller tires may mean you need a lift kit and/or flat fenders. You may also need an axle gear ratio change. You may want to add air lockers at the same time to avoid doubling the labor. Proceeding in stages can make the sticker shock a little less daunting. Some Jeep dealers offer modified JKs for sale, or they can build your JK when you purchase it. Often, the entire build can be financed. But keep in mind, the dealer may not offer the best products for a specific application. Consumer awareness pays big dividends when buying and modifying a JK.

Our goal is to guide you down the right trail so that you can enjoy the adventures and family fun that a Jeep Wrangler JK can provide. As life becomes more stressful, a Jeep becomes more important as a way to enjoy the beauty, solitude, and adventures offered in the backcountry. This book helps achieve your goals.

WHEELS AND TIRES

Tires are the most common and most important performance modification to the Jeep Wrangler JK, and an off-road JK needs tires for a specific application, such as trail driving, rock crawling, or mud. Even if you start with the Rubicon model, changing to a larger tire is often the first upgrade to a new Jeep. If you start with a Sport or Sahara, you should upgrade to a true off-road all-terrain or mud-terrain tire. All-terrain and mud-terrain tires offer a more aggressive tread pattern, softer compounds, and much improved performance when you wheel off road. But there is a downside.

Mud-terrain and all-terrain tires use a softer rubber compound. Softer tread compounds accelerate tire wear and increase rolling resistance, thereby reducing fuel economy. The more aggressive tread designs of mud and all-terrain tires increase road noise. This is most notable on mud-terrain tires. The larger tread blocks on a mud tire also increase tire squirm on the highway, which reduces handling responsiveness. Off-road performance improves dramatically, however. Moreover, the more aggressive look of the all-terrain and especially the mud-terrain tires is an integral element of the Jeep persona.

All-Terrain Versus Mud-Terrain

Which is better, an all-terrain or a mud-terrain tire? It depends upon which side of the fence are you on. While there has never been a clear winner in this argument, among the many factors to consider are highway versus off-road miles, weather conditions, terrain, and road surface, to name just a few. But with the launch of two new all-terrain tires, the Falken WildPeak A/T3W and the Mickey Thompson Baja ATZ P3 All Terrain Tire, the line between A/Ts and M/Ts is blurred. These new-generation A/T tires offer more aggressive tread patterns and sidewalls while retaining a smaller void ratio for reduced noise on the highway and harder rubber compounds for better tire wear.

Tire selection is crucial to realize the best performance from your JK, and you need to take lift, suspension setup, and, of course, application into account.

Mud-terrain tires, such as the Falken WildPeak M/T tire (left), are generally pre-ferred for serious off-road JKs. The large tread blocks and softer rubber com-pound provide increased grip on soft terrain. They also look more aggressive. All-terrain tires, such as the BFGoodrich All Terrain T/AKO2 tire (middle), appeal to milder off-road use due to better wear and a quieter ride on the highway. Although the A/T tire may have a harder rubber compound, the increased tread area due to a smaller void ratio allows most A/T tires to perform with the equiv-alent M/T tire in most off-road conditions. The Mickey Thompson Baja ATZ P3 (right) all-terrain tire blurs the line between mud and all-terrain tires. More of a hybrid, the ATZ P3 features large tread blocks, a smaller void ratio, numerous sipes in the tread blocks, and a rubber compound softer than a typical A/T tire but harder than an M/T. Many tire companies have introduced this style of hybrid all-terrain tire. This new category is often called extreme all-terrain.

The void ratio is the area of tread blocks versus the area of the gaps between the tread blocks (white in the illustration). All-terrain tires use a small void ratio, meaning more rubber is on the ground. Mud-terrain tires use much larger void ratios, meaning less rubber on the ground but more ability for the tire to grip a surface, especially soft surfaces such as mud, sand, and snow. Larger void ratios also create more noise on the highway.

Tread Design Differences

The most obvious difference between the all-terrain and mud-terrain tire is in the tread design. A mud-terrain tire has more aggressive tread blocks and a larger void ratio. The void ratio is the percentage of the total tread block area in comparison to the area of the total tire tread. The tread blocks on a mud-terrain tend to be larger and thicker than on an all-terrain tire. The thin slits in the tread, called sipes, allow the tread to flex and the edges to better grip hard surfaces such as rocks. Sipes are used in both all-terrain and mud-terrain tires. Generally, an all-terrain tire has more sipes. This improves grip on hard surfaces. The new, more aggres-sive all-terrain tires create as much or possibly slightly more grip than the same size mud-terrain tire.

Although a good mud-terrain tread design can keep rocks from

Here are four all-terrain tire designs.

Top left: The BFGoodrich All Terrain T/A KO2 tire has one of the more aggressive sidewall designs. The tire's siping allows flex for better grip. The ridges between the sidewall tread blocks are stepped to help eject rocks and debris from the sidewall.

Top right: The Mickey Thompson Baja ATZ P3 all-terrain tire has a sidewall design more like a mud-terrain tire, and it grips well on rock edges and the sides of ruts where little or no tread is gripping the surface.

Bottom left: The Falken WildPeak A/T3W has an aggressive sidewall for an all-terrain tire. The stepped ridges on the upper part of the sidewall progres-sively grip the edges of rocks and slopes for better grip. They also dig into soft surfaces for even more bite.

Bottom right: This A/T tire, the Nexen Roadian A/T Pro RA8, has a conserva-tive sidewall design, but the triangular-shaped scallops on the lower portion of the sidewall provide a surprising amount of grip on loose dirt and large, sloped rocks.

The all-terrain tire has the clear advantage on the highway. Smaller void ratios mean more rubber on the road. Harder rubber compounds reduce tire wear and help with fuel economy. All-terrain tires create less noise with their smaller tread voids. The tread blocks act like pumps or fans creating more airflow. The size and shape of the blocks along with the void ratio determine the noise level. Some mud-terrain tires are loud.

In most cases, given equal tire sizes, an all-terrain is better in rain and ice. On snow, tread design and tire pressure play a large role. Either a mud or an all-terrain tire works well in snow. But not all M/T or A/T tires perform equally in snowy conditions, so you need to determine the specific characteristics of the tire you're installing.

Mud-terrain tires have softer tread compounds, but all-terrain tires have more actual rubber on the ground. The ability of the tread blocks to grip and the sidewall lugs to hold on side slopes and rock edges determine performance. Much of this depends on the tread design and siping. The advantage goes to most mud-terrain tires, but the latest more aggressive all-terrain tires, such as the Falken AT03 and the Mickey Thompson Baja ATZ P3 work extremely well in the big rocks.

lodging between tread blocks, the design must also eject mud and snow. Some designs do this more efficiently than others. In general, the larger void ratio of the mud-terrain is better in soft surface conditions, but the tread blocks need to flex to eject snow and dense mud. Tread design plays a role but so does tire pressure. Lower tire pressure helps when the voids become filled with debris, ice, snow, or heavy mud. And some all-terrain tread designs are better in snow, but lack the ability to keep small stones out of the tread voids.

Sidewall Design

One of the most important elements of tire design is the structure of the sidewall. When four wheeling on rocks, in ruts, or on side slopes, it's critical for the sidewall tread to deliver good grip. If the tires exhibit a lack of grip, the tire can slide sideways off the edge of a rock, the slope

on a side hill, or within a series of ruts. Slipping can alter your desired path. Or you can bang a rock slider, skidplate, or bumper on a rock that you thought you could avoid. The tire sidewall needs to be able to flex to conform to the road surface and to have a design that allows rocks and snow to be ejected from the tread pattern. Most off-road tires do a better job of keeping tread voids cleared when aired down to a lower pressure.

Rubber Compound and Wear

All-terrain tires tend to have harder rubber compounds than mud-terrain tires. Therefore, the mud tire wears more quickly, all else being equal. Even though the all-terrain is harder, it has more rubber on the road or trail surface due to a smaller void ratio. This usually means that the all-terrain tire has slightly better traction on hard surfaces given equal tire sizes. The mud-terrain grips better on soft surfaces. This is best distinguished when the tire is operating "in" a surface as opposed to "on"

a surface. Think "in" sand, mud, snow, and soft, loose dirt versus "on" asphalt, ice, or hard-packed dirt.

Off-Road Tire Performance

The advantages of the A/T versus the M/T off-road are less clear. In some conditions, the mud-terrain tire provides a slight advantage. But the differences are minor. The big issue is the type of surface. For the most part, the all-terrain tire is better on hard surfaces. While the rubber compound is a little harder, the void ratio is smaller, meaning more rubber on the ground for equal size tires at similar pressures. The advantage diminishes when the surfaces are wet.

Due to deeper, larger tread blocks, the mud-terrain tire performs at its best in soft surfaces. Mud, sand, loose dirt, and snow are conditions giving the mud-terrain tire better performance. In certain types of snow, especially in slushy, sticky snow conditions, the M/T has an advantage only if the tread design (and lower tire pressures) can eject snow from the tread voids.

Tire Size, Diameters, and Ground Clearance

Increasing tire diameter allows more ground clearance and larger contact patches on the ground. Keep in mind that the low points under any Wrangler JK are the center sections of the axle housing. Suspension lifts raise the chassis/body, but not the axle housing. A suspension lift is installed mostly to gain clearance for larger-diameter tires. Going from the stock 32-inch tire in the JK Rubicon to a 34-inch-diameter tire increases ground clearance by 1 inch.

Increasing tire size increases tire weight, and off-road tires weigh substantially more than the stock 31- to 32-inch tires. Because the tread is the heaviest part of the tire and is farthest from the center of rotation, all the weight when rotating (called rotational inertia) creates large loads on ball joints, tie-rod ends, and suspension components. The inertia caused by weight away from the center of rotation increases as rotational speed (RPM) increases, as the distance from the centerline increases, and as tire weight increases. Wear in steering components leads to shimmy and death wobble on the solid-axle JK. Increasing tire size requires upgrading key steering components to ensure performance and safe operation. In addition, as tire size goes up, it is crucial to dynamically balance the tires (see the wheel and tire balancing section on page 24) to reduce the possibility of shimmy or wobble.

Exceptional tire compliance allows much easier rock crawling by sticking to a slanted rock. This rock has a 60-degree slope. Most of the tread is in contact and the sidewall is contributing some grip as well.

Tire Size and Off-Road Performance

Large-diameter and wide-tread-width tires have a larger rubber contact patch on the ground, especially at low tire pressures. This improves traction. Because taller tire sidewalls can be aired down with a greater reduction in sidewall height, ride quality is better. The downside of larger tires is increased brake and steering system wear. Fuel economy also takes a negative hit.

Tire Compliance Over Rocks and Obstacles

If you use your JK for serious rock crawling or steep hill climbs and descents, especially those with big ruts, tire compliance of the tread over road surface irregularities is extremely important. Tire compliance is the ability of the tire tread and sidewall to conform to the shape of rocks, road surface irregularities, or other obstacles. Both sidewall stiffness and tread design are factors. Tire pressures are key, but tire design plays a factor in how low a pressure you can run, especially without beadlock wheels (see the wheel section on page 22 for an explanation of beadlock wheels).

Siping

Sipes are thin cuts in the tread of a tire. They allow the tire tread to separate slightly, which improves traction on ice and snow. For off-road use, the siping can improve traction when rock crawling. Depending on the siping pattern, they can also increase lateral grip, helping to hold the tire sideways on rocks, side slopes, and ruts.

Lateral Grooves and Crosscuts

Lateral grooves and crosscuts are similar to siping but larger and allow tread blocks to flex and grip soft surfaces and uneven terrain more effectively. At lower tire pressures, grooves

Left: *Sipes are the thin cuts in the tread blocks, and this tire has considerable siping. Sipes allow tread blocks to flex and provide additional edges to help grip the surface. They are most effective on hard surfaces such as rocks and ice.* Right: *Siping is limited on this tread design. Notice the small ridges in the tread between the tread blocks. They help eject rocks and other debris from between the tread blocks.*

and crosscuts can flex to help expel snow from tread voids for better traction.

Forward and Side Grip

Tread and sidewall design play a major role in how a tire grips in low-traction situations. Good forward traction is critical for climbing and descending large rocks and hills. Side traction is crucial for holding onto side slopes, ruts, bumps, and rocks. Tire designs are a compromise. Different designs are better in certain off-road situations. A lot depends on how you use your JK.

Ply Ratings, Tire Cutting, and Slashing

Cutting or puncturing a tire tread or slashing a sidewall is fairly common off road. Areas with sharp rocks are most likely to cause problems. Two practices help reduce the possibility of serious tire damage: run only load range "D" or "E" tires and air-down to a lower tire pressure as described later.

Load range refers to the ply rating. Previously, bias-ply tires used a ply-rating system of up to 10 for light

Sidewall lettering can provide a wealth of information. This Falken WildPeak A/T3W has a load-range E rating, so it's equivalent to a 10-ply tire. The load range and sidewall design of this tire make it durable against punctures.

truck and off-road tires. With modern materials, fewer plies are needed to achieve the same strength and puncture resistance. The D rating is approximately the equivalent of an 8-ply bias tire. An E rating is nearly the equivalent of a 10-ply bias tire. Tires with D and E ratings provide the best protection off road.

Falken WildPeak M/T Test Summary

In the eight months we tested this tire, we encountered many different and demanding conditions. On the highway we tested in dry, wet, snow, and ice. We also tested on city streets, mountain roads, and interstates in wet and dry conditions. On the trails, we run in all sorts of conditions including mud, snow, ice, soft dirt, rocks (including sharp sidewall killers), hard dirt, gravel, and sand-covered rocks. We tested on large rocks and boulders, steep climbs and descents, up and down steep ledges, side slopes, and over sharp rocks in all sorts of road and weather conditions. Overall, Falken has created a tire with great compromises that allow outstanding off-road performance in areas we consider to be the highest priorities.

One of the most important elements of a great off-road tire is the ability to grip laterally on a sloped rock. The tire tread and the sidewall design contribute to this. The Falken WildPeak M/T features an aggressive tread design but has a void ratio on the low side for a mud-terrain tire. This reduces road noise and improves performance on hard surfaces. The Falken WildPeak M/T did well in our tests.

Falken WildPeak M/T Tire Specifications

Size: 37x12.50R17LT
Load Range: D/8-ply rating
Approved Rim Width: 8.5 to 11 inches
Overall Diameter: 36.7 inches
Section Width: 12.9 inches
Tread Depth: 21/32 inch
Tire Weight: 81.8 pounds
Maximum Pressure: 50 psi

Off-Road Tests

Because the market offers a wide selection of all-terrain, mud-terrain, and rock-crawling tires, the choices can be overwhelming. However, we break down the primary performance factors such as tread design, siping, and sidewall design, to help you make a sound and balanced buying decision.

Hill Climbs

Regardless of the trail condition (wet, dry, snow, ice), climbing hills puts a premium on traction. We use a wide variety of hill climbs for testing, including rutted, loose

Downhill grip means the difference between control and chaos! Or worse. This slope is 45 degrees and the Falken WildPeak M/T tires hold with little slip or wheel lock up. Tires need to instill confidence when you drop down a 45-degree slope. Tire lock up downhill when steering can lead to a serious slide and potential rollover. Note the small amount of dust. Very little sliding and tire lock up means good traction and a safe descent.

The Falken WildPeak M/T provides excellent traction for descending rocky drop offs, allowing a smooth descent and minimal spring compression. This minimizes forward weight transfer and reduces the risk of a rollover on steep drop offs.

The Falken WildPeak M/T uses a relatively stiff sidewall and therefore has little flex. The tire pressure is set at 15 psi and the grip is fine. However, lower tire pressures allow the tire to comply better with the terrain, which improves traction.

dirt, rocky ascents as well as damp dirt, muddy dirt, and snow. On our 25-degree rutted, loose dirt slope, the Falken WildPeak M/Ts climbed easily in any conditions. On a challenging 35-degree slope where turning is involved, we had no issues, even though we did encounter slight wheel spin when we didn't use lockers.

Hill Descents

Hill descents can be tricky with a lifted JK Unlimited. So much weight is already on the front tires that when you go down a 45-degree slope, little weight is left on rear tires. On a 45-degree slope, we experienced minor wheel lockup, but it was easily controlled and caused no problems.

Rock Crawling

If it's dry, we run the Falken WildPeak M/Ts at 10 to 12 psi in the rocks. This is a compromise between ground clearance and traction. The tread block design and the siping on the Falken WildPeak M/Ts allow the tread to conform to the shape of the rocks. The tough and aggressive sidewall design provides exceptional grip when climbing on the sides of steep rocks, a nice touch that minimizes the chance of sliding sideways off a rock and smashing a rock slider.

On-Road Tests

Most owners use their JKs for on-road as well as off-road service; therefore, you need to consider on-road responsiveness, noise, ride quality, and other factors.

Noise

The Falken WildPeak M/T falls on the quiet side of the spectrum; not the quietest we have tested, but far quieter than the loudest. Falken engineers worked hard to find a tread block pattern and void ratio that is not too noisy but still offers excellent performance.

Ride

Most vehicle manufacturers

suggest high tire pressures to improve fuel mileage numbers. This tends to accelerate tire wear in the center of tread and increases ride harshness. Given the sad state of our roads and highways, this can make for a less than comfortable ride. Moreover, overinflated tires reduce braking and cornering traction, which is made more significant when the tire sidewall is on the stiff side.

Summary

The bottom line is that Falken has hit a home run with its first consumer M/T tire. Great performance off road and good characteristics on road make this a great choice for the rocks and all other off-road situations.

Tire Deflators

Tire deflators are the easiest way to air-down tires when you hit the trails. In general, there are three types: First, there are tire pressure gauges that have a release valve for letting air out of a tire. These are slow and require constant attention. Second are deflators that screw onto the valve stem and depress the spring-loaded valve core. These are adjustable for minimum pressure when they shut off and usually come in sets of two or four. They aren't much faster than a

Mickey Thompson ATZ P3

While technically an all-terrain tire, the Baja ATZ P3 is actually a hybrid all-terrain tire with many features more commonly found on a mud-terrain tire; for example, the rubber compound is new and softer than normally found on A/T tires. This improves grip under all conditions. That usually means wear accelerates and the tire is more susceptible to cuts and chipping. But the new rubber compound was engineered to improve wear characteristics, reduce cutting and chipping, but still provide improved traction. The engineers also paid close attention to the groove design. The smaller void ratio on most A/T tires means that mud and snow can build up in the tread and reduce tire grip.

To determine performance, we have run the Mickey Thompson Baja ATZ P3 all-terrain tires in several situations from hardcore rock crawling to wet street and highway driving. We tested the 37X12.50R17LT on Mickey Thompson Metal Series MM366 17-inch diameter x 9 inches wide wheels. The tire section width is 13.1 inches and the tread width is 10.4 inches. These are great tires in all off-road situations and really good on the highway.

Highway and Street

If you use your Jeep on the highway, especially as a daily driver like we do, street and highway performance

is important. Living in the mountains, good handling in wet and dry conditions is critical. The design and rubber compound combined with a smaller void ratio than a traditional M/T tire makes the Mickey Thompson Baja ATZ P3 an exceptional asphalt performer. Sure, an ultra-high-performance street tire may have more grip, but would be pretty useless on the trails. We have yet to try the ATZ in the snow, but based on all the conditions we have tried, expecting good snow performance is no stretch.

The Mickey Thompson Baja ATZ P3 is possibly the best compromise between a great all-purpose trail tire and an excellent tire for the street and highway. It is perfect for the daily driver who wheels on the weekends or the hardcore wheeler who must drive his rig to work on asphalt most days. Over time, this tire could prove to be a real

game changer for the multi-use off-road vehicle.

The Baja ATZ P3 All Terrain Tire groove design improves self-cleaning and reduces wear. The void ratio is a little larger in the Baja ATZ P3, giving the tire tread a much more aggressive look. The sidewalls are also much more aggressive, featuring deep sidebiters for better traction on side slopes, rocks, and other situations where the traction of the sidewall makes a big difference.

One of our test hills incorporates a nearly 40-degree slope. Although some tires have not made it to the top at all, the Baja ATZ P3 /Ts made it with no issues and no wheel spin when lockers were used.

Off-Road Tire Test

We put six off-road tires to the test to illustrate the various characteristics in different off-road conditions. They include the Falken WildPeak A/T3W, Mickey Thompson MTZ, Maxxis Trepador M/T, BFGoodrich KO2, Nitto Trail Grappler, and the BFGoodrich Mud-Terrain T/A KM2. Each tire offers certain attributes that excel in specific driving conditions. This should help you select the tires for your particular needs and off-road preferences.

Another new tire from Falken is the WildPeak AT 3W all-terrain tire. While this tire is a more traditional all-terrain tire, it is aggressive. If you use your JK as a daily driver with long

Mounted on a 35-inch tire, the Falken WildPeak AT 3W features a tough E-rated sidewall that's resistant to cuts and punctures. Aired down, this tire does a great job conforming to rocks for improved traction. Traction climbing up steep rock faces determines the capability of any off-road tire. The WildPeak AT 3W has plenty of grip to climb steep rocks.

The BFGoodrich all-terrain tire has set the standard, and all other off-road tires are compared to it. The first on the market in the 1970s, BF-Goodrich has been a leader in off-road performance and good on-highway characteristics. The All Terrain TA KO2 is no exception, and the BFGoodrich All Terrain tire is one of the most aggressive for off-road challenges. The assertive nature of the KO2 allows great rock crawling performance, but it is still good for asphalt treks. The sidewall design allows the KO2 great side traction, minimizing the chance of sliding sideways off a steep rock or ledge.

Mickey Thompson Baja MTZ Radial offers an aggressive tread and sidewall design, a soft rubber compound, and durable construction. This tire performs extremely well on rocks, sand, mud, and loose rock hill climbs and descents. The Baja MTZ Radial instills confidence when it comes to climbing, and especially descending, steep waterfall ledges. Highway handling and noise are both good. The Baja MTZ is a little on the quiet side of the mud-terrain tire spectrum.

The Maxxis Trepador M/T tire has an aggressive tread design with a large void ratio, deep tread blocks, and a soft rubber compound. The sidewall lugs are large. This tire is best on a serious trail rig that sees minimal travel on pavement. But the wear rate is high and highway driving requires constant attention due the movement of the large, deep tread blocks.

commutes, this tire is a great choice. Except with soft surfaces such as mud and sand, this tire holds its own on any dry off-road surface and may even be better on hard-pack snow and ice than a mud-terrain tire.

With a great reputation on the rocks, the Nitto Trail Grappler is a popular tire on serious JK trail rigs. And like other high-end mud-terrain tires, it gets the job done on the squishy stuff and is decent on the highway. It provides the traction necessary to crawl up and down steep rocks without lockup or sliding. This is critical for control and safety with the front-heavy JK Unlimited.

The BFGoodrich Mud Terrain Krawler is the latest in a long line of BFGoodrich Mud Terrain tires. Every new version exceeds the capability of the last. This tire shines in the rocks and any soft surface. Tread wear and road noise are typical of most mud-terrain tires.

pressure gauge but with four and automatic shut off, you can screw them on and walk away. The third deflator also screws onto the valve stem, but it also unscrews the valve core from the stem while capturing it within the nozzle. They have a pressure gauge and an on-off pressure relief valve for accurate control of tire pressure. This allows for rapid airing down. One of these deflators is typically faster than four of the others. The downside is the need to watch the pressure as it drops.

A hybrid system called 2-Way Air uses a system of tubes plumbed into the vehicle. The tubes run to Schrader valves at each corner and to a shut off valve. The pressure relief valve is adjustable to control pressure when airing up. Tube "whips" are placed from the chassis-mounted valves to the tire valve stems. This system works for airing down and up; it can be used with a compressor or a Power Tank.

The Currie Deflator removes the valve core from the valve stem, so you can rapidly deflate tires. The gauge allows precise pressure monitoring. The Deflator consists of gauge, a plunger, which unscrews the valve core, a fitting that screws onto the valve stem, and a pressure release valve. Although the operator is a little more involved in the process, this is the fastest way to air-down four tires, even faster than the set of four screw-on deflators. The cost is about half.

The Multi-Choice Mil-Spec Deflators from Extreme Outback are high-quality deflators. These feature detents from 20 psi down to 10 psi in 2-psi increments. They adjust by rotating the knob on the top.

The Staun Tire Deflators allow all four tires to be aired down at once. They are made from brass and have an adjustable pressure relief valve. They screw onto the valve stem.

Tire Pressures for Off-Road Jeep Wrangler JKs

There are four important reasons to air-down. The first is to increase traction by increasing tire contact patch area. Reducing inflation pressures from 50 psi to 7 psi on a 285 70-17 10-ply tire increases the tire contact patch by up to 220 percent. Second, aired down tires improve ride comfort, significantly. The third reason is to reduce the chance of a sidewall puncture. Think of a highly inflated balloon. If you poke at it, it will likely puncture. A softly inflated balloon, when poked, has considerably more give and is not likely to puncture. Fourth, aired down tires reduce damage to the road surface by spreading the weight over a greater tire contact patch surface area. This helps reduce erosion over time.

Some disadvantages are reduced ground clearance due to the shorter sidewall that results from less pressure, and the increased possibility of the tire bead unseating from the wheel rim. Finally, you need to add air back to recommended highway tire pressures for your vehicle. For hard surfaces and rock crawling, higher pressures are needed to help keep the tire bead seated on the wheel rim, and to protect the sidewall and tire bead from bottoming on the rim, which would likely damage the tire or even bend the wheel rim.

Tire compliance over rocks becomes more important when the surface is slippery. The tire contact area on this rock is several times larger than it would be at full tire inflation pressure.

Airing down tires to a lower pressure allows the tire to conform to the terrain, increasing traction. This is important for rock crawling for both climbing and descending. This tire is at about 15 psi and the tire contact patch and the sidewalls conform to the rock edge, allowing a much easier climb up the rock.

The first step in determining optimum inflation for a specific tire is to inflate to maximum pressure as specified on the sidewall of the tire. Next, measure the distance from the ground perpendicular to the fender flair. Check the sidewall height. You can calculate the inflated sidewall height from the tire specs. Find the overall diameter, subtract the wheel diameter, and then divide by 2 to get the sidewall height. For this tire, the overall diameter is 36.7 inches; subtract 17 inches and then divide by 2. The sidewall is 9.85 inches as shown in the left photo. With a deflator in place, reduce the pressure so that the sidewall height drops 10 percent of the total or slightly less than 1 inch. We started at 44 inches from the ground to the fender flair edge; we want to go to 43 inches and read the pressure, which was 11 psi. This is the air pressure we use for most off-road driving, including rock crawling. In the right photo, we reduced the pressure so that the sidewall height drops 20 percent of the total or slightly less than 2 inches. We started at 44 inches; we want to go to 42 inches and read the pressure, which was 4 psi. This is the pressure we use for smooth surfaces off-road, such as mud, snow, sand, or ice as long as ground clearance is not an issue. You need beadlock wheels to run at tire pressures below 10 psi.

This "AIR UP TIMES and QUANTITY OF TIRE FILLS" Chart illustrates the speed and quantity of tire inflations of our portable high performance CO2 air systems.																
	10 PSI Increase				**20 PSI Increase**					**30 PSI Increase**					**40 PSI Increase**				
Power Tank "COMP Series"	5-15 psi, 10-20 psi, 15-25 psi inflation time TIME:	Qty. of tires.	Qty. of tires.	Qty. of tires.	5-25 psi 10-30 psi 15-35 psi inflation time TIME:	Qty. of tires.	Qty. of tires.	Qty. of tires.	Qty. of tires.	10-30 psi 20-50 psi 30-60 psi inflation time TIME:	Qty. of tires.	Qty. of tires.	Qty. of tires.	Qty. of tires.	20-60 psi 30-70 psi 40-80 psi inflation time TIME:	Qty. of tires.	Qty. of tires.	Qty. of tires.	Qty. of tires.
What's your tire size?		PT5 Tank	PT10 Tank	PT15 Tank		PT5 Tank	PT10 Tank	PT15 Tank	PT20 Tank		PT5 Tank	PT10 Tank	PT15 Tank	PT20 Tank		PT5 Tank	PT10 Tank	PT15 Tank	PT20 Tank
205/75R15	6 sec.	45	90	136	12 sec.	23	45	68	90	18 sec.	15	29	44	59	25 sec.	11	23	34	45
225/75R16	7 sec.	38	76	114	15 sec.	19	38	57	71	22 sec.	12	24	36	49	29 sec.	10	19	29	38
30 x 9.50 x 15	8 sec.	34	68	102	17 sec.	17	34	51	64	25 sec.	11	22	33	44	33 sec.	9	17	26	34
32 X 11.50 X 15	12 sec.	26	53	80	22 sec.	13	27	40	54	34 sec.	8	18	26	36	46 sec.	7	14	20	27
33 x 12.50 x 15	15 sec.	20	40	60	30 sec.	10	20	30	40	45 sec.	7	13	20	26	60 sec.	5	10	15	20
295/75R16	15 sec.	20	40	60	30 sec.	10	20	30	40	45 sec.	7	13	20	26	60 sec.	5	10	15	20
35 x 12.50 x 15	19 sec.	15	30	45	38 sec.	8	16	24	32	56 sec.	5	10	16	20	1.3 min.	4	8	12	16
325/70R17	19 sec.	15	30	45	38 sec.	8	16	24	32	56 sec.	5	10	16	20	1.3 min.	4	8	12	16
37 x 12.50 x 17	23 sec.	12	24	36	45 sec.	6	13	20	26	1.1 min.	4	8	13	16	1.5 min.	3	7	10	13
39.50 x 15 x 15	41 sec.	7	14	21	1.3 min.	3	7	10	14	2 min.	2	5	7	10	2.8 min.	2	4	5	7
42 x 15 x 15	56 sec.	5	10	15	1.9 min.	2	5	7	10	2.8 min.	1	3	5	6	3.8 min.	1	3	4	5

If your inflation / deflation requirements fall below the RED line, we suggest using Monster Valves for maximum performance from your Power Tank system.

All times are approximate based on average tire size and stem flow rates. Your times may vary due to your tire brand, rim width, and stem flow rates.
NOTE: All inflation times above can be cut by 50% when inflating through our Monster Valves!

Power Tank created an inflation time for various tire sizes at given pressure increases. The chart also shows how many tires can be inflated for various size tanks.

A simpler solution is a portable air compressor, such as the Viair unit. This economical alternative is somewhat slower than a twin compressor with air tank system (such as that system, also from Viair).

A quick and convenient way to air-up features the compressed CO2 tank and regulator system from Power Tank. This high-pressure system fills large tires quickly. The tanks come in three sizes: 15, 10, and 5 pounds. The tanks need refilling. With our 15-pound Power Tank, we can inflate our 37x12.50x17-inch tires (all four) from 10 to 26 psi in about 2.5 minutes and, in fact, we can fill about 32 tires this way (on a fully filled tank).

On a Wrangler JK Rubicon, this Viair onboard compressor mounts to the area formerly occupied by the front sway bar and disconnect mechanism. The stock bar was replaced with a Currie Antirock Sway Bar.

The two-way air system uses a yellow air line called a whip and runs from a valve mounted through the body seam to the tire valve stem. Each tire is set up this way.

The 2-Way Air System allows all four tires to be deflated or inflated at one time. The lines in the kit allow connection of all four tires to a valve that releases air, or can be connected to a compressor or Power Tank to inflate all four tires simultaneously. The valve on the left is an adjustable pressure relief valve for airing up to a pre-set pressure. The chuck in the middle allows connection of an onboard compressor, portable compressor, or a Power Tank. The lever on the right controls airflow for both airing down and up. An additional valve allows the use of a tire pressure gauge to monitor tire pressure while airing-down. The pressure relief valve is used to preset maximum pressure when airing up.

Wheels and Tires

Wheels for performance vehicles tend to be lightweight. While weight is an important consideration for off-road applications, strength and durability are more important. Moreover, for the JK, it is especially important that the wheels are the optimum size with proper backspacing and offset. Wheels for the Wrangler JK come in steel and alloy aluminum. Both materials are used on standard bead rim or beadlock versions. Alloy and steel used in the manufacturing of wheels offer their own distinct advantages. Steel is less common because

A Power Tank or compressor can be used to air-up with the 2-Way Air System. It allows for easier airing up and down, even though the time needed is about the same as deflating or inflating each tire individually.

all wheels available on Wrangler JKs are aluminum alloy. It is more difficult to maintain proper balance with steel wheels than alloy wheels. Steel is less expensive and is strong and malleable, meaning that the wheel bends on impact, instead of cracking or breaking. A bent steel wheel can be hammered back (although with great difficulty) into a reasonable shape to hold air if deformed on the trail. A cracked or broken alloy wheel cannot be repaired. Any wheel can be scratched, gouged, or more severely damaged when off roading.

Alloy wheels are lighter for the same size and strength. They also offer an extensive range of styles. Aluminum alloy dissipates heat better than steel, helping cool brakes under

Airing down in the rocks allows a tire to conform to the rocky surface for improved traction and improved ride. **Top:** *The Falken WildPeak M/T tire is inflated to highway pressure, 26 psi.* **Middle:** *This is the same passenger-side front tire at 16 psi. The tire has better compliance.* **Bottom:** *At 6 psi. The tire conforms to the rock for better traction. For this low pressure, we use Raceline Monster Beadlocks.*

extreme conditions. Aluminum is also more costly. Forging, high-pressure die casting, low-pressure die casting, and gravity casting are used to manufacture alloy wheels. Forged wheels are the toughest and strongest, but also much more expensive, as much as double the cost. Many forged wheels are not street legal and are mostly used for competition.

The Jeep Wrangler JK Rubicon comes with nice alloy wheels as standard equipment. But if you want to run larger tires, especially 35-inch or larger, these wheels are too narrow and the backspace wrong. This can cause the tire to crown, increasing wear in the center of the tread and allowing the tire to rub on the frame when turning full steering lock.

The Mickey Thompson M/T Metal Series MM 366 comes in a 17x9–inch-wide version with a 5-on-5 bolt circle and a 4.5-inch back spacing. That's perfect for the JK with 35-inch and larger tires. The Metal Series are alloy wheels with simulated beadlocks.

This steel beadlock wheel looks like a homemade modification for a standard steel wheel. The beadlock ring uses only 16 bolts to hold it in place. For a 17-inch wheel on a JK, most beadlocks use 32 bolts. This wheel is not well maintained, as shown by the rust. Beadlock wheels can be dangerous. The beadlock ring bolts need to be torqued to the proper specification regularly. Loose or broken bolts can lead to failure of the beadlock rim because the tire bead is no longer secured to the wheel. As a result, it can cause a flat tire or even injuries should the ring strike someone. It is important to use quality materials that are properly engineered. A home-built beadlock is not a sound idea. It is important to check the torque every 30 days (at a minimum) to verify the beadlock ring is secure.

Many manufacturers produce quality alloy wheels for off-road use. We have experience with several wheel companies making high-quality products, including Raceline, American Expedition Vehicles (AEV), Method, Mickey Thompson, Walker Evans, ATX, and KMC. You should select the appropriately sized wheels for your build-up plan and application. But wheels are also a personal choice, so they need to suit your tastes and carry features

The Mopar beadlock wheel for the Wrangler JK features a hybrid design that uses a standard beaded rim. It also has a beadlock rim that bolts on the wheel to secure the tire at low pressures. Without the beadlock ring, the wheel can run at highway speeds with normal on-road tire pressures.

you desire. Cast wheels are by far the most common. The casting process is less important than the quality of the materials used in the process. Cast wheels can crack or even break from hard impacts off road, even though it is rare. We recommend selecting the highest quality wheel you can afford, because a wheel failure off road can create a dangerous situation.

Standard Bead versus Beadlocks

Modern wheels and tires are manufactured to close tolerances, so wheel bead diameters are a close fit to the tire bead. For this reason, most JK owners can use a standard bead wheel, which is similar to the stock wheel on a JK. Beadlock-style wheels are available, and while these look like beadlocks, they have a standard wheel bead. A true beadlock wheel has an outer ring, which bolts to the wheel. The ring holds the tire bead in place, so it cannot become dislodged from the wheel at low pressures. We have tested many different tires on standard rims down to 10 psi for soft surface, low-speed four wheeling. This is usually a low enough pressure for adequate traction and the lower limit at which the tire does not separate from the wheel. Beadlocks are necessary for more extreme situations, such as deep snow or wet, muddy, or snow-covered rocks; these conditions require lower pressures, as do tires with a stiff sidewall. We have tested beadlocks at tire pressures as low as 3 psi in snow on soft surfaces such as sand and mud, and on snowy, muddy rocks on black diamond trails.

With the beadlock ring removed, it is easy to mount the tire on the rim. With the tire on the rim, the beadlock ring is placed over the tire so that the bolt holes line up on the rim. There are 32 bolts holding the Raceline beadlock ring on the rim, place the first 4 bolts at approximately 90-degree intervals and snug down to center the tire and secure the ring squarely in place.

The Raceline Monster Beadlock is one of Raceline's Competition Series Beadlocks. We have run this wheel on our JKs for a couple of years. They have been used hard and the only rock damage is to the beadlock ring, which is easily replaced.

The Ultra Wheels Extreme True Beadlock comes from a company with an off-road racing heritage and delivers reliable off-road performance at a variety of tire pressures. The aluminum beadlock ring attaches to the outside of the wheel and clamps the tire's bead surface between the lock ring and the machined shelf. This locks the tire's bead onto the wheel. These wheels are on Dave Luman's Rock-Slide Engineering JKU.

Torque all the bolts in two or three steps. With the Raceline beadlocks, the first torque step is about 14 ft-lbs. The final torque is 18 ft-lbs. After a few miles of driving recheck the torque. The beadlock bolts should be re-torqued every 30 days.

Insert the remaining bolts through the beadlock ring and start the bolts into the bolt holes on the rim. Snug all the bolts without tightening.

A few myths about beadlock wheels need to be addressed. The most significant myth is that beadlocks are not street legal. That is not true. Most manufacturers state that their beadlock wheels are not "recommended" for highway use. However, on-road use is not prohibited. Often the manufacturer has not had the beadlock wheels tested to DOT specifications. Given the small market for beadlocks, this costly process is usually avoided. The AEV beadlock is an exception and there may be others on the market that have also been tested. A second concern is that beadlocks are difficult to balance. Again, this is not quite true. A high-quality wheel of any design should balance without issue. Keep in mind that all JK tires should be dynamically balanced, which is covered on page 24.

Typically, most beadlocks have 32 bolts holding the outer ring in place. It's essential that beadlocks are properly installed and maintained. These bolts must be installed in the proper sequence and torqued to the correct spec. We torque in three stages starting with 12 ft-lbs, progressing to 14 ft-lbs, and ending at 17–18 ft-lbs. Beadlock manufacturers recommend torquing bolts in a star pattern. We then double check the torque of all bolts. Different wheel manufacturers may have different torque specifications. You must also check torque setting at least monthly to ensure reliability and safety. We recommend sticking with traditional bead wheels or the simulated beadlocks if you like the look. If you use your rig for serious rock crawling, mud running, or trail driving, you may need beadlocks, but then you must be willing to put in the time and money for proper and regular maintenance.

Wheel Aspects to Consider

Wrangler JKs are equipped with 17- and 18-inch-diameter wheels, although the current Sport model comes with 16-inch-diameter wheels. The optimum diameter for a JK wheel is 17 inches. This allows the maximum amount of sidewall height for most-effective airing down. Smaller-diameter wheels can have clearance issues with brake calipers. The widest wheel on many stock JKs is 7.5 inches. This is too narrow for tires more than 33 inches in diameter. The optimum width is 8.5 to 9 inches for 34- to 37-inch tires with a 12.50- to 13.50-inch section width.

Features

The JK uses a 5-on-5 bolt pattern, meaning five lug holes in a 5-inch bolt circle. (The metric equivalent of 5 x 127 can be used.)

Wheel backspace is critical on the JK. Backspacing is measured from the back of the wheel rim to the mounting surface of the wheel to the hub. Too much backspace with larger, wider tires can cause rubbing problems as the front tires are turned near full lock and at the extremes of vertical suspension travel.

Wheel weight is important, but given that off-road tires are heavy and the Jeep Wrangler JK uses solid axles, the effect of wheel weight is minimal compared to the total unsprung weight of the wheels, tires, axle housings, gears, and half the weight of suspension components. The most common wheel size for a JK with larger A/T or M/T tires is 17-inch diameter by 8.5- to 9.0-inch width. A typical steel wheel weighs about 40 pounds, an alloy wheel in the mid- to high-20-pound range, and an alloy beadlock with steel retaining ring weighs about 44 pounds.

If you use anti-theft lug nuts with splines, make sure you have the proper key socket that fits on your lug nuts. There are several sizes with

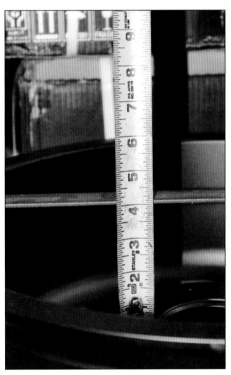

Optimal backspacing for 8.5- to 9.0-inch-wide wheels is 3.5 to 4.75 inches. The smaller the backspace measurement, the more the tire sticks out from the vehicle. The Raceline Monster beadlock has 4.5 inches of backspace.

Jeep uses dynamic wheel balancing for the Wrangler JK to remedy shimmy, death wobble, and other tire balance issues. With large tires and high rotational inertia due to the heavy tire tread located away from the center of rotation, dynamic balancing resolves most tire balance problems. The tire and wheel are spun at high speed until the location of imbalance is located on both the inside and outside of the rim.

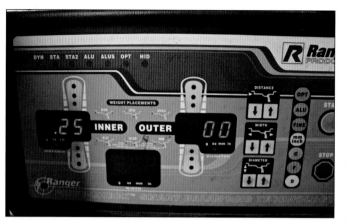

This 37-inch BF-Goodrich M/T tire and Raceline beadlock wheel measured less than 2 ounces out of balance on the first spin after mounting. After adding weights, the second spin showed nearly perfect balance at .25 ounce on the inner rim. Perfect balance was achieved on the third spin. The fallacy that beadlock wheels are impossible to balance is clearly inaccurate.

different spline patterns. Always carry the key lug socket and the socket that drives the key.

Wheel and Tire Balancing

Tire and wheel balancing is important on all vehicles. On the JK, especially with larger tires, standard static balancing is not adequate. The Jeep factory uses dynamic balancing on all Wranglers. Dynamic balancing serves to balance both the outside and the inside of the rim, which reduces wheel wobble and shimmy. The JK is prone to rapid ball joint and rod end wear. This leads to shimmy and death wobble, especially when tires greater than 33 inches in diameter are used.

Normal tire rotation is even more important with larger tires on a JK.

Choosing the Right Tires and Wheels

What is the best tire for your application? It really comes down to priorities. If you use your JK as a daily driver, and especially if you have a long commute, an all-terrain tire is likely the best choice. If you drive in mud often, a mud-terrain tire works well. If driving off-road, especially on difficult trails, takes precedence over highway driving and you want the more aggressive look, but tire wear and road noise are okay with you, then go for the aggressive mud-terrain tires.

Dozens of tires are available for the JK in a wide range of applications. Tires are under constant development and evolution, and therefore, the other newer tires may supersede the tires currently available. While there are dozens of tire choices, hundreds of wheels are available. Wheels are a critical item and need to be strong and durable for off roading. Select a good alloy wheel if you can. If budget is a consideration, go with a steel wheel if you must. And if you drive a JK in extreme conditions, a beadlock wheel is likely required.

Wheel Spacers and Adapters

Wheel spacers that slip over the wheel studs are not a good idea. Wheel adapters with built-in wheel studs that bolt onto the wheel studs on the hub work better and are safer. Check the regulations in your state, though, because they are not legal in some states.

Wheel and Tire Maintenance

Wheel lug nut torque should be between 90 and 100 ft-lbs, but check with your wheel manufacturer for the correct torque specification. Because of the more extreme conditions off road, check torque often. If you remove lug nuts, re-torque the nuts using a star pattern. After 200–300 miles of driving, re-torque the wheels. Torque on beadlock bolts should be checked every 30 to 60 days. Having an equal torque around the outer ring is important. If a bolt is broken, replace it immediately. We carry spare bolts just in case.

Keeping wheels and tires clean helps longevity and gives you an opportunity to check for cracking and chunking of the tires and scratches or cracks in wheels. The aftermarket carries many good wheel and tire cleaners.

SUSPENSION, LIFTS, AND STEERING

Suspension lift kits are a popular upgrade and almost a necessity for off-road Wrangler JKs because they are required to install larger tires for increased traction and ground clearance under the chassis. Lift kits generally fall into three categories: spacer lifts, spring lifts, and coil-over spring and shock absorber lifts. The lift kit you need depends on the type of off roading you plan to do. The majority of JK lifts use coil springs engineered for the desired lift height, travel, and ride quality; equally important is shock absorber selection. Shock valving rates need to be compatible with the springs and shock travel needs to match the travel of the lifted suspension. Many lift kits include control arms, bushings, and track bars to improve strength, reliability, and suspension geometry.

Most JK owners use suspension lifts to fit larger tires. The additional weight of big tires can cause issues with the steering system. Out-of-balance wheels and worn ball joints can cause wheel shimmy. The extra load of large tires can accelerate steering box wear. The sector shaft in the steering box is also susceptible to failure under extreme loads and heavy use. It is a good idea to upgrade these susceptible parts at the same time that you install a lift and larger tires.

Lifting for Off-Road Clearance

At first glance, it may seem that a lift kit on a Jeep Wrangler JK gains ground clearance. *While clearance is increased under the chassis, a lift does not increase clearance under the axle housings. Only taller tires increase ground clearance under the axles.* So, the real reason to lift your JK is to allow the fitment of taller tires;

Extreme Jeepin' requires excellent suspension and shocks along with strong components to handle the tremendous loads of rock crawling with 37-inch tires. I have equipped this JK with a Currie RockJock 4-inch suspension lift, Currie Antirock sway bars front and rear, and Fabtech Dirt Logic reservoir shock absorbers. Clearly, suspension travel and articulation are key elements for keeping those big 37s planted to the trail.

Extreme tilt angles such as this require great articulation. This suspension is doing a good job even though the angle looks perilous. The reality is that this JK is far from rolling, although the look on the driver's face indicates that he is not so sure. With less body roll and articulation, the passenger-side tires are more likely to unload, making the situation more tense. The body on the JK is at a 37-degree angle. The driver has about 10 degrees in hand before a roll is possible.

stock fenders. To make the jump to 37-inch-tall tires, a 4- to 4.5-inch lift is ideal, but you need aftermarket flat fenders to ensure adequate clearance at the extremes of suspension travel and articulation. Also, any lift higher than 3 inches requires driveline modifications to clear the exhaust. Spacer lifts up to 2.5 inches are available from AEV, Daystar, Rubicon Express, and TeraFlex. Well-engineered spring lifts of all sizes are available from Currie, Fabtech, AEV, Eibach, ARB (Old Man Emu), MetalCloak, and Rock Krawler. Coil-over lifts are available from Fabtech, GenRight, and Rock Krawler.

When selecting a lift kit for a JK, the most important consideration is the tire diameter you need for the type of off roading you plan to undertake. Factors to consider include ground clearance, fender and body clearance, suspension travel, and the cost of upgrading susceptible parts.

taller tires increase clearance under the entire vehicle. And, let's face it: Lifted JKs look cool!

Common lift kits come in a variety of heights and types. To determine the correct lift for your JK you need to determine your intended application and, thus, wheel size. A spacer kit provides the smallest amount of lift at 1.75 inches. Many companies offer a 2.5-inch spring lift. One of the most common lift heights is 4 inches; more than 5 inches of lift creates a stability issue by raising the center of gravity height too much. All lifts increase the possibility of a rollover.

If you have a Sport or Sahara model JK, you can upgrade to a stock Rubicon suspension system to gain 1 inch of lift. Rubicons can run a 33-inch tire with no clearance issues under the stock fenders. With

a 1.75-inch spacer lift, you can run a 35-inch tire, but there could be some rubbing against the fenders at extreme articulation angles. With a 2.5- to 3.5-inch spring lift, 35-inch tires can be used with no rubbing on

Fender and Body Clearance

Fender clearance becomes an issue with full axle articulation and tires greater than 33 inches in diameter. Axle articulation is controlled by

The 4-inch lift on this JK allows the use of 37-inch tires. In turn, the taller tires increase ground clearance. The clearance under the low points, such as the differential center section on the front and rear axle housings, increases by nearly 3 inches over the stock Rubicon 32-inch-tall tires. Clearance under the frame increases by nearly 7 inches combined with the tires and lift.

spring and shock travel with some limitations from the suspension control arms. Lift kits with shock absorbers, or aftermarket shocks with longer travel allow more axle articulation. Suspension bushings such as the Currie Johnny Joints and MetalCloak Duroflex enhance movement and help articulation. Larger tires can also rub against the stock Rubicon rock sliders. So, if you install substantially larger tires, you should install a set of aftermarket sliders. Stock sliders can also be trimmed to size by using a cutting wheel to trim the excess material flush with the fender and bodylines.

Suspension Travel

Lift kits allow for increased suspension travel as long as the spring rates are not too high. Increased travel is important when driving off road, especially in more extreme conditions such as rock crawling.

Body Lifts for JKs

In the pre-JK days of the Wrangler model, body lifts were common to create more tire clearance. On the Wrangler TJ, for example, you really need a 6-inch lift to accommodate 37-inch-tall tires, but not so with the JK. The stock fenders and frame on the JK have more clearance, so unless you are going extreme with really big tires, a body lift is really not necessary. Additionally, a body lift raises the center of gravity a little, making the JK more tippy on side slopes and large rocks.

Suspension Springs

Springs keep the tire contact patches on the road surface or terrain as much as possible, as well as pro-viding good ride comfort. If springs are too stiff, the ride is harsh and the tires often lose contact with the road surface. If springs are too soft, the vehicle wallows and feels unstable. Springs are used to lift a 4x4 for improved tire and ground clearance and more axle articulation. Spring rates should be near stock or slightly stiffer. However, if the lift springs are too stiff, articulation, ride quality, and traction over rough surfaces are all compromised.

MetalCloak offers a 5.5-inch Lock-N-Load long-arm lift. This unique package uses a telescoping radius arm on the passenger's side on the JK. Solid radius arm systems can bind, causing premature bushing wear and excessive stress on control-arm brackets. This design allows the control arm to be locked solid in a static state for on-road driving and handling or "loaded" for off road where the passenger-side control arm can extend or compress during wheel travel. (Photo Courtesy MetalCloak)

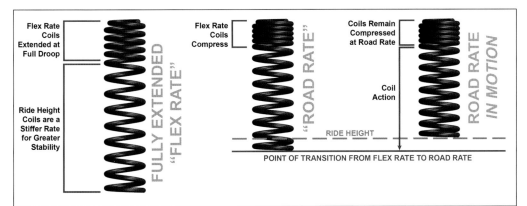

MetalCloak Road Rate True Dual Rate coil springs are wound with varied spacing between the coils. The coils at the top of the spring are wound with less spacing than the remainder of the coils. The weight of the vehicle compresses the top coils fully and the remainder of the coils slightly. This creates a spring rate for highway driving.

Off road, when a wheel is unloaded during articulation, the bound upper coils can extend, increasing wheel travel and offering more articulation. This keeps load on all four tires for a longer duration. (Photo Courtesy MetalCloak)

Currie RockJock springs are progressive-rate coils. As they compress, the rate increases more quickly than with a straight-rate spring. This reduces bottoming and limits travel. The plated discs at the bottom of each spring hold the springs in place on the spring perches on the axle housing to keep the springs from dislodging. The black cans outboard of the springs limit spring compression along with the bumpstops during bump travel. This keeps the shocks from bottoming. If shocks bottom out, they will be damaged.

Currie 4-inch lift springs lift the front of this Rubicon. Other Currie parts include the Antirock sway bar, the heavy-duty control arms with Johnny Joint rod end bushings, and Bilstein remote reservoir shock absorbers. The Johnny Joints are offered in forged, weld-on, and billet versions to give you the desired level of performance and durability for a particular application. Forged rod ends are sufficient for most applications and allow smoother suspension travel and articulation.

Dual-Rate and Progressive-Rate Springs

Dual-rate springs feature a coil design allowing some coils to bind early in suspension travel so that spring rate is increased as coils compress. A progressive-rate spring uses a design in which the coils are wound in different diameters, with different spacing between the coils, or with both different diameters and spacing. As the spring is compressed, the coil design allows the spring rate to increase throughout compression. The initial travel is softer for a more comfortable ride over smaller bumps and obstacles, but only if the soft section of the spring has not become fully compressed. As the spring is compressed, the rates become stiffer, which improves stability and control for more demanding terrain and bigger obstacles. On suspension packages designed for more than 12 inches of travel, the dual-rate springs allow the spring to stay seated in the spring perches at full extension travel. Progressive-rate springs tend to offer a smooth transition as the spring rate increases. Many companies offer dual-rate springs that are more pro-

Notice the extra bracing on the shock mount, control-arm brackets, and on the spindle. This Currie RockJock suspension is on the front of a Rubicon. The bumpstop is the light yellow knob inside the spring. The Currie kit includes the bumpstop can at the bottom of the spring. This limits travel and keeps the shock from bottoming at full compression travel. The stock rubber brake hose will be replaced with a steel braided line that is longer to accommodate the lift and increased suspension travel.

gressive than a true dual-rate spring. In most cases, a well-engineered spring for a JK lift has a spring rate close to the stock rate at static ride height. Dual-rate and progressive-rate springs are offered by AEV, Currie, Fabtech, Eibach, Rock Krawler, and MetalCloak.

Coil-Over Springs

A coil-over spring seats on perches attached to the body of the shock absorber. If the shock is a smooth body design, the installed length of the spring is fixed. If the body is threaded, the lower spring perch (also threaded) can be adjusted up or down to alter the ride height at that corner. This is beneficial to help keep the chassis level.

The primary advantages of a coil-over spring include better clearance and accessibility as well as the ability to change spring rates to fine-tune handling and articulation. Although most coil-over shocks are adjustable, you can achieve the same thing with a standard spring setup using adjustable reservoir shocks. The work involved in tuning springs and shocks is extensive. Coil-overs make it a little easier to fine tune the suspension, but for most applications, standard springs and shocks work fine, even for the more challenging rock crawling trails.

Suspension Control Arms

Suspension arms control the movement of the wheels and tires in vertical travel. They affect the amount of wheel travel and articulation. The stock JK control arms work well with stock springs, shocks, and tires for easy to moderate off-road situations. The flexible bushings on the stock control arms limit twisting and affect articulation.

For serious off roading, especially rock crawling when 35- to 37-inch tires are used, replacing the stock control arms with much stronger arms and flex bushings that facilitate easy, fluid rotation is important. Aftermarket control arms also provide increased adjustability for more precise alignment. This allows proper axle alignment and correct settings for pinion angles.

The extreme loads of larger tires and off-road activities such as rock

The stock JK track-bar brackets are formed from steel and spot-welded in place. Although they look pretty stout, in reality the brackets bend and the welds can fail when heavy loads are placed on the brackets from extreme trail four wheeling or rock crawling.

crawling place tremendous loads on the suspension bushing and mounting brackets on both the chassis and the axle housings. In addition, the brackets are exposed to and can incur damage from rocks, stumps, and other obstacles. The stock brackets often bend and break when subjected to these extreme loads. Some suspension packages include stronger brackets. In other cases, the installer can add gussets to the brackets to increase strength and reliability. Many JK builders box in the brackets with steel plate that also works as a skidplate. Mild steel plate is cut to form gussets. These are cut to fit across the bracket, rolled in some cases to fit the bracket contour, and then MIG welded in place.

Short-Arm versus Long-Arm Kits

Short-arm kits use the stock mounting locations on the JK frame. Long-arm kits have add-on brackets and crossmembers to accommodate the longer control arms, and there-

fore a long-arm kit is more expensive and more costly to install. The advantage to a long-arm kit is reduced fore and aft movement of the axle for the same amount of vertical travel. This improves ride on the highway and for high-speed off-road situations, such as desert driving. The downside of a long-arm kit in addition to the cost is clearance over rocks and other obstacles. Because the arms are longer, they are more susceptible to getting hung up on obstacles.

Long-arm suspension kits became popular with the 1997–2006 Wrangler TJ models, which have a much shorter wheelbase then the JK. The control arms on a stock TJ are fairly short. And the TJ has much less tire clearance in stock condition. To fit larger tires, even 35-inch diameter, the TJ needs about a 6-inch lift. The short control arms operate at steep angles and this affects the articulation off road and ride on pavement. The long-arm kits make a big difference on a TJ, but do not offer as much performance improvement on the JK because it has a longer wheelbase (on the two-door) and control arms that are almost 50 percent longer. The benefits to a long-arm suspension on a JK are not nearly as great as they are on the smaller, shorter TJ. The short-arm kits for a JK are suited for most applications, including the more extreme rock crawling situations. For high-speed desert driving, the long-arm kit offers some advantages of increased stability. The control arms of a long-arm kit provide less clearance over rocks. Mounting locations of the control arms on both the frame and axle make a difference in clearance.

Control Arm Joints

The stock JK control arm joints use hard rubber between the bolt bushing and the outer retainer. The rubber flexes to allow some twist in the bushing. The rubber can wear quickly with more extreme off-road driving, and it also can bind, which affects axle articulation.

Many suspension lift kits include control arms that are much stronger than stock and they use a rod–end-style joint. If you're going to

Long-arm suspension packages offer slightly better geometry over the stock geometry. Most lift kits retain the stock geometry. Long-arm suspensions became popular on the Wrangler TJ, which has short control arms. Because the JK stock arms are longer, and because only a 4-inch lift is needed to fit 37-inch tires, the geometry problems such as bump steer toe change are not nearly as severe. The long-arm kits offer improved stability and control at high speed and in desert driving conditions. MetalCloak's long-arm Lock-N-Load package has a unique design where the passenger-side front control arm compresses and extends for off-road travel and improved articulation. (Photo Courtesy MetalCloak)

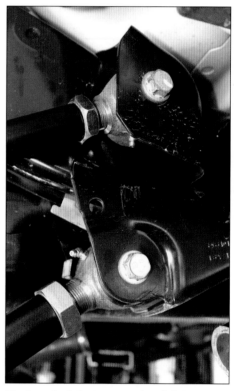

Rod-end-style suspension joints, such as these Currie Johnny Joints, offer superior strength, durability, and freedom of movement, important for quick articulation when encountering big ruts, bumps, and rocks. Threaded end joints, such as the Johnny Joint, feature urethane bushing ends and provide 30 degrees of overall travel.

The Johnny Joint is rebuildable and features a zerk fitting so it can be easily greased. This improves performance and makes this style suspension joint a good investment.

MetalCloak's Durotrak joint is low maintenance, allows high misalignment (34 degree), is self-centering, can be rebuilt, and offers an OEM-quality ride. The Durotrak joint delivers great flexibility in both transverse and rotational planes. (Photo Courtesy MetalCloak)

spend considerable time off roading your JK, a set of aftermarket control arm joints, such as the Currie Johnny Joint, Fabtech 5 Ton Joint, MetalCloak Duroflex Joint, or Rock Krawler Joint, is an essential upgrade. These joints reduce binding, allow much freer articulation, and are much stronger.

Track Bars

Track bars locate the front and rear axle assemblies laterally in the chassis. Without a track bar, the axle

The RockJock rear track bar for the JK offers increased strength. The bar is steel tube with threaded adjustable joints for perfect axle alignment. The provided bracket is also much stronger.

The RockJock front track bar is manufactured from 4130 chrome-moly 1.250 diameter .250-wall-thickness steel tubing. The axle-end Johnny Joint adjusts for precise centering of the axle housing in the chassis. Currie also makes a track bar relocation bracket to better align the track bar.

housing may walk sideways, which makes driving almost impossible. Front and rear track bars establish the front and rear roll centers, which are the point of rotation for the axles. Stock JK track bars are made from solid forgings, although aftermarket bars are usually heavy-duty alloy tubing. The stock JK track bars are not adjustable for length. They are adequate for stock applications or small lifts up to 2 inches. Larger lifts and bigger tires require beefier bars and some adjustment. The sideways adjustment allows the axle housing to be centered within the chassis. The strongest track bars use spherical rod-end-style joints, such as the Currie Johnny Joint. Other heavy-duty joints that perform in extreme off-road conditions include MetalCloak, JKS, and Rock Krawler. The stock axle housings allow vertical adjustments of the track bar, but the track bar remains as level as possible. As mentioned in the control

arm section, when running bigger tires with a significant lift, the brackets on the frame and axle housings should be reinforced with gussets to avoid damage and bending on the more extreme trails.

Shock Absorbers

Shocks control the motion and energy of the springs; essentially, shocks are spring dampeners. If the shocks are too soft, the vehicle wallows and bounces, and if they are too stiff, it is jarring and uncomfortable. Unlike on-road driving, the shock absorbers on a backcountry rig are subject to extreme loads. High-quality, aluminum internal floating piston shocks always serve you better than the low-cost, and often low-quality, steel-bodied non-rebuildable steel shocks. In addition, if a shock is too stiff, tire contact with the ground and articulation are reduced. If a shock is too short on a lifted 4x4, vertical travel is reduced along with articulation.

Shock absorber dampening rates also control how quickly weight is transferred when cornering, braking, and accelerating, and when the axles are articulating. A shock absorber with softer rates transfers weight more slowly than a stiffer shock. This affects transitional handling balance and how quickly weight moves from a tire when it encounters a rock to the tire that is still level. The thickness, diameter, and number of valves inside the shock body largely determine the dampening rate. The shock fluid flows through the valves on the shock rod, and different valve sets come into play at different shaft speeds. Some shocks use additional bypass bleed ports within the bore of the shock for improved low-speed ride comfort and control.

Different valves and bypasses control dampening rates for different shaft and piston speeds. This allows fine tuning of valving to accommodate different situations ranging from driving twisty mountain roads to rock crawling and rolling bumps in the desert. Lifted rigs need longer shocks to take advantage of the increased spring travel and articulation. When choosing a lift kit for your rig, purchase one that has springs and shocks as a coordinated package along with any necessary control arms, bushings, and other hardware. Shock travel should be limited so that the shock cannot fully extend, which can damage the piston and internal valving. In compression, bumpstops are also used to limit travel so that damage to the shock internals is avoided.

You need the correct length shock for your lift package and application. If the shock length is too short, it lim-its suspension articulation, but if it's too long, the shocks won't fit on the brackets. Fox and other shock companies have come up with a process to measure your suspension travel to help you select the correct shocks for your JK. First, install the shortest bumpstop spacers and ensure that the tires do not rub on the fenders or that the chassis or engine does not contact the steering, etc. With the JK at ride height, measure from bump stop mount to the top of the bumpstop spacer. Then measure from the bottom of the upper shock mount to the center of the lower shock mount. Next, you need to account for the stem bushings, so subtract 0.70 inch between these two points. The calculation between the measurements is the minimum collapsed length of your shocks. Choose shocks that have a slightly shorter collapsed length than your measurements.

Shock quality is important. Cheap shocks are prone to breaking near mounting points and often blow out the internal valving in extreme conditions, which renders the shocks useless.

Shock Valving

Shock valving determines how a shock absorber controls spring compression and extension during suspension travel. Inside the shock, a piston on top of the shock rod has valve shims and these slide through shock oil. The design of the piston as well as number, thickness, and width of the valve shims largely determine how quickly or slowly the shock strokes through its travel. Different valve sets come into play at different shaft speeds. Slow shaft speeds use valves to control ride and tire contact over rolling bumps and ruts as well as when rock crawling at low speeds.

Low-speed valving can affect how quickly weight is transferred from inside tires to outside tires when turning into a corner. Shock rates are also speed sensitive. The faster the shaft moves up or down, the stiffer the shock rate becomes. Shaft speeds increase when a steeper bump or rut is encountered. And the same bump hit at 10 mph has a slower shaft speed than when hit at 20 mph.

Shocks are designed with different valving rates in compression versus extension. Adjustable shocks allow quick changes to valving in bump (compression) travel and sometimes both bump and rebound (extension travel).

High-speed valving affects ride on small bumps, ruts, and washboard sections off road, and potholes and bumps on the highway. High-speed valving also comes into play if you slam into a rock too fast or drop off a rock too abruptly; for example, if you drop off a 2-foot ledge too fast and the front shock compression valving is too stiff and the rear shock extension valving is too stiff, the abrupt weight transfer from rear tires to front could cause the rear tires to lift off the ground. In extreme cases, this could make a rollover more likely.

Low-speed valving affects handling balance when turning is initiated going into a turn near the limits of traction, not something that is likely on a Wrangler JK unless in an emergency maneuvering situation. It affects the ride over rolling bumps and ruts at moderate speeds. It can also influence how the suspension reacts to articulation when rock crawling. If compression valving is too stiff, the axle articulation is limited so that the body of the JK leans more. If rebound valving is too stiff, the downhill tire may be lifted off the ground. Finding the best compromise for all conditions is challenging.

Shock Travel

Shock travel needs to allow full articulation by the suspension but should not be so much that the shock is allowed to reach full extension or compression, which can damage the internal valving and destroy the function of the shock. It is also important that the shock travel be limited in compression so that the piston cannot bottom out, which can also blow out the shock. The JK uses bumpstops to keep this from happening. When a lift is installed, it is important that the bumpstops still keep the shock from reaching full compression. Adjustable aftermarket bumpstops can be used to assure this does not happen. Hydraulic bumpstops slow the compression as full travel is reached. This further protects the shock and allows a smoother transition than a solid bumpstop.

Shaft Diameter

Shocks on modified Wrangler JKs take large loads. Most aftermarket shock absorbers designed for lift kits have larger-than-stock shafts. This increases strength and reduces shaft flex, which can lead to premature wear or failure. Although larger shafts are a great idea, the downside is a reduction of piston area unless the shock body is a larger diameter.

Piston Area

The piston area of a shock determines how much fluid the shock can move through the valves. More piston area increases the volume of fluid flowing through the shock. This allows more precise valving control of shock movements. More fluid flow can also reduce heat buildup in the

shock. If the shock oil becomes too hot, the oil foams, loses its viscosity, and the vehicle experiences shock fade. As a result, the springs are not adequately dampened and then the driver experiences poor suspension performance.

Internal Floating Piston Shocks

Monotube and dual tube gas shocks are the standard for off-road and many other applications. The dual tube design features one tube inside the other in the shock body and this design has been in use for decades. The monotube shock, a single gas-pressurized shock body, was released the 1950s, and through the decades it has been highly refined.

Bypass shocks were developed for off-road racing where high shaft speed and long travel cause considerable heat buildup. The fluid in the shock can lose viscosity with high heat causing the shock to fade or lose dampening characteristics. An additional problem with OEM replacement shocks is aeration of the fluid. Unless the shock fluid is carefully controlled, air can be introduced into the shock housing. The same effect occurs when air gets into brake fluid. Because air is highly compressible, and shock fluid is not, the shock is rendered ineffective when air is allowed inside the chamber.

Stock Replacement

When a JK is lifted, more shock travel is needed. With stock shocks, 1.5-inch spacer lifts can work adequately, but stock shocks wear quickly when larger, heavier tires are used. When larger off-road tires are used, it is best to upgrade to extended-travel, heavy-duty shocks. Aftermarket aluminum internal floating piston (IFP) shocks use high-quality components and have a much greater performance potential. These shocks absorb and dissipate heat far better than stock shocks, so you maintain control of your JK. In addition, they have much better

The Dirt Logic 2.5 reservoir shock is Fabtech's top-of-the-line shock for the JK. The body is 2.5-inch-diameter stainless steel with a 2.25-inch-diameter billet aluminum piston. Note the large-diameter shaft made of 7/8-inch-diameter steel. They also feature spherical bearings at the mounting points for quiet, smooth, trouble-free operation. Not only are these shocks tough, but also they are tuned for specific applications. We have tested these shocks for more than six months and they have endured some hard wheeling on rocks, ruts and bumps, washboard roads, whoop-de-doos, and bumpy, rocky roads. They have performed exceptionally well in all conditions including some extreme rock crawling.

Prior to running Fabtech's Dirt Logic shocks, we tested their Stealth shocks, a low-cost monotube shock. The performance is impressive in almost all conditions. These shocks are a great value, but if you run more extreme rock crawling trails or high-speed desert roads, you want a more durable high-end shock. But for less extreme four wheeling with a lifted JK, these shocks do a great job.

The MetalCloak JK Wrangler Game-Changer Mid Arm Suspension System allows travel found only in long-arm kits. This system features the 6Pak long travel shocks, MetalCloak True Dual Rate coil springs, Duroflex control arms with the patented Duroflex joint, and front and rear solid chrome-moly track bars. This system bolts onto stock mounts and has 14 inches of shock travel. (Photo Courtesy Metal Cloak)

seals to keep the gas charge separated from the hydraulic oil. This reduces the chance of aeration (foaming) and maintains consistent performance.

Remote Reservoir Shocks

Remote reservoir shocks feature an external reservoir that contains additional hydraulic fluid. The increased fluid volume promotes better cooling and the additional surface area helps dissipate internal heat. These shocks also allow for additional valve and bypass options to better tune the shock for a wider variety of situations. Remote reservoir shocks allow improved isolation of the pressurized gas from the hydraulic fluid, which reduces aeration (foaming), so the shocks effectively maintain the dampening rate. This improves shock control over extreme bumps and rocks, and in high-speed situations.

Remote reservoir shocks were developed for off-road racing but are becoming common on the more extreme JK builds. Although ideally suited for high-speed desert applications, the reservoir shock also improves performance when rock crawling by providing better tuning

options and improved cooling. Most aluminum-body shocks can be taken apart by a professional for tuning the valving. Tuning and rebuilding shock absorbers is something of an art form and a pressurized nitrogen source is needed to recharge gas shocks. Tunable and rebuildable shocks for the JK are available from Fabtech, Fox, King, Walker Evans, and Bilstein.

One of the newest shocks on

MetalCloak's Floating Shock Body Technology provides a platform featuring parallel shafts extending from a floating body, centralized by dual opposing reservoirs. This design allows for twice the usual stroke compared to typical industry shocks. Designed specifically for applications where space is limited, the 6Pak shock body extends shafts from both sides of a floating remote reservoir and allows for a much smaller compressed shock. This equates to increased shock travel in a tight space. (Photo Courtesy MetalCloak)

the market for the JK is the ARB Old Man Emu (OME) BP-51 bypass shock absorber. Most shocks are velocity sensitive, and that means the faster the shock piston travels, the greater the dampening force. This is true of the BP-51, but it also features piston bypass technology. Although most shock absorbers generate dampening based on fluid flowing through the piston, the BP-51 offers an

The new Old Man Emu BP-51 internal bypass shocks from ARB have remote reservoirs for increased oil volume and reduced temperatures. In addition, they use a shaft guard, external adjusters for setting valve rates in both rebound and compression, as well as a 6061 aluminum body with a 51-mm bore. In testing, we have found that these shocks are excellent and the external adjustments allow easy fine-tuning.

The Fox 2.0 remote reservoir shocks are some of the finest over-the-counter high-performance shocks you can buy for your JK. The 2.0 has a 2-inch-diameter main body and remote reservoir, which are made of 6061-T6 aluminum. The 5/8-inch hard chrome-plated shock shaft takes harsh impacts. High-quality seals set the Fox shocks apart from others: The main, wiper, and scraper seals defend against dirt and contamination entering the shock. If dirt and other particles enter the shock fluid, shock performance deteriorates. Pliant nitrile rubber allows for increased suspension articulation for maximum performance. The Fox 2.0 and 2.5 come in a variety of lengths for lifts ranging from 1.5 to 6 inches. These shocks are used with the Currie RockJock 4-inch lift package.

Bilstein makes a monotube remote reservoir 5160 series shock. This shock is based on the 5100 series, which has been an industry standard replacement shock for the JK since its launch. We have also tested the 5100 series non-reservoir shock. Like the Fabtech Stealth, this shock works quite well in a variety of off-road situations, even though the valving is little more biased toward high-speed desert driving. Shock absorbers fade and lose rate when subjected to high-speed driving on rough, bumpy desert terrain. Upgrading to reservoir shocks with a greater oil volume reduces shock oil overheating.

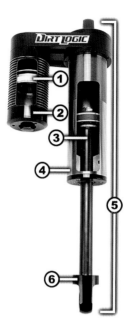

Dirt Logic offers top-quality shocks that can take on the most challenging rock crawling and trail driving conditions. The remote reservoir shock has significantly more oil capacity than a standard monotube shock and the extra oil capacity dissipates more heat and resists foaming, so the shock dampening is maintained and suspension articulation is properly controlled. If you are putting large loads on your suspension and stroking through your shock travel, remote reservoir shocks perform far better than a standard monotube shock during a day of driving. Shock valving is set up for the specific vehicle and application, so ideal control and ride comfort are attained. (Photo Courtesy Fabtech)

additional path from one chamber to the other and around the piston in the form of bypass passages. Some fluid flows through the piston and some fluid bypasses around the piston in the bypass passages. This allows the shock to adjust to varying conditions ranging from smooth roads to rock crawling and high-speed desert travel. As the piston nears the ends of travel, the bypass technology slows the piston speed to reduce the harsh impacts of the piston bottoming out at the end of travel. BP-51 shock absorber bodies are manufactured using aircraft-grade 6061 anodized aluminum to dissipate heat more efficiently than steel or alloy steel and provide superior corrosion resistance. The OME BP-51 shocks are easily adjustable by the user in both compression and rebound.

Anti-Roll Bars and Articulation

Anti-roll bars (sway bars) control body roll when cornering. On the road, sway bars effectively share cornering forces from one side of the suspension to the other. Off road, sway bars greatly reduce the ability of the axles to articulate by reducing travel. Disconnecting the sway bars helps articulation off road, but hurts handling and stability on road.

The Currie Antirock sway bars are designed to work with full articulation and no need to disconnect them. They are available with either steel or aluminum arms (aluminum shown here). The only downside is increased body roll on the highway due to the softer anti-roll bar rate. The additional roll is noticeable, but easily adapted to. Most sway bar end links, such as these Currie Antirock sway bar end links, are adjustable for length. It is important to adjust the length so that no preload is present on the sway bar when the vehicle is on the ground at rest. If you add or remove a significant amount of weight from the front or rear (as with a winch bumper and a winch), it is good practice to re-adjust the sway bar end links.

As the suspension springs compress near the maximum amount, a hydraulic bumpstop makes contact with the bump pad on the axle housing. The hydraulic piston controls the compression rate of the spring and keeps it from becoming coil bound. The Fox Shox hydraulic bumpstops feature a replaceable Delrin pad. The internal nitrogen gas charge can be adjusted with a Schrader valve for fine-tuning the compression rate.

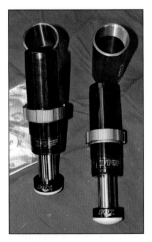

The Fox hydraulic bumpstops feature a threaded aluminum body and an adjuster ring for setting travel. The steel sleeves are threaded inside and hold the bumpstop. The sleeves can be welded into place in the frame.

The EVO No Limits On Demand sway bar disconnect allows you to bypass the computer and disconnect the front sway bar on Rubicon models. Compressed air actuates the disconnect. The sway bar disconnects at any time, in any gear, and with any amount of articulation.

The All J Hemi-powered Rubicon features the Nth Degree suspension lift. The articulation here is as good as you can get. Nth Degree created a great package for the JK. The design is now sold by American Expedition Vehicles (AEV) and is one of the best lifts on the market.

Even a moderate build with a good lift kit can provide excellent articulation. This Rubicon's stock front sway bar has been disconnected, which allows excellent suspension travel. The body is leaning very little here. It's nice for the driver but a great comfort for the passenger.

The Wrangler Rubicon comes with an electric front sway bar disconnect. Several companies make quick release kits so that sway bars can be disconnected and reconnected easily on other JK models.

Most vehicles have attaching bolts on the sway bar end links that can be removed fairly easily when going off road. Only one side needs to be removed on each bar. Make sure the end link is out of harm's way with a zip-tie or bungee. Replacement sway bars are available from Currie, TeraFlex, Addco, and Hellwig.

Articulation allows the axles of a 4x4 to move in the largest possible arc. This keeps the body more level over large obstacles such as rocks, ruts, and bumps. Good articulation improves not only vehicle stability but also tire traction by keeping all four tires in contact with the ground.

Sway bars (anti-roll bars) minimize body roll when cornering. However, they also minimize axle articulation. Axle articulation is the measure of the full vertical travel of the tire in both compression and extension travel.

Taller springs allow more travel. Shock absorbers that are too short for the springs limit travel, as does a connected sway bar. Sway bar disconnects improve travel. The Wrangler Rubicon comes with an electric front sway bar disconnect. Off-road sway bars, such as the Currie Antirock sway bars, allow full articulation without the need to disconnect the sway bars. The trade-off increases body roll on the highway when cornering. Sway bar disconnects are an easy and inexpensive way to disconnect stock sway bars on non-Rubicon JKs.

Although more body roll on the highway may feel a little unnerving, it is not a significant factor for a rollover. A vehicle's tendency to roll is largely determined the sprung weight of the vehicle, the height of the center of gravity (above ground), tire traction, and the track width of the vehicle. Cornering force or lateral

The stock steering tie-rod and drag link are not sturdy and the steering is exposed on the JK, so it's susceptible to damage in the rocks. And the tie-rod ends and drag link tend to wear quickly in rock crawling. Don Alexander's Grizzlycon is equipped with the Currie Currectlync steering. This system is made from 4130 chrome-moly 1.5-inch OD tubing. The tie-rod ends are larger and fully adjustable, can be easily replaced, and are greasable. Because all four tie-rod ends are identical, only one spare needs to be carried.

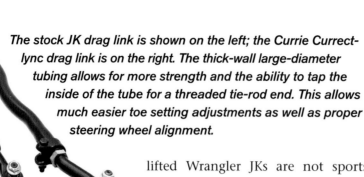

The stock JK drag link is shown on the left; the Currie Currect-lync drag link is on the right. The thick-wall large-diameter tubing allows for more strength and the ability to tap the inside of the tube for a threaded tie-rod end. This allows much easier toe setting adjustments as well as proper steering wheel alignment.

"G"s also affect the rollover potential on the highway: A lighter vehicle is less likely to roll at a given cornering speed, a lifted vehicle is more likely to roll, and a wider vehicle is less likely to roll. Where bigger tires and a lift on a JK can increase the likelihood of a rollover by as much as 20 percent, disconnected sway bars increase the risk less than 1 percent. Even with a 4-inch lift and 37-inch-tall tires, a JK is likely to start sliding before it rolls over unless the outside tires hit a curb, pothole, or something that can increase the lateral grip. In addition,

lifted Wrangler JKs are not sports cars, and on-highway high-speed cornering was never a design goal for the Wrangler.

Articulation is most important in allowing the axle housing to rotate more freely on uneven terrain when driving through ruts and over bumps and rocks. More axle articulation means keeping both driver- and passenger-side tires in contact with the ground over larger obstacles. If the axle can rotate more freely, the body of the JK stays more level. More articulation improves stability and traction. The sway bars should always be reconnected before driving any distance or at speed on the highway.

The MetalCloak high-steer system raises the track bar to correct steering geometry in conjunction with the drag-link flip hi-steer for use when lifting a Jeep JK more than 4.5 inches. This bracket also incorporates a raised mount for the steering stabilizer for added protection.

Steering System

Steering systems are not the first item anyone considers when planning upgrades on a Jeep. Nevertheless, of the things that can go wrong on the trail, steering system failure is one of the few (short of a major crash) that require repairs on the trail. Many components can break and you can still drive to a highway or at least be towed. But without steering, you are dead in the water until repairs are made. When a Wrangler JK owner comes to that realization, either from experience or education (such as reading this book), priorities change. A strong steering system means that the chance of system failure is greatly reduced. For the greatest strength and reliability in the most extreme conditions, especially when running 35-inch-or-larger tires, almost every component in the system should be upgraded. The steering system can be broken down into three categories: linkages, spindle, and hydraulics.

Steering Linkages

Steering linkages include the pitman arm, drag link, tie-rod, and the tie-rod ends, which attach the linkages to the steering arms on the knuckles. The pitman arm attaches to the steering box and the drag link. It turns the rotary motion of the steering gears into linear motion that ultimately steers the wheels.

The pitman arm on the stock JK is strong enough for most applications. When a lift exceeds about 5 inches, a dropped pitman arm can be used to keep the steering geometry in alignment. The stock drag link, tie-rod, and tie-rod ends are not up to the task when running big tires on the more extreme terrain. In fact, the stock drag link and tie-rod can bend easily if large

The JK knuckles tend to flex under extreme loads, which accelerates upper and lower ball joint wear. A brace has been welded to this hub to improve rigidity and durability. The ball joints attach the knuckle to the spindle. These are Dynatrac ball joints. The Reid Racing JK steering knuckles are extremely strong and durable and do not require bracing.

The stock JK ball joints on the left each pair wear quickly, even on stock JKs. When lifted with larger tires, wear accelerates. The wear can be bad enough to cause shimmy and wobble, not a pleasant experience. The ball joints on the right of each pair are the Dynatrac versions. They work in the stock knuckles and spindles with no modifications and are greasable, rebuildable, and much stronger than stock. They can last five times longer than the stock ball, making them more cost-effective than stock replacements even though they cost significantly more than stock replacements.

The inner C-gusset strengthens the front steering knuckle. The Artec design is strong. The gusset is MIG welded in place and sometimes a little fabrication is necessary to get the ideal fit.

Worn ball joints on the JK can cause a wheel shimmy, and this JK was experiencing a shimmy. Although shimmy, or death wobble, can occur at any speed, it is more likely at higher speeds from 35 to 70 mph, especially when a bump is encountered. Although not obvious in the photo, this ball joint feels loose and sloppy, indicating it is worn and needs replacement. New stock replacement ball joints were installed. Within about 1,000 miles, the shimmy returned. Replacing those ball joints with the Dynatrac versions solved the problem.

rocks or other obstacles are hit. Currie makes two heavy-duty steering systems, the Currectlync tie-rod and drag link as well as the Modular Extreme Duty Currectlync package. These and systems like them provide strength and reliability for most demanding off-road applications. The stock tie-rod ends wear quickly, especially with larger tires. Several aftermarket steering assemblies are available, which greatly increase durability and reliability. Most use thick-wall chrome-moly tubing and heavy-duty steel and greasable tie-rod ends. Steering linkages upgrades are worthwhile for strength and safety. Many other manufacturers offer heavy-duty steering systems as well, including Metal-Cloak, Fabtech, Rubicon Express, and Street Smart.

Spindles, Knuckles, and Ball Joints

The stock JK's knuckles and spindles are strong and work well, even with big lifts and 37-inch tires. However, the stock ball joints are another story. Even a completely stock JK sees rapid wear in the ball joints. Worn ball joints are a primary cause of shimmy and death wobble at highway speeds. Stock ball joints should be replaced when worn or if a JK has an upgrade to 35-inch tires or larger. It is good practice to use one of the aftermarket upper and lower ball joints kits, such as Dynatrac. These are durable and can be rebuilt, which over time saves money and steering hassles. As an example, the Dynatrac ball joints are made from heat-treated, billet steel bodies with chrome-moly stems and heat-treated, precision-ground stainless steel ball. They are rebuildable and easily serviced with grease fittings.

Steering a lifted JK on aired down 37-inch tires in four-wheel drive can be a chore, especially at low speeds in big rocks. Upgrades to the power steering system can make a big difference. The PSC power steering fluid reservoir is manufactured out of 6061T6 aluminum and is TIG welded. The reservoir features a 35-micron cartridge filter inside that can be serviced through the large fill cap.

Power steering fluid can get hot, especially in more extreme situations. A cooler for the fluid is important. PSC uses the Derale coolers in its power steering kit. The cooler kit uses a custom bracket to mount two coolers in front of the radiator in the JK. One cooler is for the power steering; the other is used for the transmission.

Power steering rams can create significant forces. One end mounts to the axle housing and the other end mounts to the tie-rod. This Currie bracket uses three clamping bolts to ensure that the ram does not move the bracket on the tie rod. The earlier Currie design used only two bolts.

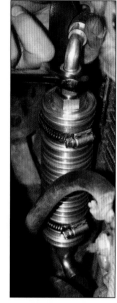

An off-road JK with large tires and high lifts places the power steering box under a considerable load, and this can generate a lot of heat. Power steering coolers are common upgrades on rock crawlers and trail machines. The relatively small Howe power steering cooler is still a tight fit in front of the radiator. A custom bracket was fabricated to mount the cooler.

Power steering systems create considerable pressure. Installing fittings into hoses is tricky, requiring a lot of force. The KoulTools hosepress is a handy device that makes the job easy and provides a leak-proof seal.

Steering Hydraulics

The hydraulic components of the steering system include the power steering box, power steering pump, power steering fluid reservoir, and a steering dampener (or an add-on power steering ram assist). The stock JK power steering hydraulics are sufficient for a stock vehicle with 31- to 32-inch tires. However, when you add big tires, the strain on the hydraulics is exponentially higher and the stock components wear quickly and often fail from the extreme loads placed on the system when off roading in extreme circumstances. In addition, the stock power steering pump does not create enough pressure to assist the steering efforts of the driver when rock crawling on aired down tires. The loads create high heat that accelerates wear and affects the other components in the system.

A higher-pressure power steering pump is needed for the more extreme conditions created by a lifted JK on big aired down tires. Aftermarket pumps usually come with new hoses and fittings designed to handle the higher pressures created by the new pump.

Most aftermarket pumps come with a fluid cooler and a larger fluid reservoir. Power steering pumps from PSC and Howe increase fluid output and flow for improved steering control and reduced steering effort. Power steering pumps such as these are needed when a power ram assist is used.

The power steering box is another weak link on modified JKs. Although the box itself provides adequate performance for off-road terrain, the increased loads can cause the sector shaft housing to flex. This binds the sector shaft (a sector shaft

Stock JK steering boxes often fail because big tires on extreme trails place a sustained and high load on the boxes. When this box was disassembled, the fluid was burned and metal bits were found. The sector shaft (the part protruding from the box on the left of the photo) was badly scarred. The snout on the box containing the sector shaft flexes, putting high loads on the shaft. This bind either wears the shaft prematurely or causes it to break. The shaft in this box was close to breaking when it started to seize.

You never want to see this on the trail. The sector shaft has been sheared at the pitman arm so there is no steering control. The only option is to replace the steering box on the trail because you cannot tow the vehicle without steering. In this case, the driver had the good fortune of being on a trail with friends and close to a highway. A replacement box was located and a couple of people on the run had the tools and skills to replace the box on the spot. It took only six hours to get moving again, not the most fun day of wheeling.

attaches the steering gears to the pitman arm), increasing loads and heat buildup as well as making steering more difficult. The accelerated wear can cause the sector shaft to seize or even break and debris from increased wear can damage the steering pump. The steering effort either becomes extreme or there is no steering at all if the sector shaft breaks. Most aftermarket steering boxes use a modified stock box to reduce steering effort in extreme conditions. Some boxes reinforce the mounting ears and the sector shaft housing to reduce or eliminate the flex that can cause increased wear or failure of the sector shaft.

The stock steering dampener is suitable only for stock JKs or mild builds; they wear quickly. One of the most effective modifications to ease steering loads in rocks and other difficult situations is a power ram assist. The ram assist replaces the steering dampener. It helps reduce steering effort by using additional hydraulic force to assist steering. You should replace the stock tie-rod with an aftermarket version with a strong mount for the ram. It is important to brace the mounting bracket on the front axle housing because the forces fed into the bracket are several times greater.

Although most aftermarket pumps and power steering boxes come with higher-pressure hoses and fittings, make sure the plumbing is up to the task. Because pressures are higher, so is heat buildup. Add a power steering fluid cooler and a higher-capacity aftermarket reservoir to the system.

The power steering ram replaces the steering dampener between the axle housing and the tie-rod. The PSC Steering ram puts out plenty of force to make steering easy even in the most difficult spots in the rocks and while the front locker is engaged.

The PSC power steering box uses a more durable sector shaft. The valving in the PSC steering box is similar to a stock JK, so that road feel is similar to stock. This design almost eliminates flex in the snout and substantially reduces the chance of a sector shaft breaking.

A higher-output pump is needed when upgrading the power steering box and adding a power ram. The PSC pump is individually tuned to work with each steering box they manufacture.

Once the ram has been bolted to the reinforced axle housing bracket and the Currie tie-rod ram bracket, custom fitted high-pressure hoses can be added.

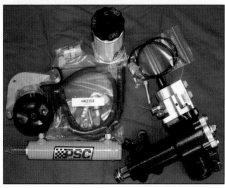

The PSC power steering system is suited for rock crawling, trail driving, and other extreme off-road conditions. It uses a custom modified power steering box, a power ram, a higher-output power steering pump, and an aluminum power steering reservoir with internal fluid filter as well as the fittings needed for installation.

Suspension and Steering Alignment

To get the best performance out of the suspension and steering, you need to consider several important alignment issues on the Jeep Wrangler JK. These include front axle toe setting, front axle lateral position, front axle square to chassis centerline, front axle caster, rear axle lateral position, rear axle square to chassis centerline, pinion angle, and steering wheel alignment.

Front Axle Toe Setting

The JK's ideal toe setting is 3/16-inch inward, although some, such as Currie, prefer 1/8-inch toe-out. Zero toe can cause wandering at speed. Toe is adjusted with the tie-rod. A simple way to measure toe is to place a mark on each front tire near the middle of the tread. Rotate the marks to the front of the tire and measure. Then rotate the marks to the rear of the tire and measure again. If the difference is greater at the rear, toe-in is present. If it is greater at the front, toe-out is present. Adjust the settings with the tie-rod until the desired setting is found.

Front Axle Lateral Position

The front axle needs to be centered in the chassis, to eliminate offset to either side. If the axle is offset, tire clearance could be an issue. Misalignment could cause a difference in handling when turning right versus left. Lateral position is adjusted with the track bar. The center of the axle housing should align with the centerline of the chassis. You can measure the distance from a hub to the chassis on each side. The distance should be equal.

Front Axle Square to Chassis Centerline

The front axle needs to be square in the chassis. To best determine this, bring the JK to a service center and place the vehicle on an alignment rack. Take a measurement from a fixed point along the frame rail to the hub or a flange on the axle. Driver- and passenger-side measurement should be equal. If the axle housing is twisted, tire scrub and tire wear accelerate. Misalignment could cause a difference in handling when turning right versus left. To square the axle, adjust the upper and/or lower control arms. The upper control arms should be the exact same

Once all the steering components are in place, it is important to check the toe setting. Marks are placed on the driver- and passenger-side front tires in line with the axle center line. The measurement is taken in the front. Then the tires are rotated 180 degrees and the same marks are used to measure at the back of the tires. If the rear measurement is greater than the front, the tires are toed-in. If the front measurement is greater, the tires are toed-out. Some prefer toe-in, others toe-out, but we usually use about 3/16 inch of toe-in.

length. The lower control arms should also be the same length. Driver- and passenger-side wheelbase measurements should be the same.

Front Axle Caster

The ideal front caster angle for the Jeep Wrangler JK is 5-degrees positive (upper ball joint trails lower ball joint). Adjust the upper and/or lower control arms to set caster. Caster can be measured with an angle finder, preferably an electronic style. An alignment rack is the best way to set caster.

Rear Axle Lateral Position

The rear axle needs to be centered in the chassis with no offset to either side. If the axle is offset, tire clearance could be an issue. Misalignment could cause a difference in handling when turning right versus left. Lateral position is adjusted with the track bar.

Rear Axle Square to Chassis Centerline

The rear axle needs to be square in the chassis. If the axle housing is rotated so the wheelbase is shorter on one side compared to the other, the tires scrub and tire wear accelerates. Misalignment could cause a difference in handling when turning right versus left. To square the axle, adjust the upper and/or lower control arms. The upper control arms should be the exact same length. The lower control arms should also be the same length. Driver- and passenger-side wheelbase measurements should be the same.

Pinion Angle

The ideal pinion angle range for the stock Jeep Wrangler JK is 4–7 degrees. The angle varies depending on the setup and equipment on a given vehicle. With CV joint driveshafts, the pinion angle is 1.5 degrees. The goal is to get the pinion shaft of the rear differential housing parallel to the output shaft of the transmission.

Steering Wheel Angle

With the front tires pointed straight ahead, the steering wheel needs to be perfectly centered. A clock spring in the steering wheel works with the electronic stability control (ESC) computer to keep the JK stable when cornering. If the steering wheel is not centered, the computer thinks the vehicle is turning. When the vehicle is turned in this circumstance, the ESC may engage the anti-lock braking system (ABS) or cut engine power because it senses that the vehicle is sliding when it isn't. This can be unnerving on the highway. You can center the steering wheel by rolling the vehicle forward so that the front tires point straight ahead. Then adjust the drag link length in or out until the steering wheel is centered.

JEEP JK PROFILE

Fabtech Motorsports's 2014 Wrangler JK Unlimited Rubicon

Fabtech Motorsports began building off-road suspension systems almost 30 years ago. The company offers a full array of suspension systems for several Jeep Wrangler models, including the JK. They offer 3- and 5-inch kits in both short- and long-arm styles. Fabtech has built several Jeeps for research and development, testing, and off-road event displays. All their Jeeps see use on extreme trails at Jeep and 4x4 events and for testing.

The Fabtech JK undergoes extreme testing at places such as Johnson Valley's notorious Hammers, Cougar Buttes, Calico, Stoddard Valley, Big Bear Lake's John Bull Trail, and the Rubicon. Some of the Jeep events attended by the Fabtech crew where the Rubicon has been put through its paces on extreme terrain include Moab's Easter Jeep Safari, Jeep Jamboree, Tierra del Sol's Desert Safari, Cal 4 Wheel's High Desert Roundup, the Big Bear Forest Fest, and Sierra Trek.

The Fabtech 2014 JK Unlimited Rubicon is equipped with a Fabtech 3-inch lift with coil-over conversion on the front and Fabtech 3-inch lift with dual-rate coil springs in the rear. Control arms are Fabtech long-arm .250 wall with "5-Ton" rebuildable joints front and rear. Fabtech Dirt Logic 2.25-inch reservoir shocks control the springs at all four corners. Front and rear axle assemblies are Dynatrac ProRock 60 with ARB air lockers. The front track bar is a Fabtech chrome-moly adjustable bar; the rear has a Fabtech track bar. Steering links are from Dynatrac. The steering box is stock; the power steering pump, cooler, and reservoir are from PSC. The hydraulic steering dampener uses a Fabtech custom cylinder. The steering dampener tie-rod bracket is a Fabtech design.

Fabtech's 2014 Wrangler JKU crawls up the rocks at the Gatekeeper on the notorious John Bull Trail during the Big Bear Forest Fest. The 3-inch coil-over long-arm lift with the Fabtech Dirt Logic reservoir shocks allows excellent articulation. Travel is good and clearances are enough with flat fenders to allow the use of Nitto 37x12.50R17LT tires on Ultra beadlock wheels.

The Fabtech 3-inch coil-over lift requires a hoop (included in the kit) to attach the coil-over spring and shock to the frame. The shocks are the tune-able Dirt Logic reservoir shocks by Fabtech. The bracket on the coil-over hoop allows the sway bar end link to be attached out of the way of the axle when wheeling off road.

The Fabtech JK uses a Magnaflow cat-back exhaust and an aFe cold-air intake. Additional skidplates are from Rock Hard. Fenders are aluminum and the front and rear bumpers and rock sliders are all from Poison Spyder. A Warn Zeon 10S winch with wireless remotes facilitates vehicle recovery. Auxiliary lighting is from Rigid and the additional roll cage bracing is a custom design from Fabtech. Like many in the Jeep JK parts industry, the Fabtech Motorsports crew actively participates in off roading. The hands-on, real-world approach translates into a better product for the Jeep enthusiast.

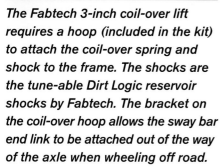

The Fabtech JK features Dynatrac ProRock 60 axles with ARB air lockers. The Fabtech Dirt Logic power ram assist helps the PSC power steering. The front bumper and rock sliders are from Poison Spyder. A Warn Zeon 10S winch and Rigid auxiliary lighting grace the bumper.

Fabtech Motorsport's Rubicon Specifications

Year/Model: 2014 Unlimited Rubicon

Engine & Transmission: Stock

Tires: Nitto 37x12.50R17LT

Wheels: Ultra Wheel

Front & Rear axle housing: Dynatrac Dana 60

Front & Rear ring/pinion: Dynatrac Dana 60

Front & Rear axles: Dynatrac with ARB Air Locker

Rear suspension: Fabtech 3-inch lift with dual-rate coil springs, Dirt Logic shocks 2.25 inches with reservoir

Front suspension: Fabtech 3-inch lift with coil-over conversion, Dirt Logic shocks 2.5 inches coil-over with reservoir

Rear control arms: Fabtech long-arm .250 wall with "5-Ton" rebuildable joints (lifetime warranty)

Front control arms: Fabtech four-link long-arm .250 wall with "5-Ton" rebuildable joints (lifetime warranty)

Rear track bar: Fabtech

Front track bar: Fabtech chrome-moly adjustable

Steering tie-rod & drag link: Dynatrac

Ball joints: Dynatrac heavy duty

Steering knuckles: Dynatrac

Steering dampener: PSC pump with Fabtech custom cylinder

Power steering pump, cooler & reservoir: PSC

Bracket for steering dampener: Fabtech

Cold-air intake: aFe

Cat-back exhaust: Magnaflow

Auxiliary switch system: sPOD

Onboard compressor: ARB CKSA12

Engine/transmission skidplate: Rock Hard

Gas tank skidplate: Rock Hard

Transfer case skidplate: Rock Hard

Evap relocation: N/A

Fenders: Aluminum Poison Spyder

Rock sliders: Poison Spyder

Auxiliary lighting: Rigid front bumper and pillar pods

Roll cage: Custom Fabtech

Recovery kit: Custom assembled/Warn

Good axle articulation allows safe descent of steep drop-offs. The Fabtech JK axles are articulated near full travel, allowing the body of the JK to remain almost level. The tree on the right features some scars where vehicles without good articulation have tipped over onto the tree. Others have rolled over a little farther down on this tricky spot on the John Bull Trail.

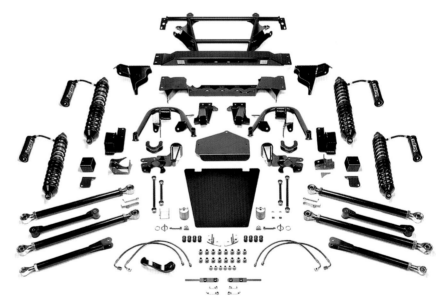

The Fabtech Crawler 3-inch Long Travel Suspension system includes everything needed for great off-road performance and articulation. Long-arm links and mounts, coil-over hoop kit for the front coil-overs, long-travel coil springs for the rear, and sway bar links front and rear are all included in the kit. Additional items in the kit include front and rear track bar brackets, a drop pitman arm, extended-length brake lines, emergency brake bracket, and front and rear bumpstop brackets.

BRAKE UPGRADES

To safely operate your JK in extreme off-road conditions, the brake system needs to lock up the tires or at least engage the anti-lock brake system under all operating conditions. When the driver presses on the brake pedal, the pedal arm pushes on a rod that compresses a plunger and a piston in the master cylinder. The master cylinder pressurizes the brake lines and pushes the piston or pistons on the brake caliper. This forces the brake pads against the brake rotors, and the friction created by this interface slows and stops the vehicle.

The amount of force the driver applies against the brake pedal is the first step in the process. The average person generates in the range of 70 to 100 pounds of force against the brake pedal. The pedal pad is on a pivot that is a fulcrum, and the rod to the master cylinder is on the end opposite the pedal pad. The distance from the pedal pad to the pivot is much greater than from the pivot to the master cylinder rod, and this creates a leverage ratio. The ideal ratio to operate a brake system with a power booster is between 6:1 and 7:1. This means that a 100-pound

force applied to the pedal becomes a 600- to 700-pound force on the master cylinder piston. If the master cylinder piston area and the total area of the caliper pistons are designed correctly for the rotor size and the friction of the brake pads, the driver can lock up the tires (or engage the anti-lock brakes) with less than 100 pounds of pressure on the brake pedal.

Increase Brake Performance

The Wrangler JK's stock brake system performs sufficiently for tires up to 33 inches in diameter, but if you mount larger wheels and tires, you overload the stock system. When you mount larger wheels and tires, you need an aftermarket brake system that provides exceptional stopping power for your off-road application. For most off roaders, the JKs with more powerful brakes are always preferred because the brakes are an essential safety device. When you add larger-diameter tires that weigh much more than the stock JK tires, the rotational forces (inertia) increase dramatically, and these overpower the stock brake system. That 100 pounds of pedal pressure

Brakes take a beating on long, steep descents. Stock JK brakes work fine with stock or slightly larger tire sizes as long as the system is maintained properly. Stock JK brake calipers are a single piston, floating design. A single piston is on one side of the caliper and the other side floats so the pad on that side can push the brake pads against the brake rotor. This system is fine for most applications, but the small piston area does not create enough clamping force to be effective with large, heavy tires on modified JKs.

Aftermarket brake calipers, pads, and rotors such as these from Wilwood use a rigid caliper design with pistons on both sides. This four-piston caliper increases piston area and raises clamping force on the pads against the rotors. In addition, the slotted, cross-drilled, and vented rotors efficiently dissipate heat to maintain performance. Wilwood offers 14-inch front and 12.88-inch rear brake discs in slotted and slotted/cross-drilled designs. Many aftermarket packages include larger-diameter rotors and bigger brake pads. Because the rotors are bigger, they better counteract the rotational inertia of taller tires. All of this translates to considerably greater stopping power. (Photo Courtesy Wilwood Brakes)

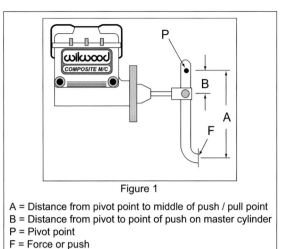

Figure 1

A = Distance from pivot point to middle of push / pull point
B = Distance from pivot to point of push on master cylinder
P = Pivot point
F = Force or push

The brake pedal ratio is fixed on the JK and is hard to modify. Pedal ratio, along with master cylinder bore area and caliper piston area determine clamping force for a given pedal pressure applied by the driver. The ideal pedal pressure is in the range of 60 to 100 pounds of push. With stock brakes on a JK and 37-inch tires, it takes more pressure than is comfortable to apply the brakes for maximum deceleration. This can be a problem in emergency situations on the highway and can make dropping off rocks and ledges difficult to control. (Photo Courtesy Wilwood Brakes)

Hard braking is necessary to control speed when crawling down large rocks. Controlling speed is crucial in these circumstances. With stock brakes, pedal effort can be high to keep speeds down. If speed is too fast, the vehicle drops down hard, possibly causing damage. In more severe situations, a fast drop-off compresses the front springs, transferring more weight onto the front tires and off the rear tires. If only one front tire drops off, and the drop is large, rollovers are possible.

to lock up tires on a stock JK must increase almost 50 percent when you upgrade to 37-inch tires. This is not only a factor on the highway, but is critical when dropping off rocks or ledges off road.

The amount of pedal pressure to control a descent on a drop-off surprises most drivers. For this reason, brake upgrades provide much greater clamping force of the brake caliper against the rotor. The diameter of the rotor is a key factor. The larger the diameter of the rotor, the more braking force the system can create, and the more heat can be dispersed. This occurs for the same reason larger-diameter tires need more braking force to reduce speed. In many brake upgrade packages, the stock pedal and booster are used, but rotors, calipers, brake pads, and in some cases the master cylinder are changed for more stopping power at the optimum amount of pedal pressure, 60 to 100 pounds, generated by the driver's leg muscles.

A good brake upgrade package, whether rotors and pads, or a complete system, takes into account all of the factors needed to properly engineer the system. When properly designed, the improved performance is significant when running larger tires.

Brake Rotors

The single most important element of improved braking performance is the rotor. Brake rotors come in two styles: vented and solid. Vented rotors help dissipate heat for better braking performance in extreme conditions. Vented rotors are used in the front of the JK, but the rear rotors are solid. Keep in mind that a JK Unlimited carries about 60 percent of its weight on the front tires on level ground. Under severe braking, another 10 percent of the weight transfers forward. This means that the front brakes do much more of the work when slowing and stopping. This occurs even more when descending hills or ledges. Add the extra weight of modifications and larger tires and the job of the brake system increases considerably, as does stopping distance. Because a large-diameter rotor increases leverage and braking force, the rotor is key to improving braking performance. Stock replacement rotors are available from Stop Tech, Power Stop, Black Magic, Omix-Ada, Crown Automotive, Hawk, and Mopar.

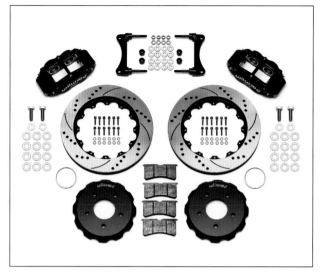

Wilwood's front brake kit for the JK includes four-piston rigid calipers with mounting adapters for the stock knuckle, vaned, larger-diameter rotors that are drilled and slotted, hats to attach the rotors to the stock JK hubs, brake pads, and mounting hardware. A kit such as this not only provides more stopping power, it also delivers longer rotor and pad life. Wilwood offers the 12.88-inch-diameter rotor that fits inside 17-inch wheels; the 14-inch rotor works only with 18-inch-or-larger wheels. (Photo Courtesy Wilwood Brakes)

The rotor has been bolted to the hat. The larger area of the rotor and brake pads increases braking power. The vanes between the braking surfaces on the inside and outside of the rotor improve brake cooling in severe situations. The slots on the face of the rotor allow gases released from the hot brake pads to dissipate more quickly. This reduces potential brake fade when the pads and rotors become hot. (Photo Courtesy Wilwood Brakes)

Dynatrac offers a brake rotor and pad upgrade using the stock calipers. The kit includes much stronger caliper mounting brackets for the stock calipers, reducing flex in the mounts. The rear rotor assembly is being installed here. The front rotors feature a vented design to improve cooling. The front rotors are 13.50 inches in diameter; the rear rotors are 14.25 inches, both significantly larger than stock. With 37-inch tires, even using the stock JK calipers, these brakes improve stopping distances in an emergency stop by up to 30 percent compared to the stock system. Because stock calipers are used, they do not need to be disconnected. Bleeding the brakes after installation is not necessary.

The Dynatrac caliper bracket replaces the stock bracket. This is necessary to move the stock caliper outward from the centerline of the hub to accommodate the larger rotor.

Dynatrac's larger rotor (right) provides a considerable performance improvement compared to the stock JK rotor (left). The increased brake pad contact area along with more leverage from the larger diameter improves the stopping capabilities of the larger rotor.

Large-diameter rotors provide more surface area for increased clamping power and heat dissipation. Compare Black Magic's big rotor (right) to the stock JK rotor (left).

The JK's stock rotor is 11.9 inches in diameter; aftermarket rotors range from 12.5 to 14 inches in diameter. A 13.5-inch-diameter rotor is about 11 percent larger, about the same increase as a 33-inch-diameter tire compared to a 37-inch-diameter tire. The larger area of a bigger rotor means the brake pad can be larger to increase the contact area and improve braking performance. The rear rotors on a JK are slightly larger at 12.4 inches, but they are a solid design and feature a built-in drum for the parking brake.

Most JK performance rotors are either cross-drilled or slotted, sometimes both. Cross-drilling allows the gases from the heated brake pads to escape. These gases can reduce friction between the rotor and the pad, which reduces brake performance. Slots in the pads help gases evacuate to maintain brake performance, but the slots also provide additional edges that help the pad grip the rotor more efficiently.

Heat buildup in the calipers, rotors, and pads is also a factor. Larger rotors dissipate heat more effectively, which reduces fade and wear. Overheating brakes can be a big problem, and safety demands reliable and powerful braking performance on descents and many other off-road situations. The pad friction material and the ability of the rotor to dissipate heat are critical. Vented rotors cool down much better than solid rotors, an especially important consideration for the hard-working front rotors. Cross-drilled and slotted rotors help dissipate heat as they remove gases and brake dust created from brake pad heat and wear. Rotors can be coated with a zinc compound that improves wear and performance.

Brake Calipers

Floating and solid calipers are available for the JK. Floating calipers have pistons on one side only with a floating bridge holding the brake pad on the other side. When pressure is applied, the piston or pistons on the inside of the caliper push against the brake pad while moving the floating bridge to put an equal force on the outside brake pad. Solid calipers have pistons on both sides of the caliper to push the brake pads when pressurized.

Brake calipers are manufactured in two different styles. The most common calipers, the floating style, are found on most vehicles as original equipment. For the JK, the stock calipers are floating cast aluminum. Solid, or fixed, calipers with pistons on both sides of the rotor are machined from billet or forged aluminum. Many aftermarket solid calipers hold four or six pistons and are much more expensive to produce. The advantages are improved clamping force, less weight, and some improvement in heat dissipation.

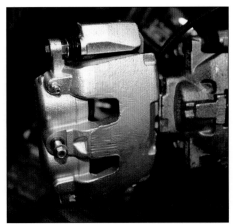

Black Magic's big-brake kit for the JK features a two-piston floating caliper design versus the single-piston floating design of the stock caliper. The larger caliper is the Black Magic version, which uses an OEM brake caliper from a larger vehicle and is machined to fit on the stock JK steering knuckle.

Large-diameter aftermarket rotors offer increased brake performance and are a crucial component of the brake system's capability, but so are the calipers. The two-piston Black Magic larger caliper (right) supplies much greater clamping force than the stock single-piston JK caliper (left). The Black Magic front caliper offers significant increases in stopping power when used with their rotors and larger bore master cylinder.

The complete Wilwood front brake system has been installed except for the brake pads. In addition to improved brake performance, a system such as this has a major "cool" factor. (Photo Courtesy Wilwood Brakes)

The Black Magic big-brake kit uses a 13.25-inch-diameter Centric rotor; the stock rotor is 11.9-inches in diameter. The hat is integrated with the rotor and has been machined to fit the 5-on-5-inch bolt pattern of the JK. The slots are directional, so there is a driver- and passenger-side rotor.

The Dynatrac caliper bracket in the foreground is much more rigid than the stock caliper bracket in the background. When increasing rotor diameter and thickness, the caliper needs to move outward and upward on the steering knuckle to properly position the caliper.

Red Loctite keeps bolts from loosening. Because of heat and vibration in the brake system, red Loctite should always be used on all brake system mounting bolts. It is common for brake hardware to loosen with use, especially during more extreme off-road driving. Most often caliper bolts work loose. Not only does this affect braking performance, making it potentially dangerous, but it also can damage key parts of the brake system. (Photo Courtesy Wilwood Brakes)

Rigid, or solid, calipers do not have to be removed from the caliper bracket to replace the brake pads, unlike floating calipers. The bolt and sleeve across the bridge is removed and the pads can be easily removed and replaced. (Photo Courtesy Wilwood Brakes)

Some aftermarket brake upgrade kits use larger cast calipers, usually modified from another original equipment application. They almost always use the floating design and two pistons on the inside of the caliper. The solid calipers used in some brake upgrade kits have either four or six pistons total. Because pistons are on both sides of the caliper, they tend to operate a little more smoothly. Multiple pistons deliver more piston area to increase clamping force and spread the force across a greater area of the pad against the rotor. The billet-machined calipers also have a cool factor, but at a price.

Brake Master Cylinders

Most JK big-brake kits use the stock JK master cylinder. These packages engineer the hydraulics by matching the piston area to the stock master cylinder. Some packages using larger floating calipers from another original equipment applica-tion upgrade the master cylinder to one with a larger piston bore. These master cylinders usually bolt in to the original mounts on the JK and are compatible with the brake power booster. The stock master cylinder works fine as long as the calipers are engineered to be compatible.

Brake Pads

A variety of brake pad compounds, such as organic, semi-metallic, ceramic, and ferro carbon, are offered for different applications. Some pad compounds require high heat to generate maximum friction and the best brake performance. Other compounds are designed to operate at lower temperatures. For highway and off-road driving, maximum friction from the brake pads is needed quickly for emergency stops and rock crawling. If you drive in areas with long, steep descents, a slightly harder compound is often preferred. Stock replacement brake pads are available from Mopar, Mopar Severe Duty, Black Magic, and EBC.

In all cases, if you upgrade your brake system, whether a complete package with rotors, calipers, and pads, or just rotors and pads, use

The Dynatrac caliper bracket remains in place to install brake pads but the caliper must be unbolted from the bracket from at least one point to swing the caliper out of the way. The caliper has yet to be mounted during this installation.

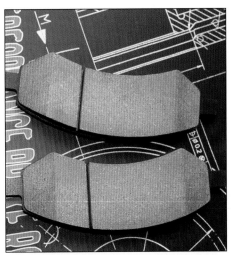

New brake pad and rotor break-in is important. Follow the procedure recommended by the rotor and pad manufacturers. The pads need to be gently heated and then cooled. This cycle needs to occur several times so maximum performance from the brake system is realized. Brake pad material is held together with a binding agent. If pads are heated too much without proper cooling, the binding chemicals cannot escape and cause green fade. The surface of the pads and the rotors glaze over, rendering the pads useless and damaging the rotors.

the brake pads recommended by the manufacturer. If you are replacing the stock pads on your JK, you can choose from many options. Most stock replacement brake pads use a compound that is slightly more aggressive than the original pads. This improves stopping power but accelerates wear slightly.

Brake pad break-in is important for all replacement brake pads. It is critical for pads on big brake kits. If you do not follow the proper break-in procedure, the pad surface can glaze over, which reduces the coefficient of friction considerably. This makes the brake pads dangerous because your stopping distances increase dramati-

cally. Follow the break-in procedure recommended by the brake system or pad manufacturer. Cleaning brake rotors is critical when replacing brake pads. Use non-petroleum cleaners such as Simple Green. Petroleum-based cleaners such as brake clean are not recommended.

Brake Kits

Big-brake kits improve stopping performance especially well when upgrading to larger tires. Big-brake kits include rotors, calipers, brackets, and other related parts to adapt the stock calipers to work with larger rotors and brake pads. Some kits include a new master cylinder. As stated before, there is no substitute for size; the bigger rotors, calipers, and brake pads simply offer more surface area and clamping power, so brake performance is improved. Wilwood Forged Narrow Superlite 4R delivers exceptional braking power for the most challenging off-road driving. The Superlite 4R front kit features slotted and cross-drilled 14-inch rotors that should fit 18-inch wheels and are obviously

compatible with larger off-road tires. TeraFlex offers a big-brake kit for the JK that delivers a significant improvement in brake performance and gives you peace of mind when taking on challenging terrain. The Black Magic big-brake kit is for the front only and includes a new master cylinder. Dynatrac's big-brake kit provides new mounting brackets for the stock calipers, which eliminate the need to bleed the brakes after installation. Other companies offering big-brake kits for the JK include Baer and Stainless Steel Brakes.

Brake Flex Lines

Brake hoses or flex lines are designed to move with the caliper during suspension travel. For optimum braking performance, steel-braided brake hoses should be used. They are more durable and the braided steel cannot flex the way a rubber brake hose does. If you upgrade to a big-brake system, replace the stock brake flex lines with steel-braided. If you have lifted your JK, chances are extended steel-braided lines are already installed.

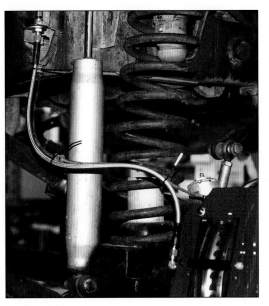

Most aftermarket brake kits do not include steel braided brake lines but many suspension lift kits do. They are needed for the increased distance between the chassis and axle and the extended wheel travel. Steel braided lines resist expansion caused by the brake fluid under pressure when the brakes are applied. Rubber brake hoses can expand, which can give the brake pedal a spongy feel. More pedal travel is required when the brake lines expand. (Photo Courtesy Wilwood Brakes)

Brake Test

When upgrading to larger tires, the most noticeable change is the brake pedal effort needed to make a normal stop. Increasing the tire size from the stock 32-inch BFGoodrich KM2 tires on a Rubicon to 37-inch tires requires about 50 percent more force on the brake pedal to make the same stop. It is common to roll through a stop sign when driving on bigger tires for the first time. The additional pedal pressure required to make even an easy stop can be unnerving.

The culprit is rotational inertia, or the flywheel effect. When you move weight away from the center of rotation, it takes more force to accelerate or decelerate the mass. Kids learn this intuitively from riding playground merry-go-rounds. A taller tire that weighs more has a higher rotational inertia, meaning it takes more power to accelerate and brake.

The formula to calculate rotational inertia is complex, but the key factors are weight, RPM, and radius from the center of rotation. The radius is key because the radius is squared in the equation. A small increase in radius translates into a big increase in rotational inertia.

It's obvious that it takes longer to stop with bigger tires, and more pedal pressure is needed to reduce speed or stop. What is the real-world difference? We tested two sets of tires with stock brakes on a JK. The first set of tires was 33-inch BFGoodrich KO2 all-terrain that weighed about 58 pounds. Speed was 45 mph on good asphalt. The stopping distance was 80.2 feet. The anti-lock brakes were engaged. With no other changes we tested a set of Falken WildPeak M/T 37-inch tires weighing slightly more than 81 pounds.

Keep in mind that almost all the additional weight is in the tread, which is the farthest from the center of rotation, in this case, a radius of 18.4 inches versus 16.4 inches. The stopping distance from 45 mph was a scary 100.2 feet. Those 20 feet translates into a big crash.

The results begged the question "Do big-brake kits reduce stopping distances"? A larger-diameter rotor with more brake pad area should provide much greater stopping power. The larger radius of the rotor works to a taller tire. A larger rotor radius creates more torque for stopping power. We installed the Black Magic Big Brake front brakes on the same JK. The Black Magic kit includes bigger rotors, new, larger calipers, and a new master cylinder to ensure pedal pressure is within a reasonable range for all drivers. After a thorough break-in, we tested the Falken 37-inch mud-terrain tires. At the same 45 mph and engaging the anti-lock brakes, the stopping distance was reduced to 81.1 feet, almost identical to the stock brakes on 33-inch tires. Pedal effort was reduced to about the same level as the stock brakes on the 33-inch tires.

For off-road driving, the bigger brakes make a similar significant improvement. When dropping off ledges or big rocks, the stock brakes do not always create enough braking force to slow the descent if you're running 37-inch tires. You should be able to lock up the brakes on a steep drop. With stock brakes, pedal effort is very high. With the big-brake kit, pedal effort is reduced and it is possible to lock up a brake, indicating that full stopping power is available to slow the descent down a ledge or large rock. ∎

Brake Fluid

Brake fluid is hygroscopic, meaning that the fluid absorbs water vapor from the air; therefore, use small pint containers of brake fluid and keep them sealed tightly when not pouring fluid into the master cylinder reservoir. Water vapor in the fluid lowers the boiling point of the fluid. This increases compressibility and can cause a spongy brake pedal, even no pedal. Clearly this can be dangerous. If the brake fluid has become contaminated it must be purged from the system and replaced with fresh fluid.

The Department of Transportation specifies three common types of brake fluid: DOT 3, DOT 4, and DOT 5. DOT 3 and 4 are the preferred types for high-performance, high-temperature use and are available in a wide range of formulations and performance characteristics. DOT 3 fluids are usually less expensive than DOT 4 fluids and are not as capable in extreme use. DOT 5 is a silicon-based fluid, which is not good for high-temperature use because it expands, becomes compressible, and makes your pedal soft and spongy. For off-road applications, DOT 4 brake fluid has a higher boiling point and may offer better performance on long, steep descents where the brakes can generate considerable heat.

Heather and Quinn Thomas's All J Products 2007 JK Unlimited Hemi

Why a JK? Back in early 2006 the rumor mill was churning about this new Jeep. I remember thinking at the time: "This sounds great for the family!" At the time we had young kids and the back seat in our 1997 TJ Wrangler was too small for our growing family. The upcoming Jeep Wrangler JK Unlimited (JKU) sounded great because it offered four doors, had room for five passengers, and had room for cargo, power windows, and door locks. We just hadn't seen a real one. Artistic renderings and spy shots were all we had seen. When the opportunity to order one came up we jumped at the chance.

By Quinn Thomas

Once it was ordered we eagerly awaited our JK's arrival. If I recall correctly it arrived late September, about a month before they started showing up at dealers for floor demos. We were part of a group of vendors who received our JKs early so we could get to the 2006 SEMA show that November with newly built aftermarket goodies. Our new JKU got attention everywhere it went.

Being one of my vehicles, it gets worked hard; no easy life for our Jeeps. In the winter it is snow-weather transportation for the family. During the rest of the year it gets to be a show-piece for our shop, All J Products: Big Bear's Jeep & 4x4 Shop. When it's not shuttling us through the snow or on display at the shop and at shows, our JK is out on the trail getting wheeled all over. Our JK is definitely not a trailer queen, and it has the bruises, dents, and stories to prove it.

Our JK's early story boasts of being wheeled bone-stock all over Southern California. We wanted to run it stock to see what it could do without any modifications. Being a Rubicon it was set up pretty well from the factory and it did a pretty good job on the trails. After about a year of wheeling it stock and having a good idea what it could do, the first things to go were the plastic bumpers. Then it received a suspension lift.

There is a saying about being in the right place at the right time. As it turns out, our friend Jim from Nth Degree Mobility needed a four-door JK to test fit a new suspension; our JK went to see Jim at Nth for some prototyping. It was there for five to six months. What came back to us was a 4.5-inch lifted JK that was the earliest prototype of the new AEV Dual Sport suspension lift. (AEV later acquired Nth Degree, and Nth's JK stuff was integrated to become the AEV dual sport lift.) Our Jeep has seen its share of mods through the years but a few of those original prototype Nth parts are still on it!

Heather and Quinn Thomas purchased their JKU sight unseen in 2006 right after Chrysler announced the launch. The first JK they saw was at Rubicon Springs in late summer 2006 when they worked at the Jeep media launch. Nth Degree installed its first JK suspension lift on this JK and later sold the design to AEV, which still produces the JK package. Since then, the All J Products JK has seen many modifications, including the installation of a Hemi engine using an AEV installation kit. Most of the original Nth Degree suspension is still in use.

All J Jeep Specifications

Year/Model: 2007 Jeep Rubicon Unlimited
Engine: 5.7 VVT Hemi
Transmission: 545RFE
Transfer case: Rock-Trac NV241 4.0 to 1
Tires: Falken WildPeak MT01 37x12.50R17LT
Wheels: Raceline 17x9 Raptor
Front & Rear axle housing: Currie RockJock 44 high-pinion/Stock JK 44
Front & Rear ring/pinion: Yukon 4.88
Rear axles: Revolution 32-spline with Factory Electric locker
Front axles: RCV CV joint 35 spline w/ ARB Air Locker
Front & Rear suspension: AEV 4.5-inch Dual Sport with OME BP-51 shocks
Front & Rear control arms: MetalCloak Duroflex
Rear track bar: AEV Dualsport
Front track bar: MetalCloak
Steering tie rod: Currie Currectlync with Johnny Joint rod ends
Steering drag link: Currie Currectlync with Johnny Joint rod ends
Ball joints: Dynatrac H/D
Steering knuckles: Reid Racing
Steering dampener: PSC ram assist
Power steering box: PSC
Power steering pump: Mopar Hemi
Power steering cooler: PSC
Bracket for steering dampener: Custom All J Products
Front & Rear brake rotors and calipers: Black Magic Big Brake/Mopar
Cat–back exhaust: AEV Custom Hemi
Auxiliary switch system: sPOD
Onboard compressor: ARB CKSA12
Radiator: AEV Hemi Conversion
Transmission cooler: Stacked Plate
Auxiliary fluid storage: AEV Fuel Caddy
Engine/transmission skidplate: Rock Hard/All J Products Custom
Gas tank skidplate: Rock Hard 4x4
Transfer case skidplate: Rock Hard 4x4
Evap relocation: All J Products
Fenders: GenRight Aluminum
Rock sliders: GenRight Steel
Auxiliary lighting: IPF Super Rallies
Roll cage: Rock Hard 4x4 Ultimate Sport Cage with Overhead Center Bars

With world-class rock crawling trails in the backyard, the All J Wrangler often tackles tough trails such as the black diamond rock garden on Dishpan Springs. The 2007 JK features an aluminum front bumper from GenRight with a Warn PowerPlant winch with a Viking synthetic winch line. Fenders are GenRight aluminum to save weight.

Through the years our JK has had its share of parts come and go: bumper changes, gear changes, etc. One of the most notable (and Heather's favorite) changes has been the addition of the 5.7-liter Hemi engine! This is the Jeep we wish Jeep had built. The engine conversion has been in the Jeep since late 2011. It's been great having the extra power and it's a lot of fun to drive. Most of the parts currently on the JK have been in use since 2010–2011, the main exception is the new front Currie RockJock 44, which was added in early 2017. The factory-installed front Dana 44 was still going strong, even

The power steering box, pump, and ram assist are from PSC. The cooler is Mopar. Front brakes are Black Magic. Steering linkages are Currie Currectlync with a MetalCloak track bar. The front axle housing is a high-pinion Currie RockJock 44 with an ARB air locker and RCV CV joint 35-spline axles.

though slightly bent, until the stock locker finally gave up. The 37-inch tires and a hard life caught up to our JK's front axle. I always assumed that the rear Dana 44 would go first with the Hemi not being nice to the rear axle, but it was the front that went first. The axle upgrade was a must after driving and wheeling the Jeep for several years with a bent front axle (the purchase needed CFO approval). The new RockJock 44 was equipped with an ARB air locker, Yukon 4.88 gears, RCV axle shafts, and Reid Racing knuckles. So here we are today with the Jeep seen in this book. It's going on 75,000 hard miles. It's been beaten and driven hard, but it has always brought the family home from an adventure safely! I am happy to thank all the companies that have helped make our shop JK the Jeep it is today.

The 5.7-liter VVT Hemi engine looks like it belongs in the JK. The AEV kit makes the swap relatively easy. The radiator is the AEV Hemi conversion and the cold-air intake is from AEV with a K&N filter. A sPOD switching box distributes electricity to numerous electrical devices without the risk of damage to the computer. An Odyssey Extreme Duty battery provides electrical power.

The suspension is the AEV Dual Sport 4.5-inch lift (formerly Nth Degree) with ARB BP-51 adjustable reservoir shocks. The front sway bar is the stock electric disconnect version with extended sway bar links. Steering knuckles are from Reid Racing. Ball joints are the rebuildable units from Dynatrac.

The rear axle is the stock Rubicon Dana 44 with the original electric locker. The ring and pinion gears are Yukon 4.88 ratio. The rear suspension is AEV 4.5-inch Dualsport with the AEV Dualsport track bar. MetalCloak Duroflex control arms replace the stock arms. The shocks are fully adjustable ARB BP-51 reservoir shocks. The exhaust system is the AEV custom system for the Hemi engine.

The Rock Hard 4x4 skidplates and the GenRight rock sliders have seen considerable use.

BUMPERS, ARMOR, AND PROTECTION

The Jeep Wrangler JK models feature some underside protection, but they need additional protective body armor to handle the rigors of demanding off-road conditions.

All JK models have stock skidplates for the fuel tank and the transfer case to protect these key components. These are sheet metal and offer good protection for moderate off roading, but other key components remain vulnerable. The JK models also feature rocker slides that protect the rocker sills from damage. Like the skidplates, they offer some protection, but for serious off-road driving, especially for rock crawling, extra protection is called for. To protect valuable and critical underside parts, the stock plates and sliders need to be upgraded to ensure reliable protection for key and expensive components.

Skidplates

When driving off road, obstacles found in even moderate conditions can damage the underside of your JK. Loose rocks, ruts, and bumps, even downed tree branches and shrubs can reach unprotected underside parts, such as the oil pan, transmission, sway bar disconnect unit (on Rubicons), and the fuel evaporation unit. Moreover, the protected areas, given a hard enough impact, can still allow damage to the components they protect. Additional and stronger underside protection is needed for serious off roading in your Wrangler JK.

Stock Sheet-Metal Skidplates

Two skidplates on the stock JK protect the gas tank and the transfer case. A plastic pan also covers the front sway bar and steering; it offers little protection but does improve aerodynamics. The rocker slides offer some protection from damage, but a hard drop on large rocks can still damage the rocker panels.

The costs to repair unprotected underside components can be major. Damage to the engine oil pan and transmission pan can be extensive. These are unprotected. Should a large

Aftermarket bumpers, fenders, and rock sliders all help enable a JK to run big tires and tackle more extreme rock crawling trails. Rock sliders also offer important protection for the rocker panels on a JK.

Underside protection is crucial when you hit the difficult trails. The Wrangler JK is equipped with stock skidplates, but they are sheet metal rather than steel plate and only offer moderate protection against obstacles. Big rocks can do big damage, and therefore aftermarket body armor is required on a dedicated off-road rig. The engine oil pan and transmission skidplate on the JK are from ARB. It is new and unscathed. Directly behind the oil-pan skid is the transfer case skidplate from Pure Jeep. It has taken a beating for about four years, as has the gas tank skid to the left and rear. It's also from Pure Jeep. All these skidplates have held up well even with considerable abuse on some serious rock crawling trails.

rock pierce the transfer case skidplate, damage can occur. The sheet-metal gas tank skid offers some protection, but a sharp rock or branch could penetrate the sheet metal, causing the plastic fuel tank to leak. Not only is this a hazmat issue; it could cause a fire with possible extreme consequences.

Aftermarket Skidplate Armor

More aftermarket parts, including skidplates and other underside armor and protection, are available for the Jeep Wrangler JK than any other model in history. In almost all cases, skidplates and underside armor are made of steel plate; heavy-duty plate offers the best protection from sharp rocks and scrapes when dragging over obstacles. The downside to heavy skidplates is added weight, but at least it is down low. Heavy-duty skidplates are available

The Wrangler JK comes with skidplates made from sheet metal; these offer some protection, but they do take a beating. Valuable underside components need more protection for serious rock crawling.

Unless you add a skidplate, the engine and transmission are unprotected. The differential cover, being the low point of the vehicle (except tires), can take some serious hits in the rocks. Several companies make much stronger differential covers, such as this one from Currie. Also note the stock tie-rod with several scrapes. There is also a small bend in the tie rod near the right of the differential cover. Aftermarket drag links and tie-rods are stronger. The stock links on this Jeep were replaced with Currie Currectlync steering.

The stock JK evaporation canister skidplate offers some protection, but the sheet-metal design does not lend itself to protection in big rocks.

Rock Hard 4x4 and other skidplate manufacturers make integrated skidplate systems such as this one. Complete systems offer great protection because the skidplates complement one another. This system includes a skidplate for the engine, transmission, and oil pan as well as the gas tank. The hole in the engine skidplate allows oil drainage from the oil pan without removing the skidplate. Note the tapered washers on some of the bolts. This design keeps the bolt head from dragging on rocks and incurring damage.

in steel plate typically with 3/16-inch thickness. Aluminum skidplates save some weight and are made from 1/4-inch-thick aluminum sheet. The Rock Hard 4x4 oil pan and transmission skidplate weighs 49 pounds in steel and 31 pounds in aluminum.

Although adding skidplates to unprotected areas such as the engine oil pan is important, consider that many skidplate manufacturers make skidplate packages that cover all-important items. They are normally designed to work together for improved fit and appearance.

Skidplates get damaged. That is why they are in place. Most skidplates are painted; some are powder-coated. They get scraped and dinged, so paint is adequate protection because it is easier to touch up painted skidplates.

Fuel Evaporation Canister Location

The fuel system evaporation canister is in a vulnerable spot. It can easily be damaged from rocks and other items under the vehicle. The evaporation canister can be relocated or a skidplate can be added to provide protection. There are many options, but it is important to do one or the other.

Gas Tank Skidplates

Although the stock JK gas tank skidplate offers some protection, the tank is large and may still be damaged when the vehicle drops onto sharp rocks or other obstacles. For serious four wheeling, adding a steel skidplate is important. Most gas tank skidplates are designed to bolt on directly over the existing sheet-metal protection.

The JK's engine and transmission are not protected. Although less vulnerable than the gas tank, they are still exposed and can be damaged,

The Rock Hard 4x4 engine and transmission skidplate bolts to the transmission and engine crossmembers but also attaches to the frame rails for added strength. The rear of the skidplate extends under the driveshaft, providing protection for the U-joint also.

even to the point of puncturing the oil pan. This is clearly not good. Adding skidplates to protect these exposed components is a really good idea for serious four-wheeling.

Although the transfer case comes with a sheet-metal skidplate, extra protection is a good idea. Some manufacturers offer skidplate kits that protect the oil pan, transmission, and transfer case. The transfer case housing is a casting and can easily crack from a severe impact.

Tailpipes and mufflers take a beating even with moderate off-road driving. Although they aren't critical components, such as a gas tank or oil pan, skidplates are available to protect the muffler. An alternative is to use an aftermarket cat-back exhaust system, which moves the muffler between the frame rails where it is protected from damage. These exhausts often have a shorter, more compact tailpipe that is also out of harm's way.

Several manufacturers offer high-quality skidplates. Rock Hard 4x4 makes skidplates that overlap, offering a seamless appearance. The company offers powder-coated laser-cut

The skidplate below the bumper protects the crash bar, and the radiator to some degree. This Hanson full-width bumper has several excellent features, such as the tapered ends that give better clearance over rocks. The winch mounts low in the bumper for improved airflow to the radiator to help maintain cooling. The light pods fit the stock JK fog lights. The tube bracing on the bumper adds considerable rigidity to the bumper. The fenders are GenRight steel with tubular edges. When you hit big rocks such as these, strong protection pays off. The stock tie-rod and drag link have been replaced with Currie Currectlync steering components that handle rock bashing much more effectively.

Fitting larger tires leads to several issues beyond a suspension lift. These rock sliders, as well as the sliders that come on the JK, are too long to provide adequate tire clearance. Properly sized sliders need to be fitted to ensure clearance through the entire range of suspension travel. The stock sliders can be trimmed for more space between the tire and the slider. Inadequate space can lead to tire damage.

We have tested the Rock-Slide Engineering slider steps under hard use for the past couple of years. The damage on the slider is from slipping off rocks while rock crawling. Although the retractable step (green panel) is scraped, it still functions perfectly. The lower section of the slider has an add-on skidplate that adds even more protection. Many believe that retractable step sliders are not tough enough for serious rock crawling, but that is not the case. The Rock-Slide Engineering slider steps are strong and offer excellent protection as well as easy entry and exit.

steel skidplates in 3/16- or 1/4-inch thicknesses. An aluminum skidplate is also available in a 1/4-inch thickness. The Rock Hard skidplates also feature tapered bolt head protectors that slide over rocks more easily with no damage to the bolt head. Other skidplate manufacturers include GenRight, Poison Spyder, ARB, Skid Row, Body Armor 4x4, Rampage, Artec, Mountain Off-Road, and Synergy.

Steering and Rubicon Electric Sway Bar Disconnect Unit

The Rubicon comes with a plastic shield below the front bumper that improves aerodynamics and fuel economy. However, it offers little protection for the steering and electric sway bar disconnect. Aftermarket skidplates are available to provide valuable protection to this vulnerable area. Many aftermarket winch bumpers come with a plate that extends below the bumper, providing good protection for some steering components and the sway bar.

Dave Luman demonstrates the durability of the Rock-Slide Engineering slider steps on the big rock on the famous John Bull Trail near Big Bear Lake, California. The passenger-side rear tire is off the ground and the passenger-side front is barely touching. Almost all of the passenger-side weight is resting on the slider step. Just before this photo was taken, the Jeep pivoted on the slider step, turning about 20 degrees. Another JK equipped with the Rock-Slide Engineering slider step pivoted in the exact same spot just before Dave.

The Rock-Slide Engineering slider steps mount to the frame and to the body panels. The frame attaching bolts carry most of the weight. The body mounts add protection to the body and reduce flex of the slider. The sliders are made from 3/16-inch formed steel. Rock-Slide Engineering offers an add-on skidplate, also 3/16-inch steel plate that bolts on over the slider but allows the step to function.

Rock Sliders

Rock sliders, also called rocker slides, protect the vulnerable rocker panels below the doors on all JK models. Damage to the rocker panels can be difficult and expensive to repair, so it's a priority to protect this area of the JK. Current JK models are equipped with stock rock sliders that offer some level of protection. More robust sliders are suited for extreme off-road activities and can take a real beating. For this reason, sliders can be made from formed heavy-duty steel plate or heavy wall steel tubing. Sliders should bolt to the frame rails; some sliders have additional mounting points on the body to help stabilize the slider. But these body mounts should never be the primary or only mounting points for a slider. Some rock sliders are designed with steps built in to ease ingress and egress. Other sliders have swing down electric steps that make getting into a lifted JK with 37-inch tires much easier. Rock-Slide Engineering uses heavy-duty material for its sliders. To illustrate how much pounding rock sliders can be subjected to, Rock-Slide has a skidplate that covers the part of the slider that takes the most abuse.

One of the issues with the stock rock sliders is their width. They are almost flush with the body. They

The Rock-Slide Engineering slider steps extend to make entry and exiting a lifted JK on big tires much easier. The step features a strip of non-skid material for better traction. An optional lighting kit helps with nighttime visibility. It takes about two seconds for the sliders to fully extend or retract. The system also uses a switch mounted on the dash to turn the step operation on and off. This is great when wheeling in the rocks where exiting and entering the vehicle could cause the steps to lower onto rocks. The built-in load sensor computer stops the movement of the step if the load exceeds a preset amount. This eliminates damage to the motor and reduces possible injury if a foot or leg was to become stuck between the step and the slider.

MetalCloak offers a unique feature on its Overland series of flip step rocker slides. These wide steps flip up when wheeling and down for entry and exit. The steps attach to MetalCloak's Overland and Hardline rocker base. MetalCloak's sliders are made from 3/16-inch cold rolled steel. The flip step is made from hot rolled steel and steel tubing. (Photo Courtesy of MetalCloak Overland)

offer good vertical protection, but little lateral protection. Sliders that extend 3 or 4 inches from the body provide the best lateral protection because they protect the Jeep in various off-road situations; for example, this design protects the rig if it were to slide sideways off a steep rock or ledge. It allows the slider to strike another rock or tree and not the floorpan of the Jeep. The stock sliders offer very little protection in these instances, but protruding sliders protect the body in many cases.

Body Armor

Several companies make body armor to protect the rear corners of the body and other vulnerable areas. Armor is made from aluminum, steel, or plastic. Taillight guards are

The MetalCloak Overland flip step rub rail provides good protection over rocks, bumps, and ruts. (Photo Courtesy MetalCloak)

The MetalCloak JK is outfitted with Overland fenders and sliders. The MetalCloak bumper design is modular, allowing several design options. This bumper starts with the JK combo bumper base, adds JK 56-inch light caps for the stock JK fog lights, the JK bull bar, and an aluminum fairlead. (Photo Courtesy MetalCloak)

The Rock-Slide Engineering Rigid Shorty front bumper is formed from 3/16-inch steel, as is its bull bar. The winch mount sits down inside the bumper for better airflow. In addition, Rock-Slide offers mounting brackets for a 20-inch light bar.

Aluminum fenders save weight, but any flat fender adds a retro look to the JK. More important, more tire clearance is gained. The GenRight design arches the fender slightly for even more clearance. GenRight also builds an all-aluminum front stubby winch bumper. (Photo Courtesy GenRight Off Road)

This JK has stock fenders. There is a downside to using a stock bumper. Notice the passenger's side of the bumper. The big dent in the plastic bumper cover is caused by an encounter with a large rock. Most likely, the right front tire slipped off a rock, allowing the bumper to impact another rock. This is common with stock bumpers when rock crawling.

also available. Although some of these products are heavy duty and can protect the body from dents, the primary job of this type of protection is to protect the paint and easily damaged components from scratching in heavy brush and tree branches.

Door Options

One of the unique elements of the Wrangler is the ability to remove the doors. This alters the trail driving experience, but also makes passengers more vulnerable. Several options are available for half doors and tubular doors; even Jeep offers half door options. Tube doors provide security while maintaining the open-air experience provided by removing the doors, and many styles are available. Mesh coverings for tube doors help keep mud, branches, and debris out of the interior. Bestop, Olympic 4x4, Body Armor, Rugged Ridge, Smittybilt, and others make tube doors. Tube door fabric covers are available from SpiderWebShade and Dirty Dog 4x4.

Fenders

Stock fenders for road use simply are not suited for off-road JKs with 2-inch lifts and 33-inch tires or larger because they do not afford enough clearance. Aftermarket fenders offer two benefits for the JK owner. First is improved tire clearance for larger tires, so your JK has full suspension articulation for scaling the most difficult obstacles. And second, with dozens of product options, JK owners can alter the look of the JK to personalize the style for individual tastes. Most of the flat fender designs not only allow more tire clearance but also have the retro flat fender look of the original World War II Jeeps. Off Road Evolution's front and rear steel-plate fenders are made of rugged 3/16-inch laser-cut steel plate and 1¾–inch 0.20-wall tube. These fenders offer exceptional wheel clearance and keep debris away from the body.

Tire Size

Stock Wrangler JKs can accommodate up to 33-inch-diameter tires with minimal tire rubbing in the fenders at full articulation. With flat fenders, 33-inch tires do not rub on the fenders. With a 2-inch lift and flat fenders, up to 35-inch tires can be accommodated. With 3.5- to 4-plus-inch lift, flat fenders allow tire sizes up 38 inches.

Flat Fenders and Tire Spray

Flat fender styles range from wide to narrow with many different looks. The narrower styles often do not extend wide enough to retain tire spray from water, snow, and mud. With large tires, the spray can affect visibility and even cover the roof. Keep this in mind when choosing aftermarket fenders for a JK. Another consideration with narrow fenders is local laws regarding spray from tires. Many states require mud flaps if the fenders do not contain the spray.

Materials

Most aftermarket fenders are either fabricated or pressure-formed steel or aluminum. Fabricated fenders often use tubing along the outer edge to add strength. Some fenders are made of flexible formed plastic compounds. Rigid fenders are strong, but if you hit obstacles with a rigid fender, body damage where the fender mounts to body panels is likely. Flexible fenders such as those by MCE, absorb much of the impact and minimize possible damage.

Modifying Stock Fenders for Clearance

Stock JK fenders can be trimmed for increased clearance with a heat knife or Sawzall. This takes a good eye, a steady hand, and patience. The vertical overhang on the fender is trimmed away, increasing clearance for larger tires and increased articulation.

Front bumpers can offer considerable utility. Not only do they provide protection, this bumper features mounts for a winch, lights on the bull bar, light receptacles in the bumper for the stock JK fog lights, and a pair of D-ring mounts. More than 400 different front bumper combinations are available for the JK.

Hanson makes a full range of bumpers for the JK models. This full-width bumper features a bull bar and extensions that add strength to the structure. The slotted skidplate under the bumper protects the electric sway-bar disconnect gear box. Both front and rear bumpers can take a beating in the rocks. Well built designs rarely receive more than cosmetic damage.

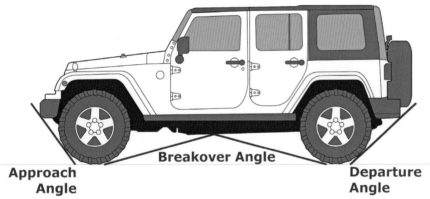

Stock Wrangler JKs offer the best approach, breakover, and departure angles of any stock 4x4 SUV. The approach angle is an indication of how steep a climb can be tackled before the front bumper hits the obstacle. The departure angle is the opposite. When going from a steep descent or drop off to flat ground, this angle will determine when the rear bumper will scrape the ground. The breakover angle determines how large a bump or rut can be navigated before the vehicle high-centers on the frame, skid plates, or crossmembers. The greater these angles are, the larger the obstacle is that can be driven over without damage or getting stuck.

Stubby bumpers offer one great advantage for rock crawling. They expose the front tires. When approaching a rock with only one front tire, much larger rocks can be climbed because the tire is the first component to hit the rock. The approach angle is 90 degrees in these cases. If the bumper extended in front of the tire treads, then the bumper contacts the rock first if the rock is taller than the bumper height from the ground. This Rock Hard 4x4 stubby bumper features a gusseted bull bar/stinger, fog light receptacles, Hi-Lift jack notches, and D-ring mounts. (Photo Courtesy Rock Hard 4x4)

Front Bumpers

Front bumpers are available in a wide range of styles but fall into two general categories: full width and narrow, or stubby bumpers. Recently, modular multi-piece bumpers have become popular. These allow a stubby bumper to become a full-width bumper or something in between by adding bolt-on sections to the narrow bumper. Some of these bumpers are designed with a locking storage compartment. Most easily accommodate winches, lights, and shackle anchors for recovery. Bumpers can be made from fabricated steel or aluminum, or can be formed under extreme pressure from either material.

Front bumpers with a bull bar, winch, light bars, and other accessories can interfere with airflow to the radiator. In hot conditions, this can cause overheating of the engine and transmission. Vented hoods can alleviate this problem. You need to determine the application or where you will be operating the JK to select the ideal bumper style.

Full-Width Bumper

As the name implies, a full-width bumper is about as wide as the front of the JK. They offer tire protection, but when encountering single large rocks, the approach angle is not as great as with the stubby bumper. Full-width bumpers are available in steel and aluminum and are suitable for most off-road situations but are not the best suited for rock crawl-

ing situations. Full-width bumpers protect the stock fenders from damage. Extreme rock crawling is better served with a stubby bumper.

Stubby Bumper

Stubby, or narrow, front bumpers have two distinct advantages that are ideal for extreme rock crawling. First, they weigh less and provide a strong mount for a winch and winch line. This can be an important consideration. Second, they have a much better approach angle when crawling over single large rocks. See the illustration for an explanation of approach angle.

Stingers

Stingers are best suited for long, steep descents and extreme ruts where rollovers are more common. Front-bumper stingers work like bull bars but also serve to help prevent a forward rollover when descending steep ledges or drop-offs. The rollover can still occur, but the stinger usually forces the vehicle to one side or the other so the Jeep rolls instead of flipping over forward. To do this, a stinger must be strong and protrude high enough so that if you run a taut

string from the peak of the stinger to the top of the roof at the windshield, the hood is below the string. This indicates that the engine compartment will be protected more in a rollover.

Bull Bars

Bull bars are an excellent choice for all off-road conditions, especially in areas with heavy brush impeding the trail. As the name implies, bull bars are intended to fend off animals, such as bulls, in a collision. In Australia they are often called "roo" bars because accidents involving kangaroos are commonplace there. Bull bars can also fend off brush and tree branches.

Both front and rear bumpers are made from plate or pressure-formed steel or aluminum in 3/16- or 1/4-inch thicknesses. The big advantage

Rock-Slide Engineering Crawler fenders are formed from 3/16-inch aluminum. They allow maximum axle articulation with no tire rub using 37-inch tires and a 4-inch lift. The shape of the fenders creates a rigid platform without adding much weight over stock fenders.

The All J Wrangler JKU is equipped with a GenRight stubby aluminum bumper with a brush guard and support tubing, sway-bar disconnect box skidplate, D-ring and light mounts, and a Warn winch mount.

to aluminum is light weight, but steel offers superior strength. Smittybilt, Poison Spyder, AEV, and many other companies offer a wide range of bumpers in a variety of styles. For optimum strength on either aluminum or steel, welds must have excellent penetration from the bumper to the frame. This is especially important on aluminum as the loads on the bumper can cause poor welds to fail.

Winch Mounts

Most aftermarket front bumpers feature mounts for winches. Some need additional plates to mount a winch. Be aware that not all winches have the same mounting bolt pattern, so check. Some winches do not fit on some bumpers. Winches place extremely heavy loads on the bumper and frame. Be sure mounting points are strong for the winch and bumper.

D-Ring Mounts

D rings, or shackles, are a critical component for winching and vehicle

recovery. Many front bumpers have D-ring mounts. Most are welded in place and are strong. Some are bolted in place. Bolt-on mounts should be steel plate with four mounting holes because the load from winching puts the bolts under enormous tension.

Rear Bumpers

As with front bumpers, rear bumpers are available in many styles. The most important feature on a rear bumper when running larger tires is a spare tire carrier. The stock spare tire carrier does not handle a tire larger than 33 inches without using an auxiliary mounting plate to gain clearance. Even more important, the extra weight of a tire and wheel of larger than 33 inches in diameter puts a large load on the stock spare mount. The stock mount bolts to the rear gate through sheet metal. The extra load over time can bend and even tear out the tailgate sheet metal.

Rear bumpers need to be sturdy for rock crawling because they often

The stock JK tire carrier bolts onto the rear door sheet-metal skin. Tires larger than 33 inches do not fit on the carrier because they hit the top of the rear bumper. There are kits to raise the lugs holding the wheel for more clearance, but the weight and vibration of larger tires causes metal fatigue in the sheet metal. This can lead to failure of the mounting points.

impact large rocks when dropping off a rock or ledge, or can scrape when climbing. Most rear bumpers are designed to provide better departure angles than stock. Stock bumpers are rarely suitable for more extreme trail conditions. Like front bumpers, rear bumpers are made from steel and aluminum and can be fabricated or formed. Light mounts and D-ring mounts are included in some bumpers and optional on others.

Tire Mounts

Most rear bumpers include a tire carrier, but not all bumpers do. Tire carriers are available as a swing out with the tailgate door; others swing out separately. Those that swing with the door are more convenient but also cost more. Both work well as long as the tire carrier mount to the bumper is strong enough to handle the heavy load of a larger wheel and tire.

The GenRight rear bumper includes D-ring mounts and a depression for spare tire clearance. The separate GenRight Swing Out Tire Carrier attaches to the rear tailgate hinges. Made from DOM steel tubing, the tire carrier offers optional mounts for a Hi-Lift jack.

The AEV tire carrier works with the AEV rear bumper or can be adapted to many other bumpers. The heavy-duty tubing and strong bushing allow all the weight of the tire and other accessories to be easily carried by the bumper. The design of the AEV bumper allows it to open and close with the rear gate. No latches or other mechanisms are needed. Accessories for this tire carrier include a Hi-Lift jack and Pull Pal ground anchor combo mount, CB or ham radio antenna mounts, and a mount for the AEV auxiliary fuel tank, which holds 10 gallons of fuel.

Other Mounts

Many rear bumpers have mounts (built-in and optional) for Hi-Lift jacks, Pull-Pal ground anchors, fuel/water cans/tanks, shovel and axes, and antenna mounts for CB or ham radios. These mounts can be convenient for quick access and to keep large, heavy items outside the passenger compartment, which enhances safety.

JEEP JK PROFILE

John and Cinde Angelastro's sPOD JK

In 2011 we decided to build a two-door JK that would represent our company and be a daily driver, rock crawler, and expedition vehicle. We had previously owned four Jeeps: a 1978 CJ-5 purchased in 1979, a 1947 CJ-2A Willys purchased in 1990, a 2003 Jeep Wrangler TJ Rubicon purchased in 2003, and a 2011 Jeep JKU Rubicon.

By John Angelastro

We contacted Airpark Dodge Chrysler Jeep in Arizona because we had heard they were able to obtain a Gecko green Jeep JK two-door Rubicon, and no one could get them west of the Mississippi! In June 2012, we made the purchase without ever being there in person and using text messages for 80 percent of the communications! We flew to Arizona, picked it up, and drove it back to California.

The first modification was to change out the bumpers and add armor. Next, we added the six-switch sPOD system to lay the foundation for electrical upgrades which included a ham radio, a race radio, a CB, and a six-port power outlet (three powered by

Falken WildPeak MT01 LT37X-12.50R17s and Walker Evans Forged Beadlock 31-Series wheels help the sPOD JK negotiate almost any terrain. The suspension comes from Rock Krawler, via the kit. Rock sliders are Poison Spyder Brawler Rockers.

John and Cinde Angelastro's sPOD JK

Year/Model 2012 Jeep JK (two-door): Component/Replacement Part

Engine & Transmission: Stock

Transfer case: NV2410R with 4:1 gear ratio

Tires: Falken WildPeak M/T01 LT37X12.50R17 D/8-ply rating

Wheels: Walker Evans Forged Beadlock 31-Series in shot peen gray

Front & Rear axle housing: Rubicon Dana Model 44/Rubicon Dana Model 44 (sleeved and gusseted using EVO

Front axle housing: Manufacturing kit; fully installed by Duval Offroad Designs)

Front & Rear ring/pinion: Nitro gear and axle 4:88 (fully installed by Duval Offroad Designs)

Rear axles: Ten Factory Axle Kit made of 4140 chrome-moly (fully installed by Duval Offroad Designs)

Front axles: Rubicon Dana Model 44

Front & Rear locker: OEM Rubicon E-locker

Rear suspension: Rock Krawler w/ Rock Krawler 2.0 RRD Emulsion shocks

Front suspension: Rock Krawler X-factor 4-inch long arm w/ Rock Krawler 2.0 RRD Emulsion shocks

Front & Rear control arms: Rock Krawler X-factor

Rear track bar: Rock Krawler

Front track bar: Synergy MFG

Steering tie-rod & drag link: Synergy MFG/Rock Krawler

Ball joints, Spindles & Steering Knuckles: Reid Racing, Inc.

Steering dampener: FOX

Power steering: Stock

Front & Rear brakes: Stock

Cat-back exhaust: Magnaflow

Auxiliary switch system: sPOD

Onboard compressor: Off Road Only Complete York Air Supply Kit driven off the engine's harmonic balancer

Interior/seat covers: Bartact front and rear seat covers with custom embroidered headrests

Rear bumper: Modified Poison Spyder BFH II with integrated AEV tire carrier (modifications by All J)

Front bumper: Poison Spyder Brawler Lite

Engine/transmission skidplate: EVO Manufacturing

Fenders: Poison Spyder narrows with integrated rear corner body armor

Rock sliders: Poison Spyder

Auxiliary lighting: Rigid, Baja Designs

Roll cage: Poison Spyder (fully installed by Duval Offroad Designs)

The sPOD JK is loaded with electrical add-ons, including radios, lights, and a winch. Of course, a sPOD is used for the wiring and power source for all electrical accessories. It isolates add-on electrical needs from the CAN-BUS computer and wiring. John also installed a dual battery system featuring Odyssey Extreme batteries. Under the hood but not visible is a York onboard air compressor driven off the harmonic balancer.

The sPOD JK is used for overlanding as well as rock crawling and off-road day trips. The centerpiece of the rear cargo area is the 50-quart ARB fridge mounted on a Tembo Tusk pullout slide. The Outback fold-down tailgate table provides a work surface for many different activities. The yellow hose is not an air line, but attaches to a 5-gallon self-contained water system made by SprayBox. Six power outlets are accessed from a panel in the upper left of the cargo area. The storage rack above the fridge is a Baja interior rack made by Synergy Manufacturing. A race radio and a ham radio antenna are mounted to the top of the tube on the AEV tire carrier, which is normally used for the AEV fuel caddy.

the sPOD and three live to the battery) installed in the rear of the Jeep for easy access and all of the lighting. The lighting additions included two rear bumper–mounted LED lights, four green LED rock lights, two front bumper LED lights, two pocket-mounted LED lights mounted into the front bumper, one 10-inch LED light bar on the bumper's stinger bar, and two A-pillar–mounted flood LED lights.

The front bumper is a Poison Spyder; the rear bumper is also a Poison Spyder, a BFH II with an AEV tire carrier. Quinn Thomas at All J Products in Big Bear modified it for us to create the perfect combination of a departure angle and a rattle-free swing-gate/tire carrier. The front bumper is a Poison Spyder Brawler Lite with the OEM-like pockets for the factory or off-road fog lights.

The Jeep went into Poison Spyder in August of 2012 for a full custom 3-inch wheelbase stretch. This included the Rock Krawler kit for the two-door Jeep Wrangler and custom rear corner armor with integrated narrow fender flares and flush-mounted LED taillights. The front fender flares are the bolt-on narrows. We added the Poison Spy-

der Brawler Rockers and body armor to help protect the lower and upper factory body panels.

We then added the wheels and tires. We went with Falken WildPeak MT01 LT37X12.50R17s and Walker Evans Forged Beadlock 31-Series wheels.

Next was our onboard air system made by Off Road Only (ORO), which is a complete York Air Supply Kit driven off the engine's harmonic balancer. We plumbed it to a small air tank mounted under the rear chassis of the Jeep.

Then we moved to the interior. We wanted a functional daily driver that had all the amenities of a rock crawler and expedition/overlanding (vehicle dependent traveling).

We started with the seats. We outfitted them with the Bartact mil-spec tactile seat covers for front, rear, and headrests. The covers include custom embroidery on the headrests and each seat has zippered pockets and MOLLE pouches along with tactical webbing built in to help with storage of flashlights, winch controls, knives, etc.

Next was the Poison Spyder roll cage that Mike Duval at Duval Offroad Designs installed for us. He integrated interior lighting and RAM ball mounts on the center portion.

The OEM grab bar was replaced with the Carolina Metal Masters billet machined grab bar with fully integrated 1-inch ball mounts for attaching and using the RAM Products mounts for phones and GPS.

Because we wanted to use this Jeep for overlanding, too, we wanted the amenities of vehicle dependent camping. We added the 50-quart ARB fridge mounted on a Tembo Tusk pullout slide, Outback fold-down tailgate table, a 5-gallon self-contained water system made by SprayBox, and a Baja interior rack made by Synergy Manufacturing.

In addition to extensive off roading in places such as Big Bear Lake, Moab, and the Rubicon, our Gecko sPOD JK has been displayed at many shows including the Off Road Expo in Pomona and the 4 Wheel Parts Truck & Jeep Fest. The sPOD JK has also been showcased at many Jeep and off-road events, including Tierra del Sol's Desert Safari, Jeep Jamborees, Big Bear Forest Fest, King of the Hammers, and High Desert Round-Up.

The sPOD 2012 Wrangler JK two-door of John and Cinde Angelastro serves many functions. Many company JKs are used for display, as is the sPOD JK. But John and Cinde are longtime Jeepers, and their JK is extensively used off road both for family fun and for product testing and development.

DRIVELINES, AXLES, AND LOCKERS

To extract maximum performance for off-road service, almost every JK needs upgraded axles, lower differential gear ratios, and stronger driveline parts. For rock crawling, trail driving, or mud operation, JKs need to be geared down for improved acceleration and torque. Selecting a lower gear ratio almost is always a requirement for modified off-road JKs because larger tire diameters demand it. Although some models, such as the Rubicons, are better equipped for off-road use, many stock trim JKs need a ratio change for safe and capable off-road service.

Climbing steep hills and rocks takes torque. Even more torque is needed with larger tires. Quinn Thomas is driving the All J Wrangler up a rocky grade using a Hemi V-8 conversion with 4.88 ratio gearing for the axles. Power is not an issue with this Jeep.

The Rubicon models have an optional axle ratio of 4.10:1 and are equipped with 32-inch tires. Pentastar 3.6-liter JKs have plenty of torque and power for good off-road performance. However, increasing tire diameter adversely affects performance unless axle ratios are changed. The Rubicon with 32-inch tires and a 4.10 gear ratio runs almost the same RPM at 60 mph as a 4.88 gear ratio and 37-inch tires. This is the ideal ratio for the Pentastar engine with an automatic transmission. The early 3.8-liter V-6 engine is underpowered

and has a higher first gear ratio in the automatic transmission. The optimal gear ratio for 37-inch tires is a 5.13:1 axle ratio. The first gear ratio in the manual transmission–equipped JKs is somewhat lower, a 4.56 axle ratio in the 2012-and-newer JKs works. The earlier JKs needed a 4.88 axle ratio for good off-road performance.

The Wrangler JK has housed several different engines since its release in 2007. Chrysler installed a 3.8-liter EGH V-6 in the 2007–2011 JKs that produced 202 hp and 237 pound force-feet of torque. It was mated to a 4-speed transmission. From 2012 on up, the new and much more powerful Pentastar V-6 was slotted into the JK engine bay, which cranks out 285 hp and 260 ft-lbs of torque. The 5-speed automatic was paired with the Pentastar and transmitted power to the wheels. The differences are significant. Most important, the two engines and transmission packages require different gearing when upgrading to larger tires.

The 6-speed manual transmission is standard on all JKs; a 4-speed automatic transmission was offered as an option 2007–2011. The 2012–present JKs offer a 5-speed automatic transmission as an option, and these

Jeep JK Gear Ratios

3.8-Liter Engine, Automatic Transmission (2007–2011)		3.8-Liter Engine, Manual Transmission (2007–2011)		3.8-Liter Engine, Automatic Transmission (2012–up)		3.6-Liter Engine, Manual Transmission (2012–up)	
1st	2.84	1st	4.460	1st	3.59	1st	4.460
2nd	1.57	2nd	2.610	2nd	2.19	2nd	2.610
3rd	1.00	3rd	1.720	3rd	1.41	3rd	1.720
4th	0.69	4th	1.250	4th	1.00	4th	1.250
Reverse	2.21	5th	1.000	5th	0.83	5th	1.000
		6th	0.797	Reverse	3.16	6th	0.797
		Reverse	4.060			Reverse	4.060

in general provide better driveability for off-road service. Most JKs use the Command-Trac part-time four-wheel-drive system with an optional Trac-Loc limited-slip differential. The Rubicon models use the Rock-Trac NV241 transfer case with 4:1 low-range gearing. Electric locking front and rear differentials are standard on the Rubicon. Below are the transmission gear ratios for JK models.

The final-drive and crawl ratios are critical for off-road driving. The final-drive ratio determines the speed of the vehicle at a given engine RPM. A numerically higher ratio means that the vehicle travels at a slower speed for a given engine RPM with all else being equal; for example, a JK with a 3.21 axle ratio and 32-inch-tall tires travels at 74 mph at 2,500 engine RPM. The same tires with a 3.73 axle ratio travel at 64 mph at 2,500 rpm. With the Rubicon 4.10 axle ratio the speed drops to 58 mph at 2,500 rpm.

The second important ratio is the crawl ratio. In two-wheel drive and in drive (1.0:1 transmission ratio), the crawl ratio is the same as the axle ratio. In four-wheel-drive low range with a 4.0:1 transfer case ratio also in drive, the crawl ratio is 16.4:1. To calculate this, multiply the transmission

The Jeep Wrangler JK Rubicon comes equipped with a 4.0:1 transfer case low range ratio and 4.10:1 axle gearing. The transmission's crawl ratio in first gear is a low 58.9:1. With the stock 32-inch-diameter tires, a Rubicon can almost idle up a climb like this, which has a 25-degree slope, in first gear. With bigger tires, it takes a little throttle opening. Even more important is having a low crawl ratio for descending. Descending this slope in first in a stock JK Rubicon is a breeze without braking. Speed is kept to about 3 mph, about the same speed maintained by the hill assist found on newer JKs with automatic transmissions.

Axle and Transfer Case Gear Ratios

The table below shows OEM and aftermarket axle ratio and transfer case ratio combinations and the overall crawl ratio.

Model	Transfer Case (4LO)	Axle	Crawl Ratio
Rubicon	4.00	4.10	58.9
Unlimited Rubicon	4.00	4.10	58.9
Sahara	2.72	3.21	31.3
Unlimited Sahara	2.72	3.21	31.3
Sport	2.72	3.21	31.3
Unlimited Sport	2.72	3.21	31.3
Optional 3.73 final drive ratio	2.72	3.73	36.4
Optional 3.73 final drive ratio	4.00	3.73	53.6
Aftermarket rear axle ratio	4.00	4.56	65.5
Aftermarket rear axle ratio	4.00	4.88	69.5
Aftermarket rear axle ratio	4.00	5.13	73.7

These calculations are based on a 5-speed automatic transmission with a 3.59:1 first gear.

New gearing for the Wrangler JK allows much improved performance on the trails. When upgrading to larger tires, lower gearing is needed to keep the same performance. Aftermarket replacement ring and pinion gears are made from high-tensile strength 8620 steel. Motive Gear offers these gears for the Dana 44 axle housing. The ratio is 4.88:1 using a pinion gear with 8 teeth and a spline count of 24 and a ring gear with 39 teeth. Gears are checked when manufactured for fit where the gears mesh. The proper pinion depth is crucial for long wear and quiet operation. A number is stamped on the gear set so that the installer can set the pinion depth in the ring gear to the optimum setting during installation. The ring and pinion gear sets for the front axle are reverse cut.

Rock crawling up steep ledges takes considerable torque. If this Jeep had stock axle ratio gearing with 37-inch tires, it would struggle to ascend the ledge. But with 4.88:1 gearing, it has no trouble even in second gear.

gear ratio by the axle ratio and then multiply the result by the transfer case ratio. A Rubicon with an automatic transmission in first gear and low range has a crawl ratio of 58.9. The higher the numerical crawl ratio number, the slower the vehicle speed will be at a given engine RPM. The higher number translates into more torque multiplication, which is important when climbing hills and rock crawling. The higher crawl ratio number also helps keep speed lower when descending steep hills.

The Pentastar 3.6-liter V-6 makes more horsepower and torque than the earlier 3.8-liter V-6, so the earlier 3.8-liter engine needs a lower axle ratio (numerically higher) to achieve similar performance on the steep climbs and rocks encountered on the trails. Increasing tire diameter to 37 inches on a Pentastar-equipped JK, for example, requires only a 4.88 axle ratio (although many people prefer 5.13 ratio), but with the earlier 3.8, the 5.13 or 5.38 axle ratio is more useful. Although not changing axle ratios does keep engine RPM down at a given speed, for most, the loss of acceleration and torque is not a good trade-off.

Tire Size Versus Ratio

Higher axle ratios (numerically lower numbers) increase vehicle speed at a given RPM. A taller tire has the same effect of increasing speed at a given engine RPM. In both cases torque multiplication has been reduced, and this decreases acceleration and hill climbing capabilities. As tire size (diameter) increases, the axle ratio gearing needs to be lower (numerically higher) to keep the road speed in the same range as with

smaller tires and stock gearing. Using 2,500 engine RPM as a baseline in the fourth gear of an automatic transmission in a Rubicon (4.10 axle ratio stock) and 32-inch-tall tires, road speed is 58 mph. Increasing the tire diameter to 37 inches (36.7 inches actual) increases road speed to 66.5 mph. But this also reduces torque multiplication and decreases acceleration. To gain back the torque and acceleration, a gear change is required, and the closest ratio to accomplish this is 4.88 axle ratio. With the 4.88 gearing,

AEV's ProCal Module plugs into the OBD II port on all JK models from 2007 to present. On 2012 to present Pentastar engine-equipped JKs, the engine goes into "limp home" mode if the gear ratios are changed and the computer is not reprogrammed. The module adjusts the speedometer and gear ratio when larger tires are installed. If the speedometer is not recalibrated, you experience a significant decrease in the performance of the electronic stability program (ESP), transmission shift points, and engine output. In addition, the Tire Pressure Monitoring System can now be recalibrated to better suit aftermarket tires without activating the dash light. The ProCal Module makes it possible to activate daytime running lamps, one-touch turn signals, enable a temporarily increased engine idle speed for winching, clear engine codes, and even has a feature to help technicians align the steering perfectly for optimal ESP performance.

speed is now back to 56 mph. This translates to a smaller loss of speed, but a slight gain in torque to the wheels compared to stock.

Resetting the Computer

Aftermarket programmers can remap the 2012-and-newer 3.6-liter Pentastar engine ignition system. If you change axle gear ratios and/or tire size, you must reprogram the Jeep computer to the new specs. Otherwise, transmission shifting, the Electronic Stability Control, and other parameters are compromised and performance deteriorates. Some programmers allow you to alter settings for the sway-bar disconnect and electric locker operation. The AEV Pro-Cal programmer, Banks OttoMind, Superchips, Diablo, and Edge all make programmers for the Pentastar computer in the JK. The AEV ProCal, for example, plugs into the OBD II port under the driver-side dash. Dip switches are used for recalibration. Other programmers, such as the Superchips TrailDash II, also plug into the OBD II port but have a touch screen with many options and easier reprogramming.

Ring and Pinion Gear Upgrades

The primary reason for changing ring and pinion gear ratios on the JK is to gain low-speed performance when larger tires are installed, as previously explained. Ring and pinion gears are a hypoid design. You need to select high-quality ring and pinion gears, such as 8620, for reliability and performance. The 8620 steel forgings machined on a Gleason gear milling machine is the most common material for gears. The 9310 steel is used for high-stress applications such as

Installing the ring gear into the housing so that the ring gear meshes perfectly with the pinion gear is tricky. Ring and pinion installation takes experience and patience.

drag racing, but these gears wear rapidly and are not intended for highway or off-road situations. The gears should be heat-treated to a Rockwell C hardness of 60 to 64. This method of heat treating creates a hard surface to resist wear but leaves the steel below the surface more pliable to resist breaking of teeth on the gears or twisting the pinion shaft. Yukon, Motive Gear, and Revolution Gear manufacture quality ring and pinion gear sets in a wide range of ratios for the JK.

Axle Upgrades

The strength and material of the axles need to match the application of the JK. Axles are one of many items that can ruin your day. The stock JK axles are adequate for use with stock tires on moderately difficult trails, but the load on the axle shafts increases dramatically with bigger tires and more difficult trails. One issue with big tires is wheelspin. Often, when tires lose traction they suddenly regain grip; this shock can cause an axle to snap and it can also twist a stock JK driveshaft. Most stock

The ring gear has been installed in the axle housing with an ARB Air Locker. Steel shims are placed between the housing and the carrier bearings to space the ring gear to the left or right. This adjustment is used to get the ring gear to mesh perfectly with the pinion gear.

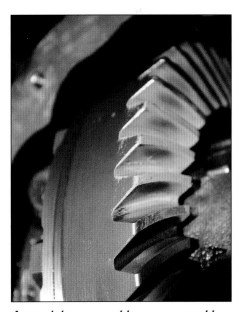

A special gear marking compound is placed on the teeth of the ring gear after initial installation. The pinion gear is then rotated. This allows the installer to see the pattern of the gears meshing, If the pattern is too deep into the gear or too shallow, spacer thicknesses must be adjusted to move the ring gear so that the optimum pattern is found, It can take several adjustments to get ideal mesh between the gears and a good pattern.

axle shafts are manufactured from 1040 or 1541 steel. High-quality aftermarket axle shafts are made from 4340 chrome-moly steel and are heat treated. Chrome-moly shafts are much more durable and less prone to breaking. High-quality axle upgrades are available from RCV, Revolution, Yukon, and Nitro.

Stock JK axles are prone to breaking under higher loads especially with larger tires. Rear axles from Revolution Gear & Axle are made from 4340 chrome-moly alloy steel. The Revolution axle is in the foreground; the stock axle is behind. Stronger materials and beefier construction combine to minimize axle failure even with the higher loads created by larger tires with superior traction. Axles are available with a variety of spline configurations. Non-Rubicon JKs come with 30-spline axles; the Rubicon is equipped with 32-spline axles. Aftermarket axles are available with up to 35 splines. More splines means more contact surface area so the load is distributed over more contact area. Also, higher-spline-count axles have larger-diameter shafts, Combined with stronger chrome-moly steel, aftermarket axles are stronger.

The stock JK front axles use universal joints to accommodate steering. Stock Rubicon axles have a 30-spline inner shaft (non-Rubicons use a 29-spline shaft) and a 32-spline outer shaft. U-joints are also prone to binding at the extremes of suspension and steering travel. Here is the RCV axle constant velocity joint. CV joints are much stronger through the full range of travel.

The RCV JK axle set on this JK is a 35-spline design to mate with ARB 35-spline air locker. This is about the strongest, smoothest operation front axle set available for the Dana 44. Although the outer shaft is still 32-spline, the inner shaft is 35-spline so strength is increased. When crawling on rocks in tight quarters where full or near full lock steering is needed, the CV axle shafts do not bind and are far less likely to fail. Reid Racing steering knuckles are cast from ductile iron and replace the stock units. The tie-rod gains 1.5 inches of clearance to minimize vulnerability to trail damage. The drag link is flipped and gains 3 inches of height to perfectly correct the steering geometry for common 3- to 4-inch suspension lifts.

Front Axle Shafts

The front axles on a JK use U-joints to allow steering, but constant velocity joints provide greater strength and improve steering response. Some aftermarket front axles use 4340 chrome-moly and are larger in diameter, further increasing axle strength, and resistance to breakage. Axles break most often when excessive wheelspin occurs and the tires suddenly gain traction. This is most common when rock crawling, especially when the surface is slick. The tires can burn through the surface and gain enough traction to put high loads on the axles. Larger-diameter axle shafts require the use of an aftermarket differential locker. In addition, the driver- and passenger-side shafts are different lengths due to the offset of the differential center section toward the driver's side of the JK.

The strongest front axle shafts use CV joints instead of U-joints. CV joints can be twice as strong as a stock front JK axle. CV joints resist binding and transfer power to the wheels much more smoothly than a U-joint.

The axle housings bend, especially in the front. The stock Dana 44 axle tubes have a 2.50-inch outside diameter. The end forgings and axle tubes tend to be weak links and the axle housing can bend under significant load in many off-road situations, and that's why many JK owners upgrade to the Dana 60 units. When the housings bend, it causes the wheels to go out of alignment and the tires to wear unevenly. In addition, this places a greater load on bearings

Installing an ARB Air Locker Differential

When building a rock crawling or trail driving JK, you often need to gear down, so your JK has more torque to scale rocks, hills, and other challenging obstacles. In addition, when increasing tire size, you need to install lower gear ratio, so your JK delivers excellent torque. You must carefully and diligently follow the proper installation and mesh procedures when installing new ring-and-pinion gears. If the ring gear teeth do not mesh perfectly with the teeth on the pinion gear, rapid wear, gear whine, and eventual failure will result.

A dash-mounted button activates an onboard air compressor to send a pneumatic signal to the ARB Air Locker, which locks-in both axle shafts for off-road driving. When the air enters the differential center section, it triggers the piston and the clutch gear to move into the locked position. Both axles are locked into position for improved traction. The differential is unlocked when the dash-mounted switch is pushed again.

It takes an experienced professional such as Oscar from Currie Enterprises about 3 hours to install ring-and-pinion gear set in a Dana 60 axle housing with the housing on a custom work stand. The process is much more difficult in a vehicle on a lift. Attempting to install ring-and-pinion gears from under a vehicle while on a creeper or your back is not recommended. You should plan on several hours to complete the process. Getting the gears' mesh pattern perfect requires installation and removal of both the ring gear and the pinion gear multiple times unless you get

You must remove the carrier from the axle housing and disassemble it before you can reassemble the differential with the required parts. The first step when installing a new ring and pinion requires careful insertion of the outer pinion bearing race into the snout of the housing. You need to position the race squarely onto the housing and properly align the bearing driver and this old aluminum shaft milled to fit the bearing race. Gently tap the race into the housing until it is fully seated in the proper position.

really lucky. Prior to installation, all parts need to be thoroughly cleaned.

Remember that ring-and-pinion gear sets require break-in. Follow the procedure recommended by the gear manufacturer. It typically takes about 500 miles for good break-in. Driving short distances to get heat in the gears then a complete cool down is part of the procedure. Failure to adhere to break-in procedures will cause rapid wear and gear failure within 1,000 to 2,000 miles. Improper break-in will lead to a whining noise as the wear increases. ∎

You need a hydraulic arbor press to perform the next procedure. Place the pinion into the correct position then a shaft presses the outer pinion bearing onto the pinion shaft.

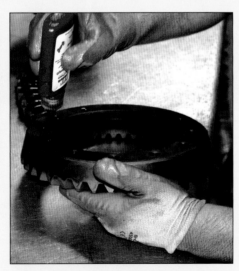

Squirt Red Loctite on the ring gear threads and bolts because these bolts must remain secured during operation.

Next, torque down the ring gear bolts to the differential case assembly on the ARB Air Locker. Although this mechanic is using an impact wrench, we recommend using a torque wrench so the bolts are torqued to the correct spec. If bolts are over-tightened, it can damage the threads.

Installing an ARB Air Locker Differential *CONTINUED*

The carrier bearing requires an interference fit on the ARB Locker housing. Align the custom bearing driver with the carrier bearing (it's the same diameter as the carrier bearing). Using a dead-blow hammer carefully drive the bearing into the carrier. Some installers heat the bearing to allow it to slide over the bearing seat.

Apply a light coat of grease to the surface of the air locker seal housing before placing it into the proper position on the carrier.

To check lash clearance between ring and pinion teeth with gear mesh compound, measure the lash, or free-play, between the ring-and-pinion gears with a dial indicator. Ten thousandths of an inch is a good lash. Lash is adjusted with shims between the pinion gear and inner pinion bearing surface.

The ARB Air Locker uses a copper air tube for locker activation, so the carrier bearing cap must be notched for the tube to fit in the housing. Secure the carrier bearing cap in a vice. A pneumatic rotary tool with an abrasive wheel grinds a notch in the cap.

Use great care when placing the ring gear and air locker assembly in the axle housing because you don't want to damage the gear or carrier housing. If the ring gear drops too quickly, fingers are vulnerable. Once the carrier is placed onto the bearing saddles, install the bearing caps and torque to the manufacturer's recommend specs.

Use shims to space the ring gear location laterally in the housing. When the correct number and thickness of shims are in place, check the yellow gear-mesh compound. The pinion gear should have a balanced mesh pattern in contact and the pinion should be in the middle of the drive and coast sides. When the gears are rotated, a pattern is left on the yellow compound. This is a good mesh pattern, but it took three attempts to get here.

The copper air tube for the air lock must be routed inside the axle housing and clear the gears. Then trim it and place it through a tapped hole in the housing. A fitting holds the tube in place and attaches the plastic air line from the air compressor.

Properly position the pinion seal and gently tap it into the axle housing snout.

Once the gear mesh has been set, we recommend using a torque wrench (not an impact wrench as is shown here) to tighten the bolt securing the yoke to the pinion shaft.

Use two Cleco pins to position the differential cover on the housing. Then place the cover over the Clecos and insert the cover bolts.

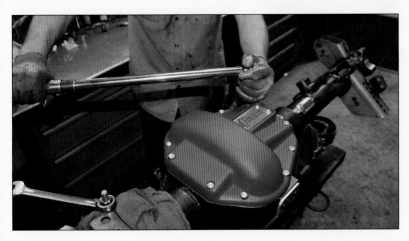

Once all of the bolts are inserted, torque the bolts to the manufacturer's specifications.

and ball joints and those also experience greater wear; the situation is compounded when 35-inch-or-larger tires are used.

Rear Axle Shafts

The rear axle shafts do not use U-joints, so they are slightly more durable than the front axles. But chrome-moly shafts still offer superior strength and reliability. Driver- and passenger-side rear axle shafts are the same length.

JKs equipped with Dana 30 axle assemblies use a 27-spline axle shaft. The stock Rubicon models use a 30-spline shaft. The 35-spline axle shafts are more desirable due to increased strength, but the carrier in the axle housing must be changed to accommodate these axles. Most aftermarket differential lockers are available for 35-spline axle shafts.

Axle Housing Reinforcements

The rigors of off-road driving, especially the more extreme trails, place considerable stress on axle housings. The Dana 44 housing and especially the Dana 30 housing are not particularly strong and are prone to bending. The front axle housing is much more susceptible to damage than the rear housing. Moreover, the larger the tires and more difficult the terrain, the more likely it is that damage will occur. For this reason, several companies offer strengthening solutions to reduce the chance of bending the front axle housing.

Trusses

Axle housing trusses are welded to the housing between the differential center section and the axle flanges. By bridging the weak areas of the axle housing, trusses increase the housing strength considerably. Because trusses are welded in place, it is critical to have the work undertaken by an experienced welder/

The RockJock track bar bracket is welded in place. These components add tremendous strength to the housing and brackets, but the welds must have proper penetration. Also by welding in the optimum sequence, the housing is less prone to warping from the high heat.

The Artec trusses and steering knuckle brace are beefy. The trusses bridge the gaps between the ends of the axle housing and the gear center section; the steering knuckle brace makes the knuckle much more rigid. This reduces flex, greatly reduces the chance of a knuckle failure, and reduces wear on the ball joints.

The stock Dana 44 axle housing in the Rubicon model is prone to bending under heavy loads. In addition, many of the stock brackets on the housing can bend or break. Artec trusses have been welded on to reinforce the stock housing. The beefier tie rod, drag link and track bar are from Currie. Also added to the housing are Currie RockJock brackets for the track bar.

Yukon Gear 4.88 ratio gears have been installed in a Currie Rock Jock 44 axle housing. The stock electric locker has been replaced with an ARB air locker with Currie 35-spline axle shafts. The copper tube is the air actuator for the air locker that will run through the center section of the differential housing and connect to the airline from an ARB compressor. It allows a steep approach angle for a single tire-rock encounter. Several companies offer very good replacement ring and pinion gear sets including Yukon, Revolution, Motive Gear, G2, and Alloy.

The RockJock track bar bracket bolts and welds to the original track bar mount on the stock axle. The new mounting hole raises the axle end of the track bar. This helps keep the track bar geometry ideal on lifted JKs. The bracket is then welded in adding rigidity to the bracket and the axle housing.

fabricator. Axle housing truss kits such as the ones from Artec Industries increase the strength of the housing and resist bending common on stock axle housing, even with the Dana 44 housing. The truss elements are prefabricated from mild steel and are easily tack welded in place. When all the truss parts are in place they can be MIG welded for a rigid structure.

Inner Support Tubes

One of the reasons the stock JK axle housing bends is the lightweight construction of the housing, especially the axle tubes. Several companies make inner tube supports that strengthen the axle tubes and housing from the inside.

Gussets and Brackets

Shock absorber and control arm brackets, as discussed in Chapter 2, are prone to damage on both the front and rear axle housing. Adding gussets to the brackets or replacing the brackets with more durable versions ensures minimal problems with

The Currie RockJock 60 is the ultimate in strength for the JK. The rear-axle assembly of the RockJock III high-pinion rear-end assembly for the 2007 and up Jeep JK includes the complete housing with the 65-45-12 ductile-iron housing center, AR400 heat-treated bottom skid plate allowing the axle to slide over rocks easily, 3 x .375–inch wall DOM steel tubes. In addition, it has red Currie ductile-iron differential cover, a 1350 yoke, custom housing ends that accept set 80 axle bearings and all factory disc brake hardware. ABS and ESP sensors are easily bolted back on. All new heavy-duty Currie Jeep JK suspension brackets are mounted and feature multiple control arm mounting holes, multiple track bar mounting holes, and adjustable shock mounting holes. Also included are the Currie Performance forged-alloy 35-spline axle shafts that are dual drilled for the stock 5-on-5-inch wheel-bolt pattern as well as 5-on-5-1/2-inch pattern. Axles feature 1/2-inch wheel studs, ABS tone rings, pressed on axle bearings, and bearing retainer plates. All you need to complete this unit is a high-pinion Dana 60 ring-and-pinion gear set, Dana 60 35-spline carrier, a center section bearing, and setup kit. Your JK's stock rotors, calipers, and caliper mounting brackets transfer over. This 66-inch-wide unit requires the use of 17-inch wheels. JKs from 2012 and up with the Pentastar 3.6-liter V-6 need a computer controller, such as the AEV ProCal Module to reset the gear ratio and tire height in the vehicle's computer. (Photo Courtesy Currie Enterprises)

The Currie RockJock 60 front axle assembly comes with all of the brackets and mounts needed for a straight bolt-in replacement for the standard front axle assembly in the JK. The Currie RockJock 60 front axle shares the same specs as the rear crate axle assembly. In addition, the tie-rod and drag link on the crate axle assembly are the Currie Currectlync heavy-duty parts. The Currie RockJock 60 features a distinctive slanted differential center section. (Photo Courtesy Currie Enterprises)

bracket bending or failure. Often gussets also act as mini–skidplates.

Full Axle Assembly Swaps

As the popularity of the Wrangler JK increases, more parts are available to solve issues when using stock components on more extreme trails. Because stock axle housings, especially the front, are prone to bending, the best solution for

The Dynatrac Pro-Rock 44 rear-axle assembly features a high-ground-clearance pinion with semi-floating axles. A step up to a Dana 44–type rear-axle assembly provides the required strength for 31-inch and larger tires. A heavy-duty nodular-iron case is used. Axle tubes are 3-inch diameter for added strength. Extreme-duty suspension brackets are included for an easy bolt-in replacement on the JK. The assembly includes a Dynatrac heavy-duty raised track bar, nodular-iron differential cover, 30-spline axle shafts, and ABS/ESP sensor mount with billet tone rings. (Photo Courtesy Dynatrac)

The Dynatrac ProRock 44 front axle assembly shares the same specifications with the 44 rear axle assembly. In addition, the Dynatrac Pro-Rock 44 front axle assembly accepts Dana 30 and Dana 40 axle shafts, Warn locking hubs, Dynatrac ball joints, Dynatrac Big Brake rotors, and dual-piston calipers. (Photo Courtesy Dynatrac)

increased strength and reliability to upgrade to one of the aftermarket axle assemblies from Currie Enterprises, Dynatrac, G2, and Teraflex. These aftermarket housings typically use larger-diameter, thicker-wall axle tubes, heavy-duty brackets with gussets for added strength and the ability to accommodate a large range of axles and differential lockers. These assemblies are designed as a bolt-in replacement for the stock Dana 30 and 44 axle housings. In addition, these axles also designed to retain the factory JK ESP, ABS, and speedometer sensors.

Currie Enterprises offers a full range of axle assemblies for a variety of applications, including mild to ultra-extreme rock crawling. The RockJock 44 is the entry-level axle in the lineup and a logical first step up from the Dana 30 axle. Fortunately, you can install many stock compo-

nents, such as Rubicon ring and pinion and locker options. This axle is suited for mild to mid JK builds using a stock powertrain with 37-inch tires and a moderate lift. This housing is compatible with stock brakes, hubs, and knuckles, so you don't have to buy aftermarket versions of these parts. The next step up in the RockJock lineup is the RockJock III 60, which delivers exceptional performance in a variety of terrain and extreme rock crawling situations. This stout unit features a 3-inch tube and accepts all the high-pinion Dana 60 ring and pinion gears. Thus, it carries the rugged 9.75-inch ring gear. For superior strength and durability, RockJock III 60 features the Ford Super Duty–type knuckles and brake setup. The RockJock 70 is the ultimate Currie axle and is more axle than many trail and rock crawling rigs need. It has 1-ton inner C knuck-

les, a rotated differential cover, provides a round bottom, and is great for sliding off rocks. Heavy throttle users and 40-inch-plus tires need to keep moving up the scale.

DynaTrac is another leader in off-road axle performance and carries a complete lineup of axle assemblies to suit almost every off-road application. Like the RockJock 44, Dynatrac's ProRock 44 accepts the factory JK Dana 44 ring and pinions, so you are afforded a wide range of gear ratio options and are not required to buy aftermarket ring and pinion gears. The unit also offers incredibly high clearance that surpasses the Dana 30. As the entry-level trail and rock crawling axle assembly, the axle is suited for up to 38-inch tires and up to 2.5-inch lift. Another welcome feature is Dynatrac heavy-duty ball joints for increased longevity and better suspension articulation. Dynatrac recommends no more than a 38-inch tire. Those with a need for bigger meats and/or tall lifts need to keep reading.

The ProRock 44 Unlimited has all the same features as the standard unit, but incorporates brackets for JKs with 3-inch-and-taller lifts. The brackets have increased caster to improve alignment and thereby enhance handling and control. Although alignment issues are sorted out with the ProRock 44 Unlimited, tire size is still a limited factor. All ProRock 44 housings use a 3-inch-diameter tube with wall thickness upgrades available. However, if you're running 37-inch-and-bigger tires, you should step up to the ProRock XD60.

The Dynatrac ProRock XD60 offers increased strength for extreme conditions, including high-speed desert driving, running 40-inch-or-larger tires, and significant power increases.

The Currie RockJock 60 delivers superior performance and rugged reliability for the JK. The rear axle assembly of the RockJock III high-pinion rear end assembly for the 2007 and up Jeep JK includes the complete housing with the 65-45-12 ductile iron housing center, AR400 heat treated bottom skidplate allowing the axle to slide over rocks easily, 3 x .375–inch wall DOM steel tubes, red Currie ductile iron differential cover, 1350 yoke and custom housing ends that accept set 80 axle bearings and allow for all factory disc brake hardware and ABS and ESP sensors to bolt back on. All new heavy-duty Currie Jeep JK suspension brackets are mounted and feature multiple control arm mounting holes, multiple track-bar mounting holes, and adjustable shock mounting holes.

Also included are the Currie performance forged alloy 35-spline axle shafts that are dual drilled for the stock 5-on-5-inch wheel bolt pattern as well as 5-on-5.5–inch pattern. Axles feature 1/2–inch wheel studs, ABS tone rings, and axle bearings pressed on, as well as the bearing retainer plates. To complete this unit, you need a high-pinion Dana 60 ring and pinion gear set, Dana 60 35-spline carrier of your choice, a center section bearing and setup kit and labor to set it up. Your JK's stock rotors, calipers, and caliper mounting brackets transfer over.

This unit is 66-inch wide. This unit requires the use of 17-inch wheels. The 2012 and newer JKs with the Pentastar 3.6-liter V-6 need a computer programmer, such as the AEV ProCal Module to reset the gear ratio and tire height in the vehicle's computer.

The Currie RockJock 60 comes with all of the brackets and mounts needed for a straight bolt-in replacement for the standard rear axle assembly in the JK. The Currie RockJock 60 is also available for the front.

The Currie RockJock 60 features a distinctive slanted differential center section. The center section comes with a replaceable lower AR400 abrasion resistant steel skidplate, carrier caps, bearing spacer to upgrade to the larger front pinion bearing to the pinion gear, and pinion seal.

The center section is built from high-strength nodular iron and provides high ground clearance. The ring gear features a large 10.1-inch ring gear and a larger carrier, increasing the overall strength compared to a stock Dana 60. The XD60 weighs about 15 percent less than the 60 but is still heavier than a stock front JK axle assembly.

Custom housings are another option. The Dana 60 and Ford 9-inch housing provide incredible strength and performance. Currie Enterprises uses the Ford 9-inch design for a complete axle assembly. Currie can build a 9-inch rear axle assembly for your JK and application. You can upgrade a Sport or Sahara model to a 4:10 gear ratio and differential

lockers, take-offs from the Wrangler Rubicon. It's a cost-effective way to improve performance and reliability.

Axle Lockers

Differentials are designed so that one wheel on an axle can freewheel. While cornering, the inside tire rotates more slowly than the outside tire. The

The ARB air locker uses a sliding ring to lock the differential. The ring (top left) is in the unlocked position. Air pressure from a compressor pushes the ring to the right to lock the differential (white arrow in lower photo). When the locker is deactivated, a spring pushes the ring back to the unlocked position.

Driveshafts take a beating on lifted JKs especially in the rocks. A seriously abused stock JK rear driveshaft (right) has a torn dust boot and dings in the shaft. The JE Reel 1350 heavy-duty rear driveshaft is much stronger and uses a CV joint that has an angularity of 32 degrees, which is necessary for lifted JKs. Although the tubing is smaller than stock, it is much stronger. The 2.75-inch outside diameter by .083-inch-wall-thickness tubing provides much greater durability and reduces the chance of binding.

The JE Reel front driveshaft (top) is much beefier than the front stock driveshaft (middle); the stock rear driveshaft is shown at the bottom. The tube of the rear driveshaft is heavily dented and the dust boot has been torn off. One of the issues with the stock driveshafts is twisting under extreme loads. This usually occurs when wheelspin stops abruptly due to a rapid increase in tire traction. Aftermarket driveshafts are strong enough to prevent much of the twisting.

differential allows this to occur without tire scrub. However, this reduces traction. A differential locker locks the driver- and passenger-side wheels together. This increases traction, but also increases tire scrub and steering effort when cornering. Differential lockers are usually associated with more extreme four-wheeling situations. But if you drive in sand, mud, snow, or ice, having at least one differential locker makes life much easier in adverse conditions because you're able to transfer power to both wheels for better traction.

The Rubicon comes equipped with electric lockers on both front and rear axles. Although electric lockers work quite well, they are prone to failure in more extreme conditions,

often due to electrical issues and actuator failure. Aftermarket E-Lockers tend to be more durable and are a good choice if you are upgrading on models with no lockers. Air lockers use compressed air from a compressor (or a compressed gas source such as the carbon dioxide in a Power Tank). Air lockers are more durable and activate more quickly. Aftermarket lockers are also easier to activate than the stock lockers found on the Rubicon and some Sahara models.

Limited-Slip and Detroit Lockers

Limited-slip differentials, such as the Eaton Detroit TruTrac, operate automatically and work well to improve traction. These traction aids are fine for easy to moderate off-road driving. Other types of traction aids such as the Detroit locker are more aggressive and work great in a straight

line, but can be difficult to drive in adverse conditions on the highway. For more aggressive off roading, most JK owners prefer selectable lockers such as E-lockers or air lockers.

Driveshafts, Yokes, CV Joints, and U-joints

In more extreme off-road conditions, the stock JK driveshafts are prone to damage from rocks, twisting, and CV joint and U-joint failure. The stock JK driveshafts use a Rzeppa CV joint. The stock front axles use U-joints. The large-diameter rear driveshaft is especially susceptible to damage. Lifted JKs also encounter clearance issues with the exhaust pipe. The solution to these issues is to upgrade the driveshafts to aftermarket products, which handle lifts and extreme conditions more effectively. The 1350 driveshafts and yokes are more durable and should be used on tubular steel driveshafts when running larger tires.

John Currie's 2015 Jeep Wrangler JK Unlimited

Owning a company that manufactures high-end Jeep parts does have perks, but John Currie needed to build the ultimate off-road JK. He embarked upon that journey a few years ago, buying and building a 2015 Wrangler JK for his personal use, allowing him access anytime. He purchased the JK in February 2015 from a local Jeep dealer in Southern California and performed all of the work himself. John's philosophy for this build was to create a Jeep that he could wheel anywhere under all conditions. Creature comfort was an important element of the build. John's highway travels have covered the West Coast from Washington to Cabo San Lucas, Mexico, all in search of great four-wheeling adventures.

John's JK made its first appearance at the Moab Easter Jeep Safari in 2015, just two months after its purchase. Since then, John has traveled to Washington for snow off roading, run the Trail of Missions in Mexico as well as pre-running for the Baja 1,000 and Baja 500. Several trips to the Rubicon and runs on the trails in Big Bear, Johnson Valley, and other 4x4 areas in California round out John's use of his JK.

John equipped his JK with 39x13.50x17–inch BF-Goodrich Krawler T/A KX tires on KMC wheels. To handle the stress of rock crawling with 39-inch tires, Currie RockJock 70 axle housings with 40-spline full floating axles are in the rear and Currie chrome-moly 1-ton 35-spline inner and outer with 1480 U-joints are used up front. The front locker is a Detroit locker with an Eaton E-locker in the rear.

John has an interesting philosophy concerning lockers. He has used a Detroit locker on the front of many Jeeps. The primary incentive is automatic locker engagement, which makes rock crawling easier. This is the same setup he used on the King of the Hammers Every Man Challenge Jeep when he won three years straight. The rear locker is electric. The caveat to this setup is the need to use a ram assist in the power steering. PSC power steering components are used throughout the system, including the PSC steering box.

John Currie loves to go Jeepin'. He has traveled all over the West coast to tackle legendary, challenging trails such as those in Moab, Utah. John selected a JK Unlimited Rubicon because of the creature comforts and highway capabilities. He wanted to be able to drive his JK to go wheeling, not tow. Even with 39-inch-tall tires, he is able to accomplish that easily. (Photo Courtesy Currie Enterprises)

John Currie's JK Unlimited Specifications

Year/Model: 2015 Wrangler Unlimited

Engine, Transmission & Transfer Case: Stock

Tires: 39x13.50x17–inch BFGoodrich Krawler T/A KX

Wheels: KMC

Rear axle housing: Currie RockJock 70

Front axle housing: Currie RockJock 70

Front & Rear ring/pinion: 5.38

Rear axles: Currie chromoly 40-spline full floating

Front axles: Currie chromoly 1-ton 35-spline inner and outer w/ 1480 U-joints

Front & Rear locker: 35-spline Detroit locker/40-spline E-locker

Front & Rear suspension: Currie RockJock 4-inch Johnny Joint suspension system w/ 2.5-inch King bypass and King air bump shocks

Front & Rear control arms: Currie billet aluminum double adjustable Johnny Joint

Front & Rear track bar: Currie adjustable Johnny Joint track bar

Steering tie-rod & drag link: Custom billet aluminum bar with Currie Modular Extreme Duty ends

Ball joints: F-350/F-450 1-ton

Spindles: Currie Extreme 1-ton-unit bearings

Steering knuckles: Currie 1-ton ball-joint style

Steering dampener: PSC ram assist

Power steering box, pump, cooler & reservoir: PSC

Bracket for steering dampener: Currie ram assist bracket

Front brakes: Wilwood 14-inch rotor, four-piston caliper

Rear Brakes: Stock

Cat-back exhaust: Magnaflow

Auxiliary switch system: sPOD

Onboard compressor: Viair

Transmission cooler: Auxiliary

Front & Rear bumper: Savvy

Fenders: MCE

Rock sliders: CRC

The front and rear suspensions use the Currie RockJock 4-inch Johnny Joint suspension system with 2.5-inch King bypass shocks and King air bumpstops. The front and rear control arms are Currie billet aluminum double adjustable with Johnny Joints. The tie-rod and drag link are custom billet aluminum bar with Currie Modular Extreme Duty ends. The ball joints come from a Ford F-350/F-450 1 ton. Currie Extreme 1-ton-unit bearing spindles and Currie 1-ton ball joint–style steering knuckles work with the RockJock 70 setup.

The ability to run world class rock crawling trails requires big tires. John uses the 39 x 13.50 x 17–inch BFGoodrich Krawler T/A KX on his JK. The wheels are KMC beadlocks. These tires and John's extensive experience including winning the King of the Hammers Everyman Challenge class multiple times makes climbing rocks and ledges a breeze. (Photo Courtesy Currie Enterprises)

The axle housings are Currie RockJock 70 with 5.38 ring and pinion ratios. The axles in the rear are Currie chrome-moly 40 full floating and an Eaton 40-spline E-locker. Suspension consists of the Currie RockJock 4-inch Johnny Joint suspension system with 2.5–inch King bypass shocks and King air bumpstops. The rear control arms are Currie billet aluminum double adjustable with Johnny Joints. Rear brakes are stock. The rear bumper is from Savvy Off Road. (Photo Courtesy Currie Enterprises)

The front brakes are Wilwood 4-piston calipers with Wilwood 14-inch rotors and Wilwood pads. The rear brakes are stock. The cat-back exhaust is from Magnaflow. A sPOD is used for additional electrical component switches. A Viair onboard compressor airs up tires after a run.

The front and rear bumpers are from Savvy Off Road, and Currie Racing makes the rock sliders. MCE flexible fenders grace the front and rear. A Warn Zeon 10-S Platinum winch with a Factor 55 fairlead system is used for the rare recoveries. Auxiliary lighting is from Rigid Industries.

John Currie has created a great trail rig and rock crawler with excellent highway manners. By keeping it simple with quality components, combined with outstanding driving skills, John can truly tackle any terrain that presents itself.

Front suspension is all Currie RockJock with the Currie Antirock sway bar. Rear axles are 1-ton 35-spline inner and outer with 1480 U-joints. Front shocks are 2.5-inch King bypass shocks and King air bumpstops. The front control arms are Currie billet aluminum double adjustable with Johnny Joints. Power steering consists of PSC steering box, pump, cooler, reservoir and a ram assist. Steering linkages are Currie custom billet aluminum bar with Currie Modular Extreme Duty ends. The spindles are Currie Extreme 1-ton unit bearings and the steering knuckles are Currie 1-ton ball-joint style. Ball joints come from a F-350/F-450 1 ton truck. Front brakes are Wilwood 14-inch rotors with the Wilwood four piston calipers and Wilwood brake pads. (Photo Courtesy Currie Enterprises)

Climbing the steep red rock ledges in Moab takes a capable rig and a skilled driver. John and his JK fit the bill. He makes it look easy! (Photo Courtesy Currie Enterprises)

ENGINES, ENGINE SWAPS, AND TRANSMISSIONS

Engine upgrades for the Wrangler JK offer more horsepower and torque. Jeep owners, especially those seeking more extreme adventures, are in search of more power. Moreover, like every other component on a JK, the aftermarket makes a superior product and it's easy to find.

Two categories of upgrades require minimal effort to install. Cold-air intakes and cat-back exhaust systems can add noticeable power gains to both the 3.8-liter and the Pentastar 3.6-liter gas engines. Engine programmers and tuners generally work on any JK, but cold-air intakes and cat-back exhaust systems are different for the 3.8 versus the 3.6 engines. A third category of upgrade, tuning programmers, may make the JK engine more responsive and can change the factory tune of the engine for added power. Programmers allow the owner to change many parameters on the computer, such as tire size and gear ratio.

A fourth upgrade category, superchargers, can add up to 100 hp and 80 ft-lbs of torque, but at a much higher cost and with far greater effort. Not all superchargers are legal in all 50 states.

Cold-Air Intakes

Cold-air intakes flow a greater volume of dense air into the engine and consequently add a little horsepower and torque while improving fuel economy. Cold-air intakes also open some space under the hood. Sometimes this extra space is needed to upgrade to a higher-volume power steering reservoir and power steering cooler. Many of the cold-air intake packages include cleanable air cleaners, saving the cost of replacement filters. Most aftermarket companies in the cold-air intake business offer systems for the Jeep Wrangler JK. These include K&N Filters, Banks Power, aFe, Airaid, Rugged Ridge, and Volant. Typical power gains range in the 10- to 15-hp range and 8 to 12 ft-lbs of torque. Fuel economy gains are typically about 1 mpg. Cold-air intakes add a nice tone to the engine, especially during acceleration.

The Pentastar 3.6-liter V-6 engine delivers plenty of power and torque for off-road driving. Many bolt-on engine accessories are available for both the 3.8-liter and the 3.6-liter Pentastar V-6 engines.

The K&N Series 63 AirCharger cold-air intake was selected for this JK build in part because of the smaller space needed for fitment. To fit the Howe power steering reservoir, extra space was needed. The K&N cold-air intake worked perfectly.

The Banks Ram-Air cold-air intake uses a large oiled filter that allows more airflow into the intake, up to 73 percent more flow according to Banks. Banks Ram-Air cold-air intakes are available for both the 3.8- and the 3.6-liter Pentastar engines.

Performance Exhausts

Cat-back performance exhaust systems typically provide better airflow out of the engine, and thus increase power and improve fuel economy. The gains are small, in the 10- to 15-hp range. Combine the exhaust with a cold-air intake and the gains are worthwhile. V-6 engines such as the Pentastar 3.6 and the earlier 3.8-liter engines sound nice. Add a performance exhaust and the exhaust tone comes alive. Aftermarket companies including Borla, Banks, aFe Power, Magnaflow, and Gibson offer a variety of exhaust systems. Each seems to have a slightly different tone to the exhaust. In addition to power, fuel economy, and sound, some systems improve ground clearance. The stock JK muffler rests laterally across the back of the JK. They get beat up when rock crawling and the exhaust tip can be crushed closed. Although many

The Banks Ram Air Intake System increases air flow allowing a gain of 8 hp and 11 ft-lbs of torque. Tuning the intake tubes reduces engine drone noise. (Photo Courtesy Banks Power)

The Borla Climber is an S-type cat-back exhaust system. The dual 2-inch pipes attach to the manifold and come together into a single 2.5-inch main exhaust pipe. The exhaust system reduces back pressure and allows free flowing exhaust, which increases horsepower and improves fuel economy. Greater gains can be enjoyed when a free flowing exhaust system is used with a cold-air intake.

The stock JK muffler mounts laterally across the chassis in front of the rear bumper. The tailpipe has been cut shorter more than once on this JK due to damage when rock crawling. The muffler has also suffered damage in the rocks. The aluminized steel muffler and tailpipe show signs of rust.

The Banks Power Monster cat-back exhaust improves flow by nearly 20 percent, and it features mandrel-bent stainless-steel construction. The straight-through muffler design delivers a more aggressive exhaust note; without it, it's overly loud. The Banks Monster Exhaust is available for all JK models. (Photo Courtesy Banks Power)

The Borla Climber muffler tucks up next to the frame rails, so that the muffler is less likely to get damaged in the big rocks. The pipes and muffler also provide additional driveshaft clearance, which is critical on lifted JKs.

The Y-pipe on the Borla Climber allows extra clearance for the driveshaft and transfer case. Note the gusset between the exhaust pipes near the frame. This increases strength by distributing vibration from the engine over a larger area of the pipes. The load on the welded joints is reduced and failure is much less likely.

of the aftermarket exhaust systems place the muffler in the stock location, some companies offer designs that tuck the muffler between the frame rails on the driver's side. Moving the muffler eliminates the potential for damage.

Engine Tuners

Engine tuners modify the program of the onboard computer. Some engine tune programmers can change settings to improve fuel economy,

The Superchips Jeep TrailDash 2 features a full-color 5-inch touch screen and an exceptional number of features. Multiple displays allow monitoring of many engine and transmission functions, including temperatures, pressures, RPM, speed, fuel efficiency, and voltage. Many computer settings can be adjusted with the TrailDash 2, including tire diameter, gear ratio, tire pressure monitoring system, and transmission performance. Different engine tunes can be programmed for improved performance or fuel mileage efficiency. An inclinometer screen monitors roll and pitch angles with adjustable alarms. Switch screens allow the operation of lockers, lights, and other accessories. Engine idle speed can be adjusted for winching. Trouble codes can be read and cleared. Gauge screens are customizable. The monitor includes a video input for a backup camera or other video feed.

The Banks Power AutoMind Flash Programmer allows adjustments to power settings, speedometer recalibration for gear ratio and tire size changes, and monitoring of engine performance and fuel economy. Trouble codes can also be read and cleared. The AutoMind features a full-color 2.8-inch screen and can be updated with a PC. (Photo Courtesy Banks Power)

Most modified JKs weigh several hundred pounds more than stock. The 3.6-liter Pentastar V-6 engine produces much more horsepower and torque than the earlier 3.8 V-6, but the extra weight of JK accessories and products reduces performance. The Edelbrock Jeep Wrangler E-Force Supercharger System is one way to get a big gain in power, performance, and towing capacity. The Edelbrock E-Force Supercharger is available only for the 2012-to-current JK with the Pentastar V-6 engine. (Photo Courtesy Edelbrock)

power, and throttle response. Other engine tuners can alter settings in the computer for tire diameter, gear ratio, tire pressure monitoring system recalibration, steering wheel centering (which helps keep the ESP working properly), engine idle speed (raises idle speed for winching), and the ability to clear engine diagnostic codes, along with a few other programming features. Some tuners, such as Superchips Trail Dash 2, offer a wide range of features via a color touch screen. These tuners use several screens for engine parameters, performance tests, and custom tuning for economy, towing, and rock crawling. Other companies making engine tuners and programmers include Gale Banks Engineering, Diablosport, Hypertech, AEM, AEV, Bully Dog, Jet Performance, and aFe Power.

Superchargers

Short of an engine swap, superchargers provide significant horsepower and torque boosts; for example, the Edelbrock E-Force Supercharger for 2012–2017 JK models increases horsepower by about 20 percent and torque by 32 percent. In a comparative dyno test, the JK 3.6-liter Pentastar with the Edelbrock E-Force Supercharger posted impressive performance compared to the naturally

American Expedition Vehicles was one of the first aftermarket companies to address computer programming issues when changing gear ratios and tire sizes on the Wrangler JK. If the speedometer is not reprogrammed, performance is severely limited by the electronic stability control system. The AEV ProCal Module easily corrects the computer program for tire diameter and gear ratio. Other reprogramming features of the ProCal Module include adjusting the tire pressure monitoring system settings, activating daytime running lights, raising engine idle speed for winching, and clearing engine codes. A unique feature assists in the wheel alignment process so that the ESP is optimized for performance. A new feature on the AEV ProCal allows transfer case calibration for non-original equipment transfer cases such as the Atlas 2-speed. The ProCal Module plugs into the OBDII port and uses DIP switches for quick, easy reprogramming.

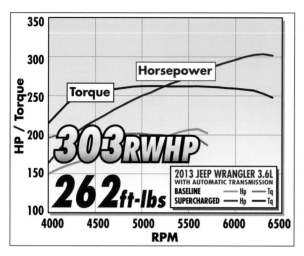

Horsepower and torque are compared before and after installation of the Edelbrock E-Force Supercharger on a Pentastar JK with an automatic transmission. Power gain is nearly 90 hp and more than 50 ft-lbs of torque. The graph compares rear wheel power, not power at the flywheel. (Illustration Courtesy Edelbrock)

Replacing the oil filter with some superchargers on the Pentastar-equipped JKs can be a major undertaking. The Edelbrock E-Force Supercharger allows easy replacement of the oil filter due to the logical supercharger housing design. (Photo Courtesy Edelbrock)

The Edelbrock E-Force Supercharger is compact, tidy, and fits under the stock hood without modifications. System components are black powdercoated. An integrated bypass valve minimizes the effect on fuel economy. The supercharger uses a self-contained oiling system with a service interval of 100,000 miles. (Photo Courtesy Edelbrock)

supercharger functions. Performance factors include power, fuel economy, throttle response, and emissions. Not all superchargers are 50-state legal. If you live in California, be aware that some superchargers are not legal there.

Turbochargers

Turbochargers also provide additional power. A turbo is driven by exhaust gas flow. Turbos operate at high RPM and a finite amount of time is needed for the turbo to spool up to create boost for added power. Turbochargers by nature do not offer advantages for low-speed off-road driving and rock crawling. A turbo is an excellent addition for improved towing and acceleration performance. In stock trim, the Pentastar engine produces 221 hp at the rear wheels. The turbo kit from Prodigy Performance almost doubles the rear-wheel horsepower. A turbo-equipped engine also offers good fuel economy by improving volumetric efficiency. Gains up to 4 mpg are common on the JK at highway cruising speeds.

The Edelbrock E-Force Supercharger was designed specifically for the Pentastar-equipped JK. The supercharger uses the Eaton Gen IV 1320TVS rotor assembly. The installation is completely bolt-on. The system is designed and manufactured in the United States. An electronic PCM programming module is included, which uses application-specific tuning. The system is 50-state emissions legal. (Photo Courtesy Edelbrock)

aspirated JK 3.6-liter Pentastar. In stock trim the Pentastar engine produced 221 hp and 219 ft-lbs of torque at the rear wheels. After the installation of the E-Force supercharger,

output climbed to 309 hp and 289 ft-lbs of torque at the rear wheels. However, the extra power does come at a price. Superchargers cost in the $5,000 to $6,000 range, and figure $600 to $1,000 for installation.

The tune on the onboard computer determines how effectively a

Prodigy Performance makes turbocharger kits for both the 3.8-liter V-6 and the 3.6-liter Pentastar V-6. The Prodigy kits are available at two levels of tune. The system features either a Precision or a Garret turbo, a large intercooler, and all the hardware and wiring necessary for the installation. Turbochargers make a lot of power at mid- to high RPM, so they are great for towing and improved acceleration. Off road, a turbo provides very little power gain. The turbo also improves volumetric efficiency for a significant gain in gas mileage.

Prodigy Performance makes two stages of turbo kits for both the 3.8-liter engine and the newer 3.6-liter Pentastar engine. The complete kits include a large intercooler that reduces intake air temperatures for maximum power. The Prodigy turbo kits come with either the Precision Turbo or a Garrett Turbo.

Air-Intake Snorkels

Clean, cool, dry air for the engine intake system improves engine performance and fuel economy.

Air-intake snorkels were originally used to ensure a dry air source for the engine when crossing deep water. Snorkels move the air intake for the engine up over the rear of the hood, usually at the top of the passenger-side A-pillar, which allows the JK to cross deep water without ingesting water into the engine air intake.

A source of clean air in dusty conditions, which are far more common when off roading, is just as important. A snorkel is more likely to draw clean air into the air intake because of its high mounting location and

avoid most of the dust present on dry and sandy trail adventures. The air is also cooler than the air passing through the grille, coolers, and radiator. This can improve power and fuel economy. Snorkels also make good cold-air intakes. AEV, K&N Filters, ARB, Rugged Ridge, and others make snorkels for the JK.

Engine Swaps

Most Jeep JK owners desire much more power output from the stock engine. A well-suited V-8 engine swap can provide that additional power and has been popular since the CJ was introduced. The early JK models with the 3.8-liter V-6 lacked power given the size of the vehicle and the weight added by modifications. The 2012-and-on Pentastar V-6 is much better. The 2012–2017 JK comes with the W5A580 5-speed

The K&N snorkel system is designed to improve throttle response and engine sound. The snorkel and cold-air box are made from rotational molded plastic. The enclosed air box provides a fresh air inlet that is separated from the hot engine compartment. The air box lid provides easy access to service the washable, reusable air filter. (Photo Courtesy K&N Air Filters)

Air intake snorkels allow cleaner air to enter the engine. The K&N snorkel works with the K&N AirCharger air intake system replacing the factory air filter and air intake housing. The snorkel allows water crossings without the risk of water getting into the engine intake system. The elevated air inlet also reduces dust flow into the air intake. (Photo Courtesy K&N Air Filters)

automatic transmission, which also improves performance. A stock JK Unlimited Rubicon weighs more than 4,300 pounds and has a maximum payload (including passengers) of 1,000 pounds. Most lifted JKs with 35-inch-or-larger tires, additional armor, bumpers, and a winch can easily add more than 1,000 pounds to the weight of the vehicle. Many modified JKs exceed 6,000 pounds, not including the weight of passengers. Performance deteriorates even more from additional aerodynamic drag with a suspension lift and rolling resistance from larger tires. No wonder engine swaps are desirable, but an engine swap is a big investment.

The Chrysler Hemi and GM LS small-block are two of the most popular engine swaps for the JK. The Hemi swap is a little less complicated because computer and wiring are more compatible. The W5A580 5-speed automatic transmission in the 2012-and-newer JKs also works with the Hemi. The GM LS engine swap is more involved due to the need to change computer systems and transmissions.

Engine swaps are a major undertaking. Installation of a V-8 in a JK most often requires removal of the entire body from the frame. This allows much easier access to all the components requiring modification or swapping. Other major items needing replacement include wiring harnesses, coolant hoses, engine and transmission mounts, computers, exhaust, fuel lines, and more. Several companies offer complete kits for owners to complete the swap on their own.

American Expedition Vehicles, Bruiser Conversions, Mopar, and Dakota Customs manufacture Hemi conversion kits. These companies

also perform the swap, and AEV sells complete hemi-powered JKs. Several companies around the country do the complete installation. On the GM LS side, MoTech, Bruiser Conversions, and RPM Extreme offer conversion kits and complete installation.

GM LSs

Introduced on the 1997 Corvette, the GM LS series of small-block engines took traditional pushrod V-8 architecture to the next level and became the most popular engine swap platform. It's compact, fuel efficient, and powerful, and that's why it's a top choice for engine swaps in the JK. The LS is offered in Gen 3

cathedral-port and Gen 4 square-port generations. As a guideline and not a rule, the Gen III engines tend to produce better low-end torque; the Gen IV engines produce more horsepower and better overall performance. Many JK owners have favored the more-torque Gen III engines for their projects.

A wide range of LS engines are available on the market today. Many used engines can be sourced from salvage yards at affordable prices. Chevy Performance, Mast Motorsports, and many other companies sell brand-new LS crate engines with a warranty. Lingenfelter Performance Engineering offers brand new LS crate

Similar to many swaps, RPM Extreme separates the chassis from the body for installation of the GM LS engine. Because a Gen IV engine is being installed, the ECU easily communicates with the CanBus wiring harness system. If you're installing a Gen III engine, you may not have full compatibility between engine and vehicle. For the swap, you need a vehicle lift to safely and securely separate the chassis from the body. To do that, you must disconnect the coolant, A/C, transmission, and fuel lines. Beyond that, you need to disconnect the electrical system harness and many other components, which takes some time. (Photo Courtesy RPM Extreme)

engines with a warranty. Options for an LS engine swap vary widely, from a budget LQ4 iron-block engine at $1,500 pulled from a salvage yard to a brand-new Chevy Performance LS9 crate engine at about $22,000. When you buy a high-mileage salvage yard engine, you should perform a rebuild, and many owners want to avoid this expense and time commitment. A new crate engine gives you a turnkey powerplant with a warranty, and that makes the swap project less challenging. You need to determine your performance target for your application, and plan accordingly. An LS engine purchase, swap kit, and extraneous parts is likely going to cost in the neighborhood of $10,000. The complexity and cost of an LS swap or engine swap in general is not for everyone. If you want V-8 power for off-road conquest, you could consider swapping in the old Gen I Chevy small-block because it costs far less than the average LS swap project.

A few of the major considerations when it comes to the LS swap project is sourcing an oil pan that's compatible with the crossmember of the chassis and offers enough ground clearance. In addition, you may have to purchase aftermarket accessory drives, so the pulleys allow enough clearance for other components. You need to be sure that you have all of the engine's electronic controls, sensors, and wiring harnesses. As such, you need the ECM and separate harness for the factory fuel injection; otherwise you must be skilled and patient to adapt the factory JK harness to the LS engine harness. Converting to carburetion does not save you a lot of money because the carbureted manifolds are expensive. Aftermarket accessory drives also significantly

increase the cost of the swap. Harmonic dampeners and water pumps must be compatible, because an LQ4 dampener does not fit on LS3 Corvette engine. To mate the engine to the Jeep transmission, you need an adapter for the bellhousing; otherwise you can use a GM transmission, but then transmission tunnel fabrication and a custom driveshaft may be required. You need to select engine mounts, adapter plates, and electrical wiring harnesses for your swap, and many of these parts are contained in a kit. Purchasing a complete kit simplifies the swap process by eliminating the need to source engine mounts, wiring harnesses, computers and computer interfaces, and all the associated parts and hardware.

The Gen 3 truck-based engine was available through 2006 with drive-by-wire technology, so the pedal's other electronic components need to be installed on a JK project. Some companies recommend using the stock JK WA580 automatic transmission found in 2012-and-newer Wranglers with the Pentastar 3.6-liter engine. In 2007 GM released the square-port Gen IV engines that have been installed in Camaros, Corvettes, and other cars, as well as trucks. The Gen IV is also offered as a crate engine with cast-iron or aluminum blocks. Some kit manufacturers use the stock WA580 JK transmission while others use the GM 6180E 6-speed automatic transmission. Gen IV engines have a wide range of displacement and power. The 6.0- or 6.2-liter engines are recommended for JKs running 37-inch-or-larger tires.

RPM Extreme, MoTech, and a few other companies offer complete swap kits, so you can install an LS engine in your JK with a minimum of hassle. These kits provide the nec-

essary parts so you don't have to custom fabricate parts and relocate underhood components to resolve clearance problems. MoTech has been offering LS swap kits for about 15 years; Gen III and Gen IV swaps are currently available. The Gen III swap kit features modules that control power modes, sensors, A/C, and more, and the modules are compatible with the A/C and Pentastar cooling fan on 2011-and-newer JKs. The harness replaces the JK's stock harness and includes PCM connectors, so it's a simple and straightforward install. The MoTech offers a basic builder kit and a premium builder kit for Gen IV engines.

The MoTech basic builder kit includes a new GM main engine harness, new MoTech interior harness, new GM Engine Control Module Pre-Programmed, new GM Body

RPM Extreme's LS3 crate engine comes complete, but you need various parts and accessories to install it. With some kits, you need to source a compatible accessory drive for the alternator, power steering, and A/C; typically a Camaro or Cadillac CTSV drive works with most vehicles. This extensive kit also includes mounts, brackets, hardware, transfer case adapter, transmission mounts, accelerator pedal and mount, EVAP vent valve and fuel tank pressure sensor, and fuel lines. (Photo Courtesy RPM Extreme)

An aftermarket rear axle assembly was installed in this JK; you need to properly measure the distance from U-joint on the tail section of the 6L80E to the U-joint of the rear end. Take these measurements to a driveshaft builder, so they can build an aluminum or chrome-moly driveshaft to your particular specifications. (Photo Courtesy RPM Extreme)

To mount the LS 3 engine to the chassis, you need to weld the motor and transmission mounts to the frame rails. So you need to carefully measure, clamp the mounts in place, and tack weld them into position. After these motor and transmission mounts have been properly tack welded, you need to stitch weld them to complete the job. When welding, alternate from one side of the mount to the other. A new aluminum radiator has also been installed in this chassis to manage the heat generated by the 6.2 V-8 LS3. (Photo Courtesy RPM Extreme)

The vast majority of the work is done. The accessory drive, exhaust manifolds, and new shocks and springs have been installed. The body is lowered into position, so the wiring harness, fuel lines, coolant lines, steering rod, and the rest of the components can be hooked up. (Photo Courtesy RPM Extreme)

Control Module Pre-Programmed, and the MoTech Module interface. Mounting hardware includes original MoTech engine frame mounts for Gen IV hydraulic mounts, MoTech transmission mount set with hardware, and a stainless-steel coolant overflow tank with mount and hardware. A MoTech powdercoated aluminum air-intake tube with mounting bracket and new Delco MAF sensor provide a fresh supply of air. A new GM EVAP vent solenoid and new GM fuel tank pressure sensor are also included. Other essential components of the kit include an EVAP canister relocation bracket, transmission cooler line drop bracket, MoTech Sanden A/C compressor bracket with powdercoated hardware, A/C lines, compressor-to-expansion block and compressor-to-condenser block, professional-grade PS lines, cooling fan spacer kit, plug-and-play nylon fuel line, 6l80 shift lever with corrected geometry, 6l80 shifter plate, supports for transmission and transfer case shift cables, adjustable-width hardware, accelerator pedal with MoTech adjustable mount, and GM ECM-Bussman mount (several configurations available).

RPM Extreme offers a variety of GM LS Gen III and Gen IV Repower Kits or swap kits, so you install a high-power and efficient LS engine

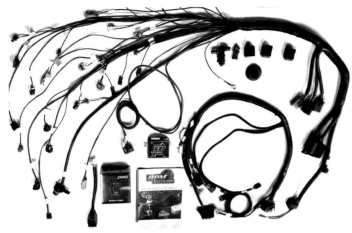

With most swaps, hooking up the electrical wiring system is not only the most time consuming it is also the most challenging. With the RPM Extreme Gen IV DIY conversion kits, the wiring harness is plug-and-play, so you don't need to have an OEM wiring modified. The electrical wiring harness for the engine easily connects to the ECU factory plug at the firewall; it wraps around behind the engine and under the fuel rails for a clean factory appearance. (Photo Courtesy RPM Extreme)

The GM and Jeep CanBus system do not speak the same digital language, so these signals are streamed through the EZ CanBus system. In this system, the GM digital language is converted to Jeep language so the engine effectively communicates with gauges and other electrical systems on the JK. (Photo Courtesy RPM Extreme)

into a JK. For this particular swap, an LS3 6.2 engine was installed that cranks out 430 hp at 5,900 and 424 ft-lbs of torque at 4,600 rpm.

Hemi

Fiat Chrysler Automotive is the parent company that produces the Hemi engine and Jeep JK, and, therefore, Hemi conversion kits are somewhat more popular because the stock JK components are more compatible with the 5.7-, 6.1-, 6.2-supercharged Hellcat and 6.4-liter Hemi swaps. The AEV kit is popular because AEV also sells complete JKs with Hemi conversion through dealers. Mopar is the latest company to enter the Hemi conversion market. Now several shops around the country are offering Hemi swap services into the Jeep JK.

Producing approximately 470 hp and 470 ft-lbs of torque to the rear wheels, the Mopar V-8 conversion kit gives Jeep Wrangler JK excellent power. The Mopar Wrangler 6.4-liter HEMI V-8 conversion kit mates to Chrysler Group's W5A580 5-speed automatic transmission, and eventually to the 6-speed manual transmission. The new 5.7-liter HEMI conversion kit also covers 2007–2017 model-year Jeep Wranglers. The engine generates approximately 375 hp and 400 ft-lbs of torque. Although these are impressive numbers, some owners have been impressed with the torque of the GM LS Gen III engines. When swapping a Hemi engine, you need to acquire the Hemi engine, bell housing, flex plate, and accessory drive. The Gen III Hemi can be adapted to the V-6 automatic transmission behind 2012–current versions. However, the older 3.8 V-6s have a one-piece tranny/bellhousing, so a compatible bellhousing is not available. When swapping the Hemi into the engine bay, the body is typically separated from the chassis. The oil pan, engine mount installation, and adapting the wiring harness are a few of the more challenging aspects of the swapping process. As with the LS engine swap, these are not inexpensive, but they are more straightforward than with the LS.

Hemi conversions are not new to the Wrangler community, and dozens of shops around the country advertise them. Choices include basic swaps working with a stock 5.7-liter Hemi all the way up to a supercharged 6.2-liter Hellcat engine. Some shops even offer stroked versions of the Hemi up to 7.2 liters or 440 ci.

The Jeep aftermarket now offers components and harnesses from companies including AEV, Burnsville Off Road, Hotwire Auto, and TeraFlex. AEV also offers a complete swap kit. The conversion components and harnesses in a swap kit help streamline the process. Modern Muscle Extreme, Arrington Performance, and Bouchillon Performance all offer the full-range Gen III Hemi crate engines. With a Hemi swap, you need to use the Chrysler big 5-speed 5R45 auto transmission or the 6-speed manual Ram transmission. Therefore, you need a customized driveshaft, and transmission tunnel modification may be required.

Compared with most LS swap kits, the Hemi swap kits have fewer components and offer a simpler, more streamlined swap process. The American Expedition Vehicles Hemi

You need to remove the stock Pentastar engine from the Wrangler JK before you swap in the Hemi. Nuthouse Industries has performed countless Hemi conversions using the AEV swap kit and they have expertly installed this 5.7 Hemi. Some engine swap projects only require removing the hood and the front clip to maneuver an engine/transmission assembly into the front subframe and transmission tunnel. But these JK bodies do not afford enough room for the engine and transmission to be slotted into place with the body attached to the chassis. So to swap in the engine, you need to separate the body from the chassis. (Photo Courtesy Nuthouse Industries)

Conversion Kit contains AEV engine mounts, AEV transmission mount, steel battery tray (OEM or Optima Group 31), AEV transmission cross-member, and AEV steering relocation bracket. Intake and cooling components include AEV air box bracket, AEV aluminum cross-flow radiator, and AEV coolant recovery bottle. Electrical parts required to complete the swap are an AEV wire harness (100-percent computer tested), AEV ProCal module, and a Custom Flashed PCM, which integrates the engine to the chassis. Plumbing and intake parts for the kit include a CNC-bent 3-piece air conditioning line set, CNC-bent 2-piece power steering line set, AEV CNC-bent fuel line, Flowmaster high-flow exhaust with catalytic converters, K&N air filter, heavy-duty transmission cooler, and front spring spacers (to correct ride height).

The New Hemi engine has been a popular engine to swap into the Jeep JK, and using the AEV swap kit, Nuthouse Industries has swapped many Gen III Hemi engines into the JKs. For this particular swap, Nuthouse Industries swaps the 5.7L Hemi into a JK for a massive boost in performance that serious off-road drivers put to effective use. The stock 3.6L Pentastar produces just 285 hp and 260 ft-lbs of peak torque while the 5.7 Gen III Hemi spools out 375 hp

Attach the engine hoist lift chains to the manifold area of the 3.6 Pentastar V-6. Remove all the motor mounts, unplug the electrical connectors from the harness, disconnect the tail section of the transmission, disconnect the steering shaft from the power steering box, disconnect all coolant and transmission lines, and be sure to attend to miscellaneous items. (Photo Courtesy Nuthouse Industries)

Once the engine has been removed from the engine bay, find a safe and secure place to store it. An engine stand can store the engine alone, but as you see here, the engine/transmission is temporarily placed on a table with wood support braces to keep it firmly in place. (Photo Courtesy Nuthouse Industries)

The AEV kit includes the motor mounts for the Gen III Hemi V-8s, so you need to align the oval holes on the frame rails, tack weld in place, and then stitch weld in the mounts. Once the motor mounts have been welded to the frame rails, spray paint the motor mounts. When finished, it looks like a factory motor mount.

The stock Jeep JK motor mounts are not compatible with the Hemi V-8 engine mounts, so you need use a cut-off wheel or plasma torch to cut off the motor mounts and then the patch plate must be MIG welded in place. Here, the patch plates have been welded in place and the welds have been ground flush with the frame rails. Mounts are inscribed with L or R for left and right side and an arrow indicates front orientation. (Photo Courtesy Nuthouse Industries)

The 5.7 Hemi has been unpacked from its crate, and the next step is to fasten the 66RPE automatic transmission to it. A rear-sump aluminum oil pan is fitted to WK and XK powertrains with a rear-sump aluminum oil pan; a plastic pan was installed on 2011 and later models. These pans often rupture during off-road use and must be changed to Dodge Ram steel pans.

The 5.7 Hemi V-8 has much bigger cooling requirements than the Pentastar V-6, so a new aluminum radiator must be installed to provide adequate cooling to the latest generation Hemi engine. (Photo Courtesy Nuthouse Industries)

Before you bolt the bellhousing of the 66RFE transmission to the engine block, you need to transfer the clutch assembly and fluid pump from the Pentastar V-6 to the 5.7 Hemi. Your Hemi may not have the correct spacer ring for the crankshaft's rear flange, so you may need to source the correct spacer. (Photo Courtesy Nuthouse Industries)

Using the engine hoist, the engine and transmission have been lowered onto the front subframe. The kit comes with AEV wiring harness, so you must plug in all the connectors. In addition, you need to reconnect wiring harness, cooling system hoses, transmission lines, accessories, and many other components. (Photo Courtesy Nuthouse Industries)

You have many other steps to perform before the project is complete. The Hemi battery tray, fuel lines, power steering lines, A/C lines, transmission, and cooling lines all need to be installed. In addition, the steering rod needs to be relocated. One of the most important steps is reattaching the body to the chassis. When all these crucial steps have been completed, the New Hemi 5.7 engine looks as if it were installed at the factory. (Photo Courtesy Nuthouse Industries)

and 400 ft-pounds of torque. When rock crawling or trail driving, this engine carries JK to new performance heights.

Transmission and Cooling Systems

Transmissions on the JK are durable units, but do require frequent maintenance when used in more extreme off-road environments. The

Rock crawlers and trail machines generate a lot of heat in extreme conditions. In low-speed operation airflow is limited, so engine temperatures can soar in the JK. Flow through the radiator is only part of the solution for maintaining normal coolant temperatures. Hot air needs to exit the engine compartment easily to allow cool air to pass through the radiator. Daystar makes hood vents and these allow hot air to easily exit the hood. Although rock crawling at low speed is not usually an issue, long steep climbs in summer heat can cause overheating, especially when light bars, winches, and winch bumpers obstruct the grille.

manual transmission on the JK is strong, but the clutch assembly experiences accelerated wear especially when rock crawling. The JK does experience some overheating in high ambient heat conditions and steep uphill grades, especially when towing. Adding a winch, a bumper with a bull bar, and light bars in front of the radiator can increase the possibility of overheating by disturbing the airflow into the radiator. Cooling aids can help to alleviate cooling issues.

Heavy-Duty Clutch Kits

The manual transmission in the Wrangler JK is the NSG370 6-speed,

which was also used on the earlier Wrangler TJ models. The transmission seems to be durable but the stock clutch system is another story. The stock JK clutch, pressure plate, flywheel, and throwout bearing provide adequate durability for highway driving and moderate off-road use. More extreme off-road activities accelerate wear on the clutch system. Although the skill of the driver plays a role, hard use wears the clutch, pressure plate, throwout bearing, and flywheel pretty quickly. When the clutch begins to slip or fails completely, the time is perfect to upgrade to a high-performance clutch and flywheel assembly.

One of the problems with a stock clutch and flywheel is stalling when going slow in the rocks. Often, to crawl in rocks with a manual

transmission, slipping the clutch is required. One solution to this is to use a heavier flywheel. A heavier flywheel has more inertia and is less likely to stall at low RPM as the momentum from the flywheel keeps the engine running. Unlike high-RPM situations where a light flywheel is best, when off roading at low speed the heavy flywheel offers advantages.

Aftermarket clutch and flywheel assemblies are not common for the JK. In part this is due to the overwhelming popularity of the automatic transmission in the JK models. Centerforce makes kits for both the 3.8 and the 3.6 Pentastar engines that have different and heavier flywheels. Kits include clutch plate, pressure plate, flywheel, throwout bearing, pilot bearing, and pilot shaft. The flywheel is made of billet steel weighing about 50 pounds,

The majority of JKs are equipped with an automatic transmission. Modern automatic transmissions have improved to the point that the manual is no longer the preferred transmission for off roading. But many longtime Jeep owners still prefer the manual transmission. For rock crawling, the stock clutch assembly is a weak link, often needing replacement before 20,000 miles. Centerforce Clutches offers a great package for the manual transmission–equipped JKs. The kit includes the clutch disc, pressure plate, flywheel, pilot bushing, and release bearing. (Photo Courtesy Centerforce Clutches)

The Centerforce flywheel for the JK is made of billet steel weighing about 50 pounds, about 50 percent more than the stock JK flywheel. Most car enthusiasts must wonder why a heavier flywheel is even a consideration. Racing and high-performance street applications always look for lightweight driveline components to reduce rotational inertia. Although a heavier flywheel reduces acceleration slightly, in the rocks, more rotational inertia translates into less stalling of the engine at the slow rock crawling speeds found on the more extreme trails. (Photo Courtesy Centerforce Clutches)

B&M Racing manufactures a new shifter for the manual transmission JKs. The Precision Sport Shifter for Jeep Wrangler JK models equipped with the NSG370 6-speed manual transmission features a billet aluminum blue anodized case, which houses internal components made from super tough 4140 chrome-moly. The shift throw has been reduced by 35 percent compared to the factory shifter, and the detent pressure has been significantly increased, creating a noticeably stiffer shift feel. (Photo Courtesy B&M Racing)

about 50 percent more than the stock JK flywheel. Installing the entire kit makes sense if you wheel hard and have experienced excessive wear with the stock clutch assembly.

Automatic Transmissions

The 2007–2011 JKs are equipped with the 42RLE 4-speed automatic transmission. The 2012–2017 JKs come with the W5A580 5-speed automatic transmission. Both transmissions seem to be durable with a reasonable life expectancy. It is important to service the automatic transmission (all years) regularly. The owner's manual recommends every 60,000 miles for heavy-duty use. If you do considerable rock crawling, then changing the fluid and filter every 40,000 miles is a better bet.

Automatic Transmission Coolers

The automatic transmission coolers in the JKs are mounted in front of the radiator. Although the stock cooler can handle the heat buildup of typical road driving, extreme off-road conditions can overheat the transmission. Towing, hot desert environments, and slow rock crawling can cause the transmission to overheat. Overheating accelerates wear considerably. Transmission fluid fires have occurred when the JK automatic transmission becomes excessively hot. An auxiliary automatic transmission cooler will improve transmission

By replacing the stock radiator with an all-aluminum high-flow radiator, cooling and reliability can be improved. C&R Racing manufactures a wide range of aluminum radiators, including radiators for most of the NASCAR teams. They also make an all-aluminum bolt-in replacement for the JK. All the radiator brackets line up with the stock mounts, making installation easy. The C&R Racing radiator flows about 50 percent more coolant than stock.

fluid cooling as well as reduce stress and wear to the transmission. Mopar, Derale, Mishimoto, and Flex-a-Lite make coolers for the JK.

Cooling Systems

For typical highway driving and moderate off-roading, the stock JK cooling system provides sufficient performance. Overheating can become an issue when towing or driving on steep grades. When larger tires, armor, bumpers, and other accessories are added, overheating becomes more likely. We have experienced overheating with modified JKs when climbing steep mountain roads where speeds vary from slow to fast. Part of the problem is getting hot air evacuated from the engine compartment. Mopar and AEV offer vented aftermarket hoods. Daystar, GenRight, and Poison Spyder make

The Derale transmission and power steering coolers are mounted on a custom bracket made by PSC. The trans cooler is inline with the stock transmission cooler to provide additional transmission cooling. This helps increase the life span of the automatic transmission.

add-on hood vents that help get heat out of the engine bay.

Removing hot air is not the only issue for managing engine and transmission temperature. Adding weight is a factor, but so is blocking airflow through the grill into the radiator. Bull bars, winches, and light bars are often installed in front of the radiator opening. This reduces flow to the radiator and creates turbulence, which disturbs airflow.

Keeping an engine running cool is all about getting heat out of the water. Two factors contribute to this: airflow through the radiator fins and water flow through the radiator tubes. Too little airflow leads to overheating and so does water that is inadequately cooled. This can happen when the volume of water in the system is not adequate but also when the water flow occurs too quickly through the radiator cooling tubes. Bent or clogged cooling fins on the radiator can restrict airflow, a problem when wheeling in deep mud. Heavy mud and small stones can bend the cooling fins.

High-Flow Radiator

The efficiency of a radiator depends upon the coolant capacity or volume and its ability to extract heat from the engine. Larger capacity improves cooling. Cooling also improves when the flow of coolant stays in the radiator core longer. The stock JK radiator uses 35-mm tubes in a single row; aftermarket radiators use up to a two-row design with 42-mm cooling tubes. More volume comes from the larger tubes and multiple rows. The radiator core is thicker to accommodate the increased capacity. C&R Racing, Flex-a-Lite, Mishimoto, and Mopar offer high-flow drop-in radiators. The C&R Racing JK radiator has helped with cooling issues in our test JK. Stock replacement water pumps are available from Mopar, Omix-Ada, and Crown Automotive.

Radiator Cooling Fans

Good airflow through the radiator improves cooling. When bumpers, winches, and lights are added to the front of a JK, airflow is disturbed. A more powerful cooling fan can increase

airflow and keep the engine running cooler in more extreme conditions. For increased airflow through the radiator, a puller fan (the stock fan is a puller fan) with at least a flow rate of 2,000 cfm improves cooling. GC Cooling, SPAL, Mishimoto, and Flex-a-Lite are among the companies making high-flow fans for JK applications.

Hood Vents

A large volume of air needs to flow through a radiator to maintain cooling capacity. Airflow is a function

of air speed and the volume of the fan when engaged. But the air must be able to exit at a rate equal to or greater than the air entering the radiator. If exit flow has been restricted, adequate air cannot enter the radiator. Hood vents and cowl hoods help evacuate hot air exiting the radiator from under the hood. Daystar makes add-on hood vents and cowls, which help reduce heat in the engine compartment. AEV, Mopar, Rugged Ridge, and DV8 Off Road make complete vented hoods for the JK.

The Daystar hood cowl and hood vents allow hot air a freer exit path from under the hood. The hood cowl also increases air space in the engine bay. Installation of both the cowl and the hood vents requires cutting the hood sheet metal. Daystar provides an accurate template for perfect alignment. The cowl is black but can be easily color-matched for a nice finishing touch.

Flowing more air through the radiator is the key to good engine and transmission cooling in low-speed off-road conditions. The air volume of the fan is one important aspect. The stock 16-inch JK fan pulls about 1,400 cfm, the 16-inch fan from GC Cooling pulls 2,067 cfm, about 50 percent more airflow. (Photo Courtesy GC Cooling)

JEEP JK PROFILE

Norbert "Nobby" and Deanna Schnabel

Our first Jeep was a used stock 1999 TJ with a manual transmission. We thought we'd enjoy driving fire roads and exploring scenic areas. Off-road driving quickly turned into a passion, however, when we joined the Bear Valley 4x4 Club and discovered challenging drives that allowed us access to extraordinary environments. Our once-stock vehicle soon gave way to bigger tires and beefed up equipment. A decade later, we sold our TJ for a JK Unlimited Rubicon with an automatic transmission and a few more creature comforts.

Nobby and Deanna Schnabel's 2017 JK Unlimited Rubicon

Year/Model: 2017 Jeep Rubicon

Engine & Transmission: Stock

Transfer case: Rock-Trac NV241 4.0:1

Tires: BFGoodrich KM2 35x12.50R17

Wheels: AEV 17 x 9 Salta

Rear axle housing: Stock JK 44

Front axle housing: Stock JK44 with Artec truss and C-gussets

Front & Rear ring/pinion: Stock 4.10

Front & Rear axles: Stock with AEV differential cover

Front & Rear locker: Factory Electric

Front & Rear suspension: AEV 4.5-inch Dual Sport

Front & Rear shock absorbers: Bilstein

Front & Rear control arms: Stock

Rear track bar: AEV Dual Sport

Front track bar: Stock

Steering tie-rod & drag link: Stock

Ball joints: Dynatrac H/D

Steering dampener: Old Man Emu SD48

Power steering box & pump: Stock

Power steering cooler: PSC

Bracket for steering dampener: AEV Dual Sport

Front & Rear brakes: Mopar

Cold-air intake: Banks

Cat-back exhaust: Banks

Auxiliary switch system: sPOD

Radiator: Stock

Transmission cooler: Stock

Rear bumper: AEV

Tire carrier: AEV with Hi-Lift jack and Pull-Pal mounts

Front bumper: Rock Hard Patriot aluminum

Engine/transmission skidplate: Rock Hard 4x4

Gas tank skidplate: Rock Hard 4x4

Transfer case skidplate: Rock Hard 4x4

Evap relocation: Rock Hard 4x4 Evap skid

Fenders: Stock

Rock sliders: Stock

Auxiliary lighting: Procomp light bar

By Deanna Schnabel

Our Jeep JK has a Duo braking system so we can flat tow it behind our truck with a slide-in camper. We enjoy traveling all over the United States visiting national parks, historic sites, and bird watching, sometimes in remote areas. This RV-Jeep setup allows us to travel and explore these areas in comfort. Moreover, when the Jeep isn't in tow, we can camp in rural environments thanks to the Dometic Refrigerator we've installed in the rear. The refrigerator allows us to keep food cold without worrying about ice lasting the length of our stay.

The Gobi-colored 2017 JKU was built at All J Products with only 800 miles on the odometer. The stock Dana 44 axles were retained with an Artec truss and C-gussets welded on the front axle housing to improve strength. Because 35-inch tires were part of the build, the stock front ball joints were replaced with Dynatrac ball joints. A Currie mini-skid control-arm bracket protects the vulnerable control arms. An AEV differential cover adds protection for the housing and improves the appearance.

Rock Hard skidplates protect the underside of the JK. A JE Reel front driveshaft replaced the stock unit for improved exhaust clearance and greatly improved durability on the rocks. At the rear, an AEV rear differential slider reduces hang-ups on the housing in the rocks.

We replaced the stock suspension with the AEV 4.5-inch Dual Sport lift, which offers a great highway ride as well as excellent off-road performance. BFGoodrich T/A KO2 tires, 35x12.50R17 are mounted on AEV Salta 17 x 8–inch wheels.

A Rock Hard Patriot Series aluminum front bumper replaces the stock bumper and saves some weight as well. Customized Blue Ox tow bar mounts were added for towing the JK behind a camper. The Warn

A Rock Hard Patriot Series aluminum stubby front bumper with a bull bar graces the front of the Gobi-colored JKU. The only remnant of the owner's previous TJ is the Warn 9.5 XP winch with a synthetic winch line.

9.5 XP winch with synthetic winch line was pirated from our previous TJ.

An ARB twin air compressor on a TeraFlex bracket is mounted under the passenger seat. An air chuck is mounted to the front bumper for quick and easy airing up. Under the hood is a Banks Ram Air Intake, a winch fuse, and a sPOD electronic power source. An AEV rear bumper with tire carrier with an AEV 10-gallon fuel caddy and a mount for the Hi-Lift jack finish the build.

Going from a short wheelbase that can turn on a dime to a long wheelbase takes some getting used to on trails. However, the longer wheelbase allows us to easily climb areas that were once difficult. Purchasing the JK Unlimited Rubicon and equipping it as we have was the right choice for us at this time to enjoy retirement.

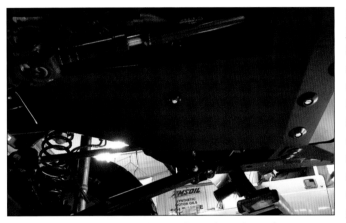

Rock Hard skidplates add protection and convenience. The engine skid features a trap door to allow easy oil changes. Many engine skidplates require removal to access the oil drain plug. The recessed buttons under the bolts keep them from hanging up on rocks and protect the heads from damage. A JE Reel front driveshaft replaced the stock unit for improved exhaust clearance.

An AEV 4.5-inch Dual Sport lift works great in the rocks but is also one of the best lifts available for a good ride and handling feel on the highway. Artec truss and C-gussets were welded on the front axle housing at All J to improve strength. The stock front ball joints were replaced with Dynatrac ball joints.

STYLING AND STORAGE UPGRADES

The Jeep Wrangler JK aftermarket provides a multitude of styling upgrades. In fact, aftermarket companies offer more choices for the Jeep JK than for any other vehicle in history. One online and mail order retailer produces quarterly catalogs exceeding 300 pages just for the Jeep Wrangler JK. And those catalogs only scratch the surface of available parts and gear for the JK. Jeep now offers many stylish options to its customers as well. Jeep and the aftermarket offer hundreds of customizing options for the JK owner.

From aftermarket tops to half doors, styling upgrades allow the individual JK owner to personalize their Jeep to an extent previously unknown. And many of the options offer performance and lifestyle advantages. Two of the many product lines provide good examples. Aftermarket tops and tube or half doors alter the driving experience as well as the looks of a JK. Given the budget, a JK owner could change a few accessories every year or two and completely alter the look and personality of a JK. New JK goodies hit the market almost daily.

Aftermarket Tops

Almost every vehicle sold in the world comes equipped with a top. The Wrangler JK can be ordered with both soft and hard tops. The original equipment Jeep soft-top uses a metal tubular frame to support the fabric. The shape of the top mirrors that of the hardtop. Several aftermarket companies, such as Bestop, Mopar, Rugged Ridge, and Smittybilt, offer other options. Bestop makes the premium-quality original equipment soft-tops for Jeep. Aftermarket companies sell stock replacement soft-tops with or without the metal bow and window. If a stock soft-top needs replacement, owners can purchase just the fabric. If your JK never had a soft-top and you want one, you

Hundreds of styling options allow JK owners to customize the look of a Wrangler. Custom hoods and hood accessories create a distinctive look for a JK, but some of the modifications are also functional. Daystar makes a hood cowl and hood vents for the JK. These require cutting openings in the hood, but they assist engine cooling by allowing hot air easier passage from the engine compartment. Hundreds of possibilities make creating a custom look for a JK easy. But the task can also be daunting.

The Wrangler JK is available with several roof options, from hardtop to soft-top. The hardtop panels can be removed to provide a sunroof effect. The front Freedom Panel take a couple of minutes to remove and store. Bestop offers a different solution. The Sunrider for Hardtops replaces the Freedom Panels over the driver's compartment. The installation is simple and so is the operation of the top. Opening and closing the Sunrider top is similar to the operation of a traditional convertible top. After it's installed, the Bestop Sunrider for Hardtops makes going from an enclosed compartment to open air and back easy and quick. Capturing spectacular scenery is a big part of the open-air experience. (Photo Courtesy Bestop)

can purchase an entire kit. The abundance of options makes selection a challenge.

Options for replacement tops offered by aftermarket manufacturers include the frameless soft-top, which provides a different look with its innovative fastback design. Some of the frameless soft-tops allow removal of the side windows and rear curtain for the open-air experience of a bikini or bimini top. Some frameless soft-top models feature a fold-back sunroof over the forward compartment without removing the top completely. Bestop is the leader in soft-top innovation, but other companies making soft-tops include Rampage, Rugged Ridge, and Smittybilt, among others.

Several aftermarket companies offer replacement hardtops as well. The hardtop on the JK removes in three segments. Two panels cover the forward cockpit area and can be removed with the larger rear section remaining in place. The bulky rear section includes the top, rear window, and side windows. This section

The soft-top on the stock JK can be a little cumbersome to operate, but the Bestop Trektop NX Glide is much easier to put up and take down. This replacement top's innovative folding frame design lets the Trektop NX Glide function like a convertible top by folding the top behind the rear seat for a total open-air ride. For full coverage, the Trektop NX Glide is fast and simple to close. Zipperless side and rear panels allow for easy slide-in and slide-out operation. Bestops TrekTop Glide features the popular fastback look. The TrekTop Glide includes the soft-top premium 30-ounce Black Twill fabric, window panels, and bows for a no-drill installation. Zippered mesh pockets are integrated into the Sunrider panel for storage of small items. (Photo Courtesy Bestop)

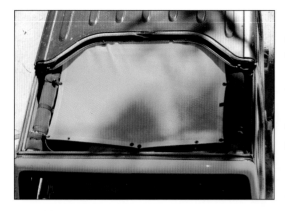

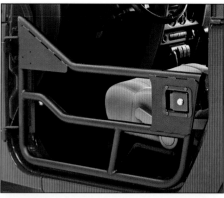

The SpiderWebShade offers protection from the sun while allowing the top-off, open-air experience. The SpiderWeb-Shade blocks up to 90 percent of the harmful UV rays and keeps the open passenger compartment cooler. The Spider-WebShade is easy to install and, when it is in place, can remain under hardtops and soft-tops.

The Element tube doors from Bestop are constructed from 1.25-inch steel tubing. The front doors are equipped with mirror mounting plates for the original JK mirrors or Bestop replacement mirrors. Using the door enclosure kit, the doors can be converted to half doors. The door enclosures are made from steel and are paintable.

requires more than one person to remove. To make the job easier, several hoists or lifts are available. Hardtop storage racks keep the valuable hardtop protected and allow easy transport. Storage bags for hardtops keep the glass and finish protected.

Sun Shades

Sunshades are available in two versions: mesh screen and solid. Mesh sunshades provide some shade but allow some light in. The solid versions block sunlight and offer some protection in rain. Many of the shades can remain in place when the factory hardtop is installed. Sun-shade designs come in a wide range of styles ranging from full to partial coverage. Tube door covers provide some protection from debris. Other mesh products range from storage bags to trash bags. Rugged Ridge, SpiderWebShade, Dirty Dog 4x4, Bestop, Smittybilt, and other companies manufacture sunshades.

Tube Doors

One of the great features on the Wrangler JK is that stock doors can be removed easily by unplugging wires and lifting the door off the hinge pins. On the Unlimited (four-door), the rear doors are also removable.

This creates a unique open-air experience. However, there is no protection from the elements or debris. Some owners do not like the unprotected feel of doors-off four wheeling. Enter the aftermarket. Seizing a marketing opportunity, the Jeep aftermarket created tube doors.

As the name implies, tube doors replace stock doors with much lighter tubular structures. Tube doors lack glass windows. Most tube doors require an aftermarket mirror because stock mirrors do not work. Although all tube doors have latch mechanisms, not all have locks. Nevertheless, tube doors give the open-air experience along with improved visibility for both driver and passenger. This helps when crawling on rocks or other obstacles. Some tube doors, such as the Bestop Highrock 4x4 Element Doors, include mirrors. These doors have several optional features. Steel skin enclosures turn the tube door into a half door and can also be removed. Bestop also offers storage bags that can mount on the inside or outside of the tube door. To further enhance versatility, the Element Upper Door features an insert fitting the stock doorframe and a clear, zippered window that can be opened for nicer weather conditions.

Tube doors are popular and the aftermarket has responded with

The Element tube rear doors are equipped with door latches, restraints, and a dome light shutoff bracket. Both front and rear Element doors can be fitted with an upper door made from the same fabric as the Bestop Supertop. The upper doors use hook and loop fasteners for a tight seal and easy removal of the window panel.

Half doors offer a different off-road experience and most come with upper doors and windows. The Mopar half doors grace the Premier Warehouse Jeep. The Premier Warehouse is part of Premier Jeep in California, the oldest Jeep dealer in the state. Originally called Don-A-Vee, the dealership was started by legendary Jeeper Brian Chuchua in 1963.

MOLLE (Modular Lightweight Load-carrying Equipment) use PALS webbing for many types of attachments, and several styles of MOLLE equipment and accessory bags can be used on Jeeps. Smittybilt, Bartact, and several other manufacturers produce MOLLE storage. The Smittybilt Gear Tailgate Cover holds several MOLLE bags. Covers are also available to fit over roll-cage bars and seat backs.

many variations and styles. Several companies offer tube doors, including Rugged Ridge, Smittybilt, Warrior, Olympic 4x4, and Bestop. To suit individual preferences, many tube door accessories, such as the Spider-WebShade ShadeSkins, a mesh cover over the tube frame, are available.

Half Doors

Half doors for the Jeep Wrangler JK allow increased open-air experiences while reducing weight. Like tube doors with an add-on outer skin, half doors provide some protection from the elements but do not have glass windows. Several companies offer half doors for the JK, including Bestop, Mopar, JCR, and Rugged Ridge.

MOLLE System Soft-Bag Storage

Modular Lightweight Load-carrying Equipment (MOLLE) provides a means of carrying and storing gear primarily for the armed forces and police. Using the PALS webbing system to attach modular bags and other storage utilities, MOLLE system storage offers many options for the Jeep enthusiast. Smittybilt offers a series of MOLLE system attach-

ments called GEAR. MOLLE panels hold gear pouches in a wide range of shapes and sizes. Smittybilt makes systems that attach to the rear tailgate, the overhead console, and a seat cover with PAL webbing for MOLLE gear. Many companies make storage pouches and bags, which attach to MOLLE webbing. Roll bar padding with the MOLLE attachments offers a great option for carrying gear and bags, such as first aid kits.

Metal Storage Boxes

Topless and doorless four wheeling makes the Jeep Wrangler unique. The open-air experience adds to the utility of the Wrangler JK. However, doing so creates security issues. Security solutions abound in the Jeep aftermarket. Companies including Tuffy, Bestop, Smittybilt, ARB, Garvin, Warrior, and others offer metal locking storage boxes and security enclosures. Lock boxes offer protection for valuables such as purses, wallets, and electronic devises. Gun lockers are also available. Storage boxes fit under seats, in the center console, and in the rear storage compartment. Some boxes use locking lids; others have drawers that slide on tracks for improved accessibility. Locking lids

Secure storage is hard to come by in a stock JK. With the top down or Freedom hardtop removed, the only lockable storage is in the glove box and center console. Tuffy makes a line of locking security boxes for added secure storage. This under-seat version is made of 16-gauge black textured powdercoated steel. Other boxes mount in the rear cargo area and include multiple compartments that can be configured in several styles.

cover the rear cargo area and provide a low-cost, lightweight solution for protection of larger items.

Interior Storage

At first glance, interior storage seems limited in the JK, but so many storage solutions are available that the storage area becomes plentiful. Under-seat storage boxes, overhead consoles, roll bar packs and bags, as well as storage racks add considerable storage to the JK interior. Secur-

Interior storage racks increase usable storage area and add a level of safety. Olympic 4x4 Products's Mountaineer Rack fits in the rear storage compartment of both the Wrangler and Unlimited. The rack removes easily if space is needed for large items and is designed so that lighter items can be strapped or bungee corded in place for security. Large, heavy items can be placed underneath. The rack keeps items stowed below in place should collision or rollover occur.

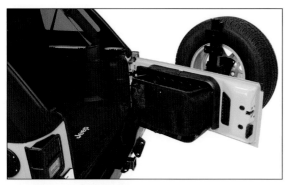

The Bestop Roughrider Tailgate Shelf deploys from an upright position with one hand. The shelf features a removable polyester mesh basket that's perfect for stowing damp items. The removable mesh basket allows the shelf to be used for tailgating or as a work surface. (Photo Courtesy Bestop)

Rightline Gear makes a functional "trunk" storage bag that straps to the back of the rear seat on both two- and four-door models. The trunk features four compartments to keep gear separated and easy to locate, and a carry handle. Each compartment zips shut on the sides and uses a hook and loop closure along the bottom. Stowing gear and tools keeps heavy items from bouncing and flying around the interior when wheeling on rough terrain. An End of the Road Super Quick Fist One-Piece Rubber Clamp holds the Power Tank in place.

The Jeep Wrangler JK provides its owner with unlimited options for exploration. Stowing gear is always an issue. When camping or picnicking in the backcountry, towels, tablecloths, and blankets often become damp or dusty. Storage for such items away from the passenger compartment is a great feature. The Bestop Roughrider Tailgate Shelf mesh basket is the perfect solution for stowing damp or dirty items. (Photo Courtesy Bestop)

In addition to the Rightline Gear trunk storage bag, Rightline offers the 4x4 side storage bag with a zipper opening on top, a shoulder strap, an additional small zipper pocket, and a mesh storage pouch. The vertical bag is a Rightline Gear 4x4 roll bar storage bag. This bag attaches to the rear roll bar and features a large zipper opening. This is a perfect bag for stowing recovery straps, tree savers, and other items needing quick access.

Cam Can. RotopaX also makes fluid storage containers, including flammable fuel cans. Both allow the stacking of two cans on mounting brackets.

ing items safely solves a bigger issue. Jeeps bounce off road. Onboard items fly around over bumpy terrain, rocks, and whoop-de-doos; even worse, flying cargo takes on missile-like qualities in a rollover or collision. Keeping cargo secure is a major priority, especially heavy items. Most aftermarket interior storage solutions are designed to secure cargo. Some, such as rear cargo-area racks, do not, so tie-down straps are needed.

Fluid Storage

Some fluids, such as drinking water, bottles of oil, transmission fluid, and cleaners, can be carried inside a JK as long as they are secured in a storage bin or bag. Large volumes of fluid, especially gasoline, need to be transported outside the vehicle. The old standby, the jerry can, offers one readily available solution. Daystar makes a nifty setup called the

Door Hinges and Stops

JK doors pivot on pins to open and close. A fabric strap restrains the door from opening too far. But nothing holds the door open, so a stiff breeze or parking on a slope can cause the door to close unintentionally. Star Fabricating and Armadillo make doorstops featuring detents allowing two stops as with standard car doors. These hold the door in

Exterior fluid storage allows easy access, and if the fluids are flammable, a much higher degree of safety. The Daystar Cam Can uses a cam lock system to stack two Cam Cans on their mounting kit. The kit attaches to the rear-mounted spare tire or any flat surface. Each can holds 2 gallons of nonflammable fluids. The attachment on this Jeep is off the spare tire carrier. A Can Cam storage trail box is also available. The trail box Can Cam holds small tools or recovery straps.

RotopaX fuel storage containers are rotational molded and both EPA and CARB compliant for carrying fuel. The fuel cans have a plastic barrier material that meets the latest government low permeability requirements.
In addition to fuel cans, RotopaX makes a line of other fluid and storage containers. Several different mounting solutions are offered for these containers that hold from 1 to 4 gallons of fluids.

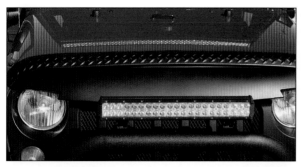

The leading edge of the JK hood is susceptible to rock damage. Wind hitting the square edge of the hood creates air turbulence that decreases fuel economy and can cause roof-mounted light bars to whistle. Rugged Ridge produces a wind deflector and a hood guard to minimize these issues. These parts are made from UV-treated thermoplastic and attach to the body with 3M tape.

With a roof rack the JK can carry enormous amounts of gear for overlanding or expedition-style travel. Roof racks can also hold rooftop tents for camping. Gobi Racks manufactures sturdy racks that mount to the chassis and the A-pillar windshield frame. An add-on ladder makes roof access easier. Several brackets are available for auxiliary lights, trail tools including a Hi-Lift jack, and canopies. The sturdy frame mounting allows the Gobi rack to carry more weight than a roof-mounted rack.

place at full-open and partial-open positions. The detents are strong enough to hold the doors open against wind and gravity. The Star Fabricating stops are also available for the rear doors of the JKU.

Mirrors

When JK front doors are removed or replaced with tube or half doors, mirrors must be replaced. About 20 aftermarket companies, including Rugged Ridge, Bestop, Smittybilt, and Olympic 4x4, manufacture replacement mirrors. Some of these aftermarket mirrors are designed for specific half door or tube door applications. Some use relocation brackets; others mount to door pivot tubes, which are exposed when the stock doors are removed.

Be aware of state regulations regarding mirrors. Most states require a driver-side exterior mirror and a second mirror, either a passenger-side exterior mirror or a windshield-mounted rearview mirror. The interior mirror must allow the driver to have an unobstructed view to the rear. Passengers creating obstructions are okay, but cargo is not.

Roof Racks

Roof racks provide vastly increased storage space. The most common roof racks come from Yakima, Gobi, Garvin, Warrior, Smittybilt, and Fab Fours. Several rack manufacturers offer a wide selection of rack styles. Roof racks allow great storage as well as a platform for rooftop tents. If overlanding and expedition-style four-wheeling are a high priority, roof racks are a necessity. For rock crawling and extreme trail driving, the additional weight on the roof can contribute to rollovers.

Some roof racks use attachment points bolted to the hardtop roof. Other racks use a wide variety of mounting locations. Tubular structures bolted to more substantial mounting points (such as the A-pillar windshield mount in the front and bumper mounts in the rear) allow great load carrying capacity. Storage bags that mount to roof racks protect gear from the elements. Straps and netting hold gear securely in place.

Mud Flaps

Mud flaps keep mud, stones, and water from hitting vehicles following you. Nearly half of the states require mud flaps on vehicles if the tires protrude outside the fender edge. Some mud flaps disconnect quickly but most are permanently mounted.

The TeraFlex Transit mud flap kit provides significant protection from gravel, mud, road spray, and debris while resisting extreme environmental temperatures. The Transit mud flaps are constructed from UV resistant and flexible injection molded high-density polyurethane. The mud flaps disconnect with a quick release removal system, designed as a simple procedure for the trail. The frame-mounted cam system allows the flap to be oriented at an angle for maximum tire clearance. This mud flap kit ensures that you stay compliant with state and federal laws and regulations requiring fenders or mud flaps over the tires to reduce spray and debris coming off the tires. (Photos Courtesy TeraFlex)

JEEP JK PROFILE

GenRight *Terremoto* Jeep JK

In the summer of 2013, the *Terremoto* was built to be the all-conquering, all-around Jeep JK. We chose this Jeep for its long wheelbase and ability to hold four people. Our idea was to get rid of the stock V-6 and transplant in a big-horsepower Chevy LS3 V-8, a strong drivetrain, and lower the center of gravity while still maintaining an excellent breakover by using a completely flat belly skidplate.

By Tony Pellegrino

Next, we gutted the entire Jeep of its stock interior (including the dashboard) and eliminated all the overriding electronic systems found in today's Jeep JKs. We then designed and built a full race-inspired interior with alumi-

The GenRight Terremoto *JK is one of the most unique street-legal JKs ever built. Tony Pellegrino has wheeled the* Terremoto *all over the United States, not only to test and showcase GenRight products but also because Tony loves to go Jeepin'! Not much of the* Terremoto *is stock. And even with the GM LS3 V-8 engine,* Terremoto *weights only 4,900 pounds, about 2,000 pounds less than most high-end JK builds. (Photo Courtesy GenRight Off Road)*

GenRight's *Terremoto* Jeep Wrangler JK

Year/Model: 2014 Rubicon

Engine: 640-hp Chevy LS3 V-8

Transmission: 4L80, full manual-shift automatic

Transfer case: Atlas 2 twin stick with a 3:1 ratio

Tires: Falken WildPeak MT 38x13.50x17 inches

Wheels: KMC Machete 17 x 8.5–inch beadlocks

Rear axle housing: Currie RockJock 70 full-float hubs

Front axle housing: Currie RockJock 70 with WARN locking hubs

Front & Rear ring/pinion: 5.38:1

Front & Rear axles: 35-spline/40-spline chrome-moly

Front & Rear locker: ARB

Rear suspension: GenRight four-link Rear Elite coil-over conversion

Front suspension: GenRight three-link Front Elite coil-over conversion

Front & Rear shock absorbers: FOX 3.0-inch IBP coil-over

Front & Rear control arms: Summit Machine 7075 aluminum

Rear track bar: None

Front track bar: GenRight Elite

Steering tie-rod: GenRight CrMo

Steering drag link: GenRight

Spindles: Currie Unit Bearing

Steering knuckles: Currie Hi-Steer

Steering dampener: PSC Ram Hydro Assist

Power steering box, pump & reservoir: PSC

Power steering cooler: GenRight four-pass cooler

Bracket for steering dampener: GenRight

Rear brake rotors/calipers: Factory JK/ TBM Modified

Front brake rotors/calipers: TBM Wave/TBM F4

Cat-back exhaust: Magnaflow

Radiator: Griffin, custom aluminum

Transmission cooler: Griffin, large universal

Front & Rear bumper: GenRight aluminum (RBB-8220 & FBB-8355)

Engine/transmission skidplate: GenRight 7075 aluminum

Gas tank and skidplate: GenRight 33-gallon aluminum tank w/ aluminum skidplate

Transfer case skidplate: GenRight aluminum

Fenders: GenRight aluminum (TFF-8640 and TFR-8020)

Rock sliders: GenRight aluminum (RCG-8104)

Auxiliary lighting: VisionX light bar, driving lights, and rock lights

The heart of the Terremoto is a 640-hp GM LS V-8 engine. The electronic fuel injection Holley Dominator EFI rests on an Edelbrock manifold complemented by a Holley LS engine wire harness, Race Pack Gauges, and Smart Wire switches. Keyless entry is through a handheld remote (which also activates interior lighting at night). A four-person intercom with headsets ties into race radio and can play music. The cooling system is custom and uses a custom Griffin aluminum radiator. All steering is the PSC with a PSC hydro-assist ram and PSC steering box and pump. The power steering cooler is GenRight's four-pass cooler. (Photo Courtesy GenRight Off Road)

The Terremoto JK features the GenRight Elite JK suspension for the JKU. The front suspension is 3-link and the rear is a double-triangulated 4-link setup. All control arms use Currie Johnny Joints and are fully adjustable. King 2.5-inch coil-over shocks with remote reservoir, springs, and hydraulic bumpstops control axle movement. All necessary hardware and brackets are included. This Elite kit is the equivalent of a 3- to 4-inch lift. It is recommended for Jeep JKs with up to 42-inch-tall tires. (Photo Courtesy GenRight Off Road)

The complete interior of the Terremoto *is custom. The roll cage is made from 2-inch-diameter steel tubing. Ostrich skin PRP seats, Momo steering wheel, Racepak digital display, a Lowrance GPS, and an iPad display provide digital information. A Rugged Race radio/intercom system, SSV Bluetooth sound system, and a Cobra CB radio provide communications and entertainment. (Photo Courtesy GenRight Off Road)*

GenRight manufactures many components from aluminum to save weight. The Terremoto *features GenRight aluminum bumpers, rock sliders, and a flat aluminum skidplate, which attaches to the frame and crossmembers. The axle housings are Currie RockJock 70s with chrome-moly axles and 5.38:1 gear ratio. The scrapes on the suspension arms and skidplate show that Tony does not baby the* Terremoto. *(Photo Courtesy GenRight Off Road)*

num digital dash, four PRP bucket seats, and a completely new heavy-duty 2-inch-diameter tubing roll cage. Tony worked with Chrysler engineers to design the cage.

Then we CAD designed a long-arm link suspension with long-travel coil-over shocks to convert the suspension system into what we call the GenRight JK Elite Suspension. This new suspension was designed around the Currie RockJock axles for maximum up travel (also keeping the vehicle low). This suspension system also moved all the spring and dampening control (which are huge high-quality racing-style shocks) out to each of the wheels for a smooth ride and predictable performance on and off road.

Lastly, we kept the Jeep as lightweight as possible. We used aluminum panels and half doors, fiberglass hood, and nothing that was not 100 percent essential to off roading. This Jeep weighs in at only 4,900 pounds; it is almost 2,000 pounds lighter than most built JKs.

This is a "driver's" vehicle! It is fun to drive and does everything you want when you want as fast or slow as you want!

Since Terremoto's debut in 2014 it has been at the SEMA show in Las Vegas, Nevada, once; the Hump 'N Bump in Logandale, Nevada, four times; the Jeep Jamboree in Parker, Arizona, four times; Tierra del Sol's Desert Safari at Ocotillo Wells, California, three times; and the Easter Jeep Safari in Moab, Utah, four times. We have used the *Terremoto* as a pre-runner for the King of the Hammers race at Johnson Valley, California, the past three years. I also lead a Jeep run after the King of the Hammers called the KOH Experience. This event has occurred the past three years.

Other events around the country include Jeep Beach, Daytona Beach, Florida, three years; the High Desert Roundup in Barstow, California, the past four events; the Big Bear Forest Fest, twice; Jeepers Jamboree on the Rubicon, four times; Topless for TaTas at Rauch Creek, Pennsylvania, once; and Off Road Expo, Oklahoma City, Oklahoma, once. We use the *Terremoto* for testing and just to go have fun running trails at venues such as Hammers.

ELECTRICAL AND LIGHTS

Off-road JKs are built for extreme service and carry many accessories that require electricity. As a result, electrical improvements are often required. The onboard computer mostly controls the electrical systems on the JK. High-amperage-draw accessories such as a winch can be wired directly to the battery. Other items, such as auxiliary lights, compressors, lockers, and cameras, should be wired through a standalone junction box that isolates the wiring from the JK wiring harness and the computer system.

Simply splicing wires into a convenient hot wire to power add-on accessories can cause damage to the computer and the wiring harness. The complex CAN-BUS electrical systems on the JK make it increasingly difficult to install electrical upgrades. The sPOD from Precision Designs makes it easy for the Jeep owner to add upgrades without damaging the power system or cutting into factory-installed wiring. Several sPOD models are available and the kit includes wiring and a switch panel.

Battery Upgrades

The original equipment battery provided in the JK works well until high-amperage accessories, such as winches and light bars, are added. The high loads from add-ons can cause premature battery failure. Aftermarket batteries such as the Odyssey Performance and Extreme Series and the Optima Red Top batteries pack more power and are designed to be more durable in the extreme conditions of off-road activities. Vibration resistance is especially

All of the circuitry of the sPOD is contained under a cover easily removed with over-center clips. The sPOD mounts under the hood with a custom bracket for the JK using two existing fender-mount bolts.

The sPOD comes with a switch panel that mounts to the upper trim panel between the sun visors. This switch panel is designed for the JK and is a perfect location for easy access to control a variety of electrical components. Many colors are available for the switch lights. The six switches here control the rear locker, the ARB air compressor for the lockers, the front locker, A-pillar lights, grille light bar, and the master power switch for the Rubicam camera system.

Wrangler JKs use a CAN-BUS electrical system. Adding electrical components by splicing accessory wires into wires in the JK wiring harness can cause damage to the electrical system and the computer. The sPOD uses a sophisticated system to bypass the computer and eliminate the need to tie into the wiring harness. The black cubes are removable relays. Behind the relays (out of view) are six accessory attachment terminals and the negative battery terminal. Fuses are in front of each relay and these need to be compatible amperage for the accessory. A 2-amp switch panel fuse and a low-voltage-detection circuit fuse are mounted to the circuit board. The wire bundle connects to the six accessories. The positive battery terminal is to the right of the wire bundle.

important. Automotive batteries are generally a lead-acid design. The lead plates within the battery can be made from lead that is almost pure or a lead alloy. The pure lead provides more power. The more plates and plate surface area in the battery the more power the battery can produce. More plates can mean that the battery weighs more. One of the common measures of battery power is the Cold Cranking Amps (CCA) number. The higher the CCA rating, the more power the battery puts out. Replacing the original equipment battery when accessories are added, especially a winch, offers a high level of security in the backcountry. The last thing you want is a battery failure when trying to winch out of a difficult situation.

Battery Cables and Terminals

Battery cables are commonly 4-gauge wire, but winches are usually wired to the battery and ground with 2-gauge wire. Tight, solid, clean connections are important, especially when adding high-current-draw items such as winches and lights. Any weak link in the electrical system can cause shorts and starting issues. Battery cables and terminals can corrode or become loose. The original equipment sheet-metal terminals are prone to loosening and can often be rotated by hand with minimal effort. Add a winch to your JK and the problems can become worse. If you upgrade to an Odyssey battery, it is important to upgrade the terminals. The stock cables are good, but the terminal posts on the Odyssey battery are slightly smaller than the stock battery terminals. The original battery terminals do not tighten enough on the Odyssey battery. Solid-lead battery terminals such as the Quadratec Extreme Duty Battery Terminal feature solid-brass accessory busses for winches and a sPOD junction.

Loose Battery Terminal Problems

The stock JK battery terminal clamps are made from sheet metal. They have a limited range for tightening. The terminal clamps tend to become loose even on the original equipment battery or OEM replacements. When the battery is upgraded to an Odyssey or Optima battery with smaller-diameter terminals, the terminal clamp cannot be tightened adequately for good contact. It may work to start the JK, but under heavier electrical loads, the connection may fail. The answer is to upgrade to high-quality battery terminal clamps.

Dual Battery Systems

Dual battery systems offer several advantages for the extreme-duty JK. If one battery should fail or lose its charge, the second battery can be switched into action. For winching, the extra capacity can help for extended operation. With the addition of lights, refrigerators, CB and ham radios, cameras, and navigation systems, considerable electrical power is needed. A dual battery system can provide that power. Genesis Off Road, Rugged Ridge, and Painless Wiring offer wiring kits for dual battery systems on the JK. Mountain Off-Road, Genesis, and Rugged Ridge offer dual

This dual battery system features two Odyssey Extreme Series batteries mounted on a Mountain Off-Road Enterprises dual battery tray. The solenoid and wiring kit comes from Painless Wiring. Dual batteries help provide electrical power for extended use, such as overlanding, general camping, and winching.

battery mounts. Dual battery wiring kits include cables, solenoid, and a three-position switch that allows use of the primary battery only, both batteries all of the time, or both batteries only when the ignition is on.

Auxiliary Lighting

Auxiliary lighting graces many JKs; a full spread of light is necessary in demanding off-road driving situations. If you wheel at night, adding lights is a wise and popular option. Dozens of lighting options are available, but beware. Some lights, such as LED light bars, are not legal in some states.

HID and Halogen Lights

Possibly the most common modification to the JK is auxiliary lighting. The most common types of lights are halogen. Halogen lights are found on most vehicles and have been for many years. High-intensity discharge (HID) lights use a tungsten lighting filament housed in a fused quartz or similar tube. Some HID lights are called Xenon lights because a small quantity of xenon gas is used in the tube. HID lights are more efficient, making more light per unit of electricity used. Both halogen and HID lights tend to fade over time, with HID lasting longer.

LED Lights

LED lights are the newest technology and are also the most popular for auxiliary lighting on a Wrangler JK. LED, or light emitting diode, lights offer several advantages. Most significant of these is greatly reduced power consumption. LED lights allow greater flexibility in lens and reflector design. The small size of LED lights allows the uses of several lights in a light bar or other fixture. LEDs with different lenses and reflectors allow varying light patterns within the same housing. LEDs also outlive the other styles of light by a wide margin. High-quality LEDs can perform up to 50,000 hours before losing significant performance. That's nearly six years of continuous operation.

Several factors affect LED light performance. The color temperature (measured by the Kelvin Color Temperature Scale) affects visibility and eye fatigue. If the color is too intense, details become washed out. If the temperature is too low, details are darker. The human eye processes light best under noonday sunlight, which is approximately 5,000 K on the Kelvin scale. LED lights at or near 5,000 K provide the lighting that gives the eyes the best detail and reduces eyestrain and fatigue.

Heat management in LED lights is an important design characteristic. Heavy-duty heat sink housings help direct heat away from LED lights. Most LED light pods and bars use aluminum plate for the circuit boards to help move heat from the LEDs to the housing. Others use copper plate, which is about 50 percent more efficient in removing heat compared to aluminum. The more efficient the design in allowing heat removal from the LEDs, the more efficient the lighting. More cooling means that the LEDs can operate at almost full capacity. This improves light output and efficiency. Excessive heat can cause LEDs to lose light strength and cause premature failure. Vibration resistance is another factor for off-road lighting.

Light output is measured in lumens and candlepower. Lumen ratings are the more common measurement and offer information about lighting power. Both measurements give an indication of how much light output is available, and although

The stock JK headlights with high beam provide a good light spread and illuminate a good portion of road and the surrounding forest. This is adequate at 5 mph, but these are not powerful enough for high-speed driving.

The Baja Designs XL Sport LED Auxiliary lights are mounted to the winch bumper. Only the LED lights are on, without the stock headlights and high beams. Clarity up close is much better but long-range vision is vastly improved. Just a pair of the Baja Designs XL Sport LED Auxiliary lights makes night off roading less fatiguing and much safer.

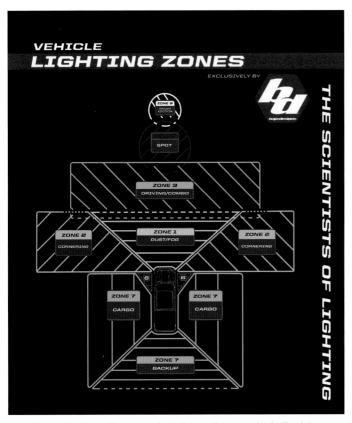

VEHICLE
LIGHTING ZONES
EXCLUSIVELY BY

THE SCIENTISTS OF LIGHTING

Off-road lighting covers a wide range of lighting needs. This chart from Baja Designs shows the various zones different styles of lights cover.

Zone 1: This zone illuminates the area directly in front of the vehicle. Mounting these lights low on the bumper eliminates glare from dust and fog.

Zone 2: This zone provides cornering light so you have adequate visibility at speed. By spreading out these lights by 10 to 15 degrees an even field of light is provided.

Zone 3: This zone is your primary driving light. These lights are mounted in the middle of the front bumper to avoid glare off the hood or from dust and fog in front of the vehicle.

Zone 4: This zone provides long-distance lighting, so you have comfortable visibility at higher speeds. Combined with zone 2 lighting, a smooth transition is achieved, creating less stress on your eyes.

Zone 5: This zone provides illumination for triple-digit speeds or wanting to see miles down the road. This is the only forward projection pattern we recommend mounting along your roofline.

Zone 6: This zone offers wheel well lighting and is ideally suited for truck, jeep, and buggy.

Zone 7: Excellent work light or "scene light" with an extremely smooth 60-degree pattern. This pattern is not suitable for forward projection applications. (Photo Courtesy Baja Designs)

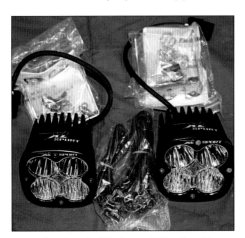

Baja Designs's XL Sport LED Auxiliary lights produce 1,800 lumens per light using four Cree XP-G2 LEDs. Each light produces 20 watts of power at 1.2 amps. The light color is daylight 5,000K, which simulates true daylight. The LED light life is nearly 50,000 hours. The front lens is made of hard-coated polycarbonate and the housing is powder-coated cast aluminum.

Baja Designs's XL Sport LED Auxiliary light kit comes with two lights, stainless-steel brackets and hardware, and a wiring harness. The lights and all connections are waterproof and submersible to 9 feet. The Baja Designs XL Sport LED Auxiliary lights on this JK used the wiring harness tied into an available socket on the sPOD.

The IPF extreme Sport 900XS lights from ARB are available in spot or driving beams. The bulbs are 100-watt H9 halogen. The lens is hardened glass and the body is steel.

Roof-mounted light bars are popular on the JK because they put out tremendous amounts of light and are great for high-speed desert driving. The downsides are considerable. Many states, including California, have outlawed roof-mounted driving lights. So, covering them is important. Even then, citations are possible. Roof-mounted light bars also create considerable glare off the hood, making driving more difficult.

KC HiLites's C20 20-inch light bar uses 36 3-watt LEDs for a total of 108 watts and an output at 7,800 lumens. The beam pattern is a combination for spot and 30-degree spread. This light bar is ideal for most off-road low-speed driving conditions. Mounting the light bar on the bumper or bull bar eliminates glare off the hood and provides excellent lighting for night four wheeling.

Small, compact LED lights mounted to the A-pillar offer great lighting for the edges of a trail and while cornering. We angle these lights a few degrees out to get the best side and cornering coverage for night wheeling. This KC HiLites bracket mounts to existing fasteners on the A-pillar. To keep the installation neat and tidy, the wires run through a grommet in a hole drilled into the fender.

standards for testing are rigid, they may not translate into how well the lights perform on the trail. The only real test is to compare lights side by side.

A big factor in LED light selection is the light beam distance and shape. Fog lights are close-in light patterns near the front of the vehicle. This pattern is also good in heavy dust. Cornering light patterns illuminate the edges of the road to the inside and outside of corners. Cornering lights are generally angled away from the vehicle by about 10 to 20 degrees. Combo light patterns are the most common for normal off-road night driving. Combo lights should be bumper mounted to avoid glare off the hood. Spotlights are generally found in light bars and are intended for high-speed driving where visibility is needed for longer distances. Because this pattern is projected well in front of the vehicle, spot pattern light bars are often mounted on the roof or on a rack.

The 50-inch roof-mounted light bars are popular on JKs. Most states do not allow the use of auxiliary lights on the highway. Some states do not allow roof-mounted lights under any circumstances. Be sure to check your local regulations. In some cases, covers can be put over lights, which may make them legal. Covers can also reduce or eliminate hum from wind.

Numerous companies worldwide make LED lights for off-road applications. Many companies in the United States manufacture LED lights for off-road applications, including Baja Designs, KC HiLiTES, Rigid Industries, and Vision X. Lights from ARB, IPF, Lightforce, and PIAA have excellent reputations.

Ray Currie's 2007 JK Unlimited

When the Jeep Wrangler JK was first introduced in 2007, Ray Currie figured that the aftermarket parts business would be minimal due to the price of a new JK. Ray purchased a 2007 JK that his son Cody used while attending California State University San Bernardino. Cody's Ford F150 pickup was too big for parking spaces at school, so the JK was selected as a daily driver and slated for occasional off-road excursions; Cody drove it for two years. It was one of the first JKs delivered by Victorville Motors in Victorville, California.

Ray Currie's son Cody used the 2007 JKU while attending California State University San Bernardino. The silver JK had a full body wrap when Monster Energy sponsored Ray's older son Casey for his off-road racing and rock crawling efforts. All the Currie guys are accomplished drivers and build great Jeeps. Rock crawling with Ray is an education in sound techniques. (Photo Courtesy Currie Enterprises)

Ray's JKU currently runs a GM LS3 Vortec engine producing 440 hp. The transmission is the GM 6L80 6-speed automatic with a stock transfer case. Airaid makes the cold-air intake. An Odyssey Extreme-Duty battery provides electrical power. The radiator is from CBR Performance. (Photo Courtesy Currie Enterprises)

Ray Currie's 2007 JKU

Year/Model: 2007 Wrangler Unlimited

Engine: GM LS-3

Transmission: GM 6L80 6-speed automatic

Transfer case: Stock

Tires: 37x12.50x17-inch BFGoodrich Mud Terrain KM2

Wheels: Walker Evans beadlocks

Front & Rear axle housing: Currie F9 9-inch

Front & Rear ring/pinion: 4.56

Front & Rear axles: 31-spline RCV/Currie 35-spline

Front & Rear locker: 31-spline Detroit locker/35-spline ARB

Front & Rear suspension: Currie RockJock 4-inch Johnny Joint suspension system

Front & Rear shock absorbers: 2-inch King bypass/ 2-inch King bypass; also King air bumps

Front & Rear control arms: Currie adjustable Johnny Joint control arms

Front & Rear track bar: Currie adjustable Johnny Joint track bar

Steering tie-rod & drag link: Currie Modular Extreme Duty bolt-on

Ball joints: Synergy

Spindles: N/A; stock unit bearings

Steering knuckles: Reid

Steering dampener: PSC ram assist

Power steering: PSC

Bracket for steering dampener: Currie ram assist bracket

Front & Rear brakes: Stock w/ Hawk Friction pads

Cold-air intake: Airaid

Cat-back exhaust: Magnaflow

Onboard compressor: ARB

Radiator: CBR

Transmission cooler: CBR

Rear bumper: Savvy

Front bumper: Savvy

Fenders: MCE

Rock sliders: CRC

Auxiliary lighting: Rigid

Roll cage: N/A

It didn't take long for Currie to make parts for the JK. The first part from Currie was a 1-inch-spacer leveling kit. In 2007, Ray took the JK to SEMA with the leveling kit and 33-inch tires on stock wheels. The JK heavy-duty steering was developed on this Jeep, as were the Antirock sway bars. The original prototype parts are still on the Jeep.

The rear axle housing is a Currie F9 9-inch with Currie 35-spline axles and an ARB air locker. The ring and pinion ratio is 4.56. Rear suspension is all Currie RockJock 4-inch lift with Johnny Joint rod ends. Rear shocks are 2-inch King bypass. Currie Antirock sway bars control body roll. (Photo Courtesy Currie Enterprises)

The front suspension is all Currie RockJock 4-inch lift with Johnny Joint rod ends. Front shocks are 2-inch King bypass with King air bump-stops. Power steering features PSC power steering box, pump, ram assist, reservoir, and a Currie/PSC cooler. Steering linkages are Currie Modular Extreme-Duty components. The rear bumper is from Savvy Off Road. (Photo Courtesy Currie Enterprises)

The Currie F9 9-inch front axle housing uses RCV constant velocity joint axles, Reid Racing steering knuckles, Synergy ball joints, and a Detroit locker. (Photo Courtesy Currie Enterprises)

better than earlier 44 axles, and modifications to those picked up the slack. Interestingly, the original Ford 9-inch housings are still in the 2007 Currie JK with almost 100,000 miles on the odometer. About 20,000 of those miles are with a GM LS engine that produces 440 hp; it is harnessed by 37-inch BFGoodrich KM2 mud-terrain tires.

Several years ago, Ray's JK appeared on the cover of *Four Wheel and Sport Utility* magazine after a four-wheeling adventure in southern Utah. The Currie JK has attended the Easter Jeep Safari in Moab every year since it was new. It has also pre-run for the Baja 1,000 and 500 races numerous times. Ray and his JK were at the King of the Hammers event in Johnson Valley when the trails were still suitable for street-legal Jeeps, before those trails turned into rock-crawling buggy terrain. The JK has extensive trail time on most of Big Bear Lake, California's, rock crawling trails, including John Bull, Gold Mountain, Holcomb Creek, and Dishpan Springs.

Naturally, Ray's Jeep is equipped with everything Currie makes for the JK. Notable exceptions are the complete PSC power-steering system that includes the steering box, pump, ram, and reservoir. It uses an ARB air locker with a Detroit locker in front. Front axles are RCV with Reid Racing steering knuckles. The big BFGoodrich mud-terrain tires are mounted on Walker Evans beadlock wheels.

Like many company owners in the Jeep aftermarket, Ray Currie is a true Jeeper, hitting the trails as often as his busy schedule allows. He knows what his customers need because he's tested all of the Currie products personally.

The Currie family has a long association with BFGoodrich tires and Walker Evans. Ray runs 37x12.50x17–inch BFGoodrich Mud Terrain KM2 on Walker Evans beadlock wheels. (Photo Courtesy Currie Enterprises)

After Cody left school, the JK saw more desert-style use. Ray wanted to equip it with 9-inch axle assemblies front and rear when most Jeep owners were opting for the RockJock 60 axle housings. Currie was well known for bulletproof Ford 9-inch axle housings, so the high-pinion version was installed in the Wrangler, in part to accommodate 37-inch tires. Sales of the Ford 9-inch were strong until some bad press on an off-road forum hurt the image. However, the Dana 44 axles in the Rubicon were much

WINCHES, VEHICLE RECOVERY GEAR, AND TRAIL TOOLS

No one wants to get stuck, but getting stuck is inevitable. It happens to everyone who goes four wheeling sooner or later. Experienced off-roaders always try to avoid getting stuck, but it happens. The key to getting unstuck is being prepared with the right equipment and the knowledge necessary to use it safely. Most aspects of vehicle recovery involve high loads on the equipment. And that can make getting unstuck risky business.

Winches make most vehicle recoveries much easier. Most modified JKs are equipped with winches even if they never see the dirt. A lifted Jeep just doesn't look right without one. If hitting the trails is not in your future but a winch is a must, price may be more important than quality. However, if you plan to go wheelin' seriously on challenging trails, then quality is everything. In the winching classes we teach, we have seen several of the low-cost winches fail. Electrical components are the most common issues. Some winches fail on the first use. A winch needs to perform when needed. Failure is not an option in extreme conditions.

Premium-quality winches come at a premium price. But rest assured,

The electric winch is most often the tool of choice for getting unstuck. Winches are an integral component in the modification package found on JKs. You need to consider many factors when selecting a winch. Pulling power and reliability are the two most important aspects when selecting a winch. The ideal pulling power for modified JKs ranges from 9,000 pounds up to 12,000 pounds, but most common is 10,000 pounds. The power ratings are not necessarily equal on all winches. As always, it's much safer and more convenient to have more capacity than required. And we have learned that reliability is usually proportional to price.

Warn makes an extensive line of winches for the serious off-roader. Often the winch of choice for the Wrangler JK, the Warn Zeon 10-S electric winch is rated to pull up to 10,000 pounds, which it does easily. It is also fast for its size. The S designation refers to the uses of a synthetic winch line as opposed to a steel cable. Warn winches come with a remote controller, but a wireless remote is also available. Winch bumpers are designed with the space and strength to accommodate most winches.

the low-cost winch that fails you in a time of need will not seem like a bargain. We have never had any problems with Warn, Superwinch, Ramsey, Mile Marker, or Viking.

Selecting a Winch

The first factor in winch selection is the line pull rating, or winching power. A winch needs a line pull rating of about twice the weight of the vehicle being winched. A stock JK weighs up to 4,800 pounds with no added equipment. With modifications, the total weight can near 6,000 pounds. A 9,000-pound winch would barely be adequate. The most common pull rating needed for a JK is 9,000 to 10,000 pounds. The Warn Zeon 10 is one of the most popular winches on the market for the JK. Winches require paramount reliability. We have used many winches, and those that instill confidence over long periods of use include Warn, Superwinch, Ramsey, and Mile Marker.

How much pulling power does it take to get unstuck? Usually the answer is more than you think. A pull on a flat, level hard surface requires only about 100 pounds. The power needed to pull a JK up a 45-degree slope with a smooth hard surface is equal to the weight of the vehicle; in the case of a JK, up to 6,000 pounds. If that surface happens to be deep sand, snow, or soft dirt, you can double the pulling power necessary. With a 9,000-pound-rated winch, you need to add a snatch block pulley to double the pulling power of the winch. We have conducted winch and snatch block pulls in which the estimated pull exceeded 20,000 pounds. Traction becomes an issue with large loads. A 20,000-pound

Winch manufacturers use a variety of attachments for the winch line to the winch drum. The Warn Zeon winch uses a sturdy wedge that passes through a loop on the inner end of the winch line and secures the line into the winch drum. At this point, there are no wraps of the winch line around the drum. At least five wraps of the winch line around the drum are required for a safe winch pull under heavy loads.

After the winch is installed on the bumper, the winch line is fed through the fairlead onto the winch spool. The winch line uses a thimble on the outer end of the line to attach the winch line to a hook or end link. The link allows the winch line to be attached to a D-ring shackle at the anchor point for winching.

Electric winches draw considerable amperage from a battery. A heavy-duty battery is important. So is the wiring. All J Products uses a battery terminal extension with an integrated fuse block when wiring a winch into the system. The fuse protects both the winch and the battery. A winch can drain a battery quickly. For this reason, running the engine at a high idle speed while winching keeps the battery charged.

Most winch lines feature an indicator showing when the end of the line is unwrapping from the spool. Many steel cable winch lines use red paint on the line, but not all winch lines have such an indicator. This synthetic line does not, so make sure to keep at least 5 wraps on the spool when under heavy winching loads. When upgrading to a synthetic winch line on an older winch, be aware that the spool drum designed for a steel winch line may not be up to the task with a synthetic line. A synthetic winch line can pull so tightly that crushing the drum is possible.

The Warn Zeon 10-S uses a hawse fairlead for smooth winch line spooling with synthetic winch line. The rounded corners of the fairlead minimize fraying of the Warn Spydura. The Spydura winch line is a dark gray color except for the last 10 feet or so. The red cover over the winch line warns the user that the tail of the line is approaching. Use caution so the winch line maintains at least five wraps around the spool drum.

pull will likely pull the winching rig rather than the stuck vehicle. We have used up to five Jeeps strapped together to make a heavy pull possible. We have also strapped a Jeep to a tree to keep the winching Jeep from moving and allow the stuck vehicle to be freed. Keep in mind that maximum pulling power of a winch occurs when the winch line is almost fully unspooled with only one layer around the winch spool. When the winch line is fully wound, most winch lines have four layers around the spool. The least pulling power occurs with the most layers of winch line on the spool. With four layers on the spool, pulling power is reduced nearly 50 percent, or about 12 percent per layer.

Another factor to consider when selecting a winch is the clutching mechanism. The ability to both pull and release loads under power is helpful. Sometimes you may need to lower a load down a grade, and some winches do not allow you to do that. This can happen with a rig that is broken down; for example, a rig with power brakes may lack a working braking system if the engine won't run and you may not be able to safely back down a steep slope. Lowering the vehicle with a winch gets the job done, but the winch must power the load in and out. You also should have an automatic locking device when the winch is not in operation but still under load. The locking should be 100 percent.

Sealed motors and electrical connections are desirable for use in severe weather and if you drive in muddy conditions or ford streams or other water areas. Series-wound electric motors seem to be more reliable, and the gear drive on the winch runs smoother with a planetary gear set. When shopping, compare features and performance. Compare line speeds at different loads and make note of the amperage draw at varying loads. Make sure you have a battery up to the task because winches can place significant loads on batteries.

Steel versus Synthetic Winch Line

Winch lines are an integral part of safe vehicle recovery. Steel cable winch lines have been the standard for many decades and are still a viable option. Synthetic line absorbs shock load better, softening the abrupt loads as slack is taken up. The synthetic line is much easier to handle, especially when rewinding

Synthetic winch line offers several advantages over steel cable winch line. It is much lighter, does not store kinetic energy as much as steel cable so it is safer to use, and is much safer when it frays. In fact, when synthetic line frays, it is still smooth winch actuation. When cable strands break on steel winch line, the barbs can cause serious cuts. On the downside, synthetic line is more expensive and the winch drum cannot store the same length of synthetic line. Steel cable typically yields about 120 feet of line on a 10,000-pound winch. The Spydura synthetic line on the Warn Zeon 10-S is 100 feet long. This winch line uses a closed link rather than a hook, so it allows for a closed winching system.

Winch Accessories

After you have selected a specific winch, be sure to acquire the accessories you need to take full advantage of the capabilities of the winch.

Winch Controllers

A remote control is a must. You do not want to be near the winch when it is under load, just in case a winch cable or attachment should snap. In addition, you do want to be

Warn offers a simple two-button wireless remote winch controller. The receiver plugs into the socket for the wired remote controller. The wireless controller operates up to 50 feet away from the winch for safety and convenience.

on the winch drum. It is considerably lighter in weight. Moreover, should a line or anchor point fail under load, the energy in the synthetic line is dissipated more quickly with little or no recoil compared to a steel cable winch line. This adds a major safety margin compared to steel cable. Synthetic line is slightly more prone to fraying, so extra precautions are in order, such as protection under the line if it will be sliding across the ground while pulling. For a given drum capacity, the synthetic line will have reduced length compared to wire rope. When steel winch line frays, the broken steel strands become barbs and can cause serious cuts if gloves are not used.

Synthetic line is thicker than wire rope line. An 80-foot-long synthetic line has the strength equivalence of a steel line that is 125 feet long. You can always carry a winch line extension with the synthetic line, just in case. However, the biggest disadvantage of synthetic is cost. An equivalent synthetic winch

line costs two to three times more than a steel wire rope winch line. Nevertheless, the synthetic line has significant advantages and should be seriously considered. Winch manufacturers offer synthetic winch line as an option. Viking, Tactical Recovery Equipment, and Master Pull sell synthetic winch line for upgrades and replacements.

Winch controllers allow operation of the winch during recovery operations away from the winch itself. This winch has a wireless remote unit plugged into the winch. The wire runs to the controller, allowing winch operation, usually by the driver from the driver's seat. Most controller cables are in the 15- to 20-foot-long range.

able to control the winch from the driver's seat so you have access to all your rig's controls, whether you are pulling your Jeep or another rig free. A wireless winch controller makes winching easier, especially when the person operating the controller is outside the vehicle.

Roller Fairlead versus Hawse Fairlead

Roller and hawse fairleads assist the winch line to feed onto the winch spool, sometimes with considerable forces acting on them. A roller fairlead has four steel rollers that reduce drag on the winch line as it spools in. Roller fairleads are heavier, but if you select a steel cable winch line, you need to have a roller fairlead. An aluminum hawse wears quickly with a steel cable, and could damage the cable over time. An aluminum hawse is ideal for synthetic winch rope because there is much less drag and you save a little weight.

The hawse fairlead is used with synthetic winch line. Note the smooth, rounded edges of the hawse. This allows smooth winding of the winch line. A steel-cable winch line wears this Factor 55 aluminum hawse quickly. The Factor 55 hawse fairlead is hard anodized for better wear resistance.

Attachment Points

A snatch block or pulley increases the pulling power of a winch. Snatch blocks also alter the direction of the winch line if necessary. Most winch manufacturers offer accessory kits along with winches that include tree saver straps, pulley blocks, shackles, and gloves. These kits are a good idea because all items are compatible with their winch brand.

A winch is useless unless you have the gear to attach it to something against which you pull. Every connection needs to have a load rating exceeding the pulling power of your winch. You really do not want a shackle, strap, or chassis attachment point to fail. A failure can easily catapult deadly projectiles through the air that can cause serious damage, injury, or even death, so be aware. If you have a 9,000-pound winch capacity, you need accessories that exceed that rating. Using the 9,000-pound winch example, you should use a minimum of a 3/4-inch bow (or D-ring) shackle that has a 9,500-pound load rating with an ultimate strength of more than 47,000 pounds. Bow shackles should be used to attach the winch line to an anchor point or another vehicle. We prefer domestically manufactured bow shackles because we have more confidence in the materials and the actual strength.

Vehicle attachment points should be on the chassis. If you have a good, strong winch bumper or rear bumper designed for four wheeling, and it has a built-in attachment for shackles, by all means, use those. JKs come with tow hooks on the chassis, but beware; these tow hooks are not ideal for winching. Tow hooks can also bend or fail and it is possible for the winch hook or link to slide off the tow hook. A closed winching system allows enhanced safety. A closed

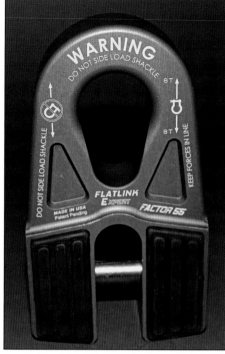

Winch line end links allow a closed winching system, so hooks cannot become disengaged during winching operations. Factor 55 makes a series of end links. The flatlink folds flat against the fairlead. At 1.75 inches thick when folded flat, the flatlink can be used with most roller fairlead license plate mounts. The flatlink mounts to the winch line thimble with a stainless-steel, double-shear pin held in place with an internal snap ring.

system refers to winch-line attachment points that are closed, such as a shackle or link, but no hooks. If your rig has a tow hitch receiver, use a bracket that is designed to fit into the receiver and that holds a bow shackle.

Attachment points away from a vehicle, such as a tree, large rock, another rig, or other object require strength and stability. Use care when selecting a winching point. The most common attachment point in the backcountry is a tree or rock. Never loop a winch line around a tree trunk

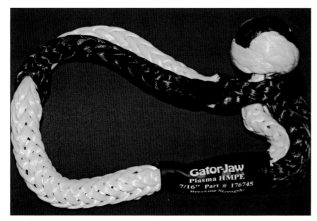

Not all shackles are steel. The Gator Jaw shackle from Bubba Rope is made from Plasma Rope, the strongest synthetic line available. This shackle features a breaking strength of 32,000 pounds. It is flexible, so it can be used in places no other shackle works, and it floats.

To extract a stuck vehicle, an anchor point is needed. A common anchor point is a tree. The tree must be sturdy. A tree saver strap should always be used around the tree, usually near the base. The tree saver strap protects the bark of the tree from damage. The wider the strap, the more the pulling load is spread out and the less the possible damage to the tree. The tree saver strap here is 4 inches wide. The looped ends of the strap are joined by a D-ring shackle, which then attaches to the winch line hook or end link. Never run a winch line around the tree. It will damage the bark and could destroy the tree. And it does the winch line no good as well.

A D-ring or bow shackle is an integral part of the winching system that must be stronger than the winch pulling power of the winch line. This 3-inch D-ring uses a 7/8-inch pin that's rated at 9,500 pounds and has a breaking strength exceeding 25,000 pounds. Many shackles have part numbers stamped into the shackle body, so ratings are easily identified. Raised letters and numbers typically indicate a domestically-made shackle with greater strength than a similar sized imported shackle. Note the shackle attachment point welded to the Rock-Slide Engineering bumper. This is a strong attachment point and ideal for the extreme loads needed when winching.

The Factor 55 Shorty Strap offers several versatile vehicle recovery and trail repair uses. The soft strap can be used on a vehicle with no shackle attachment points by wrapping around a frame member to create an attachment point for winching. The Shorty Strap can also be used to straighten bent steering components, such as a drag link or tie-rod.

or rock. You will damage the tree, often destroying it, and a winch line could pull under a rock, dislodging it and causing a serious problem. In either case, use a winching strap around the tree trunk or rock and not a chain or cable. Better yet, use a 3- or 4-inch-wide tree saver strap. Wide tree saver straps increase strength and spread loads over a larger area; they protect the tree bark and reduce

The Factor 55 ProLink shackle mount is machined from 6061 billet aluminum for exceptional strength. It can be used with steel cable or synthetic winch line and attaches to the winch line thimble with a stainless-steel pin held securely by an internal snap ring. The face of the ProLink has a rubber protector to minimize damage to the aluminum fairlead. This style end link offers a closed system winching setup, unlike a hook. This makes winching safer.

When you see a Wrangler JK on the highway sporting a Hi-Jack, it's safe to assume that rig is used off road. Of all the products available for the JK, a Hi-Lift jack is likely the most common accessory after tires and wheels. The Hi-Lift jack shown here is the 48-inch All-Cast model; other models include the Cast/Steel and the X-treme models. Jack lengths range from 32 to 60 inches on the X-treme model. Most common for the JK is the 48-inch model. Two important accessories are in use here. The Hi-Lift base provides a stable and secure platform for jacking. The Lift-Mate attaches to the nose of the jack and uses two rubber-coated hooks to grab the spokes for lifting the tire off the ground. This minimizes how high the jack must be raised for the tire tread to clear the ground. This accessory is great when high-centered and ground clearance is needed. The Lift-Mate allows the tire to be lifted so rocks or other objects can be placed under the tire to gain ground clearance.

chafing on large rocks. Many companies, including ARB, Hi-Lift, and Warn, make wide tree saver straps.

Snatch blocks perform two important vehicle recovery tasks. First, they can be used to double the pulling power of a winch, which will reduce the line speed of the winch line by 50 percent. Second, the snatch block can be used to alter the direction of the winch line to facilitate a straight pull, so that the side of the fairlead is not overloaded. This also helps prevent winch line from stacking up on one side of the winch drum. ARB makes a massive snatch block for vehicle recovery that comes in their recovery kit or as a stand-alone item. The model 9000 shown here has a breaking strength of 38,500 pounds.

A bow shackle is then used through the loops at the ends of the tree saver strap. The winch line link or hook attaches onto the bow shackle.

Often, no attachment point is available, meaning no other vehicle, rock, or tree trunk,. A winching ground anchor, such as the Pull-Pal, which digs into the surface, provides a secure anchor point against which to pull.

Hi-Lift Jack

The Hi-Lift jack is one of the most versatile tools available for use in the backcountry. In addition to jacking the vehicle for tire replacement or underside repairs, the Hi-Lift can be used for road building under the tires if the vehicle becomes high-centered, for winching, clamping, or spreading. The jack is durable and easy to use, and with accessories it does many tasks for a small investment. Remember to use a wheel chock to stabilize the rig when jacking and use a jack stand if you need to work under the vehicle.

JKs with larger tires and/or lift kits require lifting heights beyond the ability of the onboard jack. Even the Hi-Lift jack can become unstable when raised near the top of the climbing bar. The Lift-Mate is designed to operate in a manner that allows the vehicle to be lifted directly from the wheel, greatly reducing the amount of travel up the jack bar needed to lift the wheel to an adequate and safe height. The Lift-Mate is also the quickest way to lift a vehicle that is high-centered on rocks or logs. By lifting the appropriate tire off the ground enough to free the chassis or axle housing from the obstacle, you can then place rocks, boards, or a bridge ladder under the tire so that when the jack is lowered, the obstacle is cleared and the vehicle can be driven away.

Use the Lift-Mate and a jack stand to change a flat tire if you have no other jacking point available. Raise the tire with the Lift-Mate

Winching Basics and Safety

Carefully and diligently follow these procedures to avoid any risk of personal injury and damage to your JK. Never use a winch designed for off-road use as a hoist for lifting vertical loads. You need to always wear gloves, especially when working with wire rope, because cable can fray and cause nasty cuts.

Pull out the winch line from the spool by hand with the clutch lock released just in case the line was doubled over when rewinding. When the line is doubled over it will suddenly reverse direction and give the person pulling out the line quite a tug. The exception to this may be on a steep slope where the winch being used for recovery is on the rig that is stuck on the slope. The driver should stay in the rig if possible to hold the brake and ensure the rig remains stationary while someone else draws out the winch line. After the line is pulled out, the slope must be descended again to engage the clutch lock. In this case, it may be easier and safer to slowly ascend the slope as the winch operator runs the line out with the winch control.

Keep everyone away from the swing zone of the winch rope. This is the radius in which the winch line could swing if the connection breaks at either end. This zone actually has two radii, one at each end. The best place to be is to the side of either the rig being pulled or the anchor point, whether it's a tree, rock, or another rig. Anyone within the winch line swing zone is at great risk if the winch line or any attached component fails. Synthetic winch rope is much safer than the more common steel winch rope, which, when under tension, can act like a powerful slingshot. Be very careful.

After putting a little tension on the winch line, place a line dampener on the winch line. This is important when using steel winch rope; it is not self-dampening as is synthetic winch line. A winch line dampener is any fabric weighing at least 4 to 5 pounds that can be draped over the winch line. Should the line snap, the dampener minimizes the snapping effect of the broken line and reduces the flinging of the line or items attached to it. A dampener could be a large towel, jacket, blanket, sleeping bag, or a special winch line dampener designed for this purpose. Even tow or recovery straps can be looped over the winch line as a dampener. Although synthetic winch line is much less dangerous, it is a good idea to use a dampener with synthetic as well.

Assign tasks to all who are available. A spotter should be positioned to watch the vehicle being winched to make sure there are no binds or other potential problems. Someone else can watch the anchor point, especially if it is another rig. Make sure everyone is on the same page for communication both verbally and with hand signals. Keep it simple, such as thumbs up and verbal "okay" for pulling and "stop" with a balled fist thrust into the air to stop winching. The driver of the rig with the winch that is doing the pulling should organize the communications. In addition, make sure the observers are out of harm's way; do not begin the winching operation while anyone is in danger.

Always have at least five wraps (one layer) of winch line around the drum before winching. This is the minimum to prevent slippage of the line on the drum.

A winch design follows the laws of physics. As layers of winch line accumulate on the winch drum, pulling power decreases. Winch power can be reduced by nearly 50 percent from the maximum when the drum has five layers of line wrapped on it compared to the initial one layer. If you have a difficult pull, play out the winch line as much as possible to maximize the pulling power. If necessary, use a snatch block to play out more line. The pulley also doubles the pulling power while halving line speed.

Most 4x4 electric winches are rated for an intermittent-duty cycle, so if you have a long, hard pull, give your winch and battery a break once in a while. Let the motor and battery cool for a few minutes, and then resume the winching process. If the winch line is dragging on the ground over a slope breakover, use a piece of carpet or towel to minimize the wear on the line as it drags on the dirt or rocks. After checking all connections, tension the winch line lightly, and then recheck connections and make sure everyone is in a safe location and ready to start pulling. ■

attachment, place a jack stand under the axle housing or frame, lower the jack, change the tire and wheel, then use the jack with the Lift-Mate to remove the jack stand.

The rugged polyurethane Handle-Keeper holds the Hi-Lift handle to the upright steel bar, keeping it in place when not in use and eliminating "rattling" during transportation and storage.

Before you use your Hi-Lift jack, you need to consider the following: The Hi-lift jack is not self-lubricating,

The Hi-Lift jack is bulky and heavy, but many sturdy vehicle mounts are available for it. AEV makes a nice mount accessory for their tire carrier for the JK. The bottom of the jack sits in a holder while a clamp through the standard holds the jack securely in place. The AEV tire carrier can also hold a Pull-Pal ground anchor.

so it needs proper lubrication to operate safely. Before you use your Hi-Lift jack, lubricate the jack with white lithium grease, light penetrating oil, or a silicon spray.

Always place the handle against the steel standard, which is the upright vertical bar, with the handle clip holding it up before moving the reversing latch. This prevents the handle from moving up and down rapidly, which could cause serious injury or death if it comes into contact with any part of your body. Always keep your head out of the travel path of the handle. During lowering, the weight of the load pushes *up* against the Jack's handle. If your hands slip off the handle, or if the handle is horizontal when you move the reversing latch, it may move up quickly. If your head is in the handle's travel path, it could strike you.

Jacking involves heavy loads, which can create dangerous situations; therefore, you need to follow these rules for safe and effective operation. Chock and block (stabilize) the vehicle to prevent it from moving or falling. Make sure the load cannot slip, roll away, or fall. Never go underneath a raised vehicle supported with just a jack. Use a jack stand or blocks if you need to work under the vehicle. Never push a raised vehicle off the Jack. Make sure everyone is clear of the load before lowering. Keep in mind that conditions on the trail can be difficult, requiring you to work on inclined and side slopes, loose and soft surfaces, and possibly with inclement weather conditions. Practice using the Hi-Lift jack at home or some spot where you can familiarize yourself with its operation in an easy situation and environment. This saves time on the trail and minimizes the chance of problems.

The Hi-Lift jack is designed to work on rigid, flat jacking points, such as a rock slider, flat bottom bumper, or a bull bar–style bumper with notches designed for use with a Hi-Lift. Do not use this jack on curved or tubular vehicle bumpers. The vehicle could slip off the jack and fall, causing serious injury or death. Do not raise an inflated tire more than 2 inches above the ground. Never attempt to lift more than one wheel at a time.

When using a chain or tow strap in conjunction with a jack, the working load of each (chain or tow strap) must be greater than the strength of the jack. If a chain or tow strap breaks while winching, the load could shift or the chain or tow strap could snap back. When used as a winch, the top clamp supports up to 5,000 pounds. If you exceed this limit, the top clamp could bend or break, causing the load to shift or the chain or tow strap to snap back, which could result in damage or injury.

Do not use the jack to support a vehicle. Securely chock and block the vehicle to be lifted. Never get under a raised load without properly chocking and supporting the load. If a raised load falls, it can cause serious injury or death.

Straps

A tow strap can be used for pulling a stuck rig out of trouble, towing a disabled vehicle back to a paved road (why two rigs traveling together is a good idea), or assisting a vehicle with inadequate traction through a slippery spot. The most common straps are 20 to 30 feet long by 3 inches wide. Straps equipped with steel hook attaches should not be used for recovery or towing. Use straps with stitched loops at each end. Longer straps can

Hi-Lift Jacks recently entered the recovery strap market with the Hi-Lift Reflective Loop recovery straps. The straps are available in 2-and 3-inch widths at 30 feet long and a 3-inch by 15-foot–long tree saver. The 15-foot-long tree saver allows use on larger trees.

The ARB Premium Recovery Kit includes all the straps needed for comprehensive vehicle recovery, as well as other key accessories. The orange strap is a 17,500-pound-load snatch strap that does allow some stretch for kinetic vehicle recovery. The purple strap is a 66-foot-long winch line extension rated at a 9,900-pound load. The green strap is a tree trunk protector rated at 26,500 pounds. The snatch block is rated at 20,000 pounds. Also included are a heavy-duty winch line dampener, a 10,540-pound-rated 3/4-inch-pin D-ring shackle, a pair of leather work gloves, and a sturdy recovery bag.

The JK Unlimited (not shown) is the tow vehicle being used to pull the white Wrangler TJ, which lost its clutch on a Jeep run. The loads on a tow strap are typically small unless really steep hills or large rock crawling sections are encountered. Tow straps should be looped at the ends for attachment with a D-ring shackle to a solid mount at each end, Metal hooks are not used on tow straps in the backcountry. It is also important to minimize slack in the strap while towing.

The ARB Snatch Strap is in use for towing. The Snatch Strap does have some stretch so it can be used for getting unstuck. The degree of stretch is slight so it can also be used as a tow strap, Up to 30 feet is good length for a tow strap. In tight quarters, longer straps can get caught on obstacles. Shorter straps can contribute to potential collisions.

The OKoffroad Mega Kinetic Recovery Strap comes in 1.25- and 1.5-inch versions. The 1.25-inch-diameter version is rated at 52,300-pound breaking strength; the 1.5-inch version is rated up to 74,000 pounds. Both are 30 feet long and can stretch about 20 percent at full load. These are designed to stretch under load. By leaving about half of the strap as slack, the pulling vehicle can get a running start. When the slack is gone and the strap begins to stretch, the kinetic energy of the stretching strap adds to the pulling power of the strap and makes extraction easier.

get caught up on obstacles in tight quarters. Shorter straps can contribute to possible collisions. A snatch strap does have some stretch, so it can be used for getting unstuck. The degree of stretch is small, so it can also be used as a tow strap. Up to 30 feet is a good length for a tow strap.

Kinetic Yanker Straps

A kinetic strap is much like a large bungee cord. When stretched, it stores energy. Unlike chain, cable, or a nylon tow strap, which do not stretch much at all when a pulling force is applied, the kinetic strap is designed to store energy as it is stretched; then, when snapped back, the effective pulling force is increased because the strap snaps back faster than it was stretched.

Kinetic straps, also referred to as "yanker" straps, are used to do just that, yank a stuck rig to freedom. You need strong mounts on both rigs to use a kinetic strap. The mounts must tie in to the chassis, as when winch-

ing. Tow points, if really substantial, work well. A hitch receiver bracket with a bow shackle works well, as do shackle mounts on off-road-style winches and rear bumpers. Keep in mind that the force is substantial, even though the kinetic shock absorption characteristics of the kinetic strap soften the shock. Attach the yanker strap to a secure point on each rig with a bow shackle.

The kinetic, or yanker, strap is a great tool for a quick pull out of a stuck situation. They are best used when the wheels are stuck in sand, snow, mud, or gravel. It is not recommended to use a kinetic strap when a vehicle is high-centered or on any underside component. However, a rig resting on rock sliders can easily be pulled free using a yanker strap.

D-Ring Shackles

Shackles are used for attaching winch line or tow straps to a vehicle. Shackles must be rated stronger than the strap or winch line with which

A shackle bracket mounted in the hitch receiver for a trailer hitch provides a strong and secure attachment point for a D-ring shackle at the rear of a JK. A standard hitch pin holds the shackle bracket in place.

they are being used. Shackles should not be used to attach straps or lines together; if the shackles or the strap fail, the heavy steel shackle becomes a dangerous projectile. Use shackles only to attach a strap or line directly to a vehicle. Shackle anchor points must be strong. Good examples are a trailer hitch receiver bracket, a mount on a heavy-duty winch bumper, or rear bumper. Shackles should be tightened only until the pin bottoms out, then back off the pin about a quarter turn to ensure that the shackle pin does not bind after the load is released and you want to unscrew it.

The markings on a shackle offer some information about strength. If the numbers are stamped into the shackle, they are likely not as strong as shackles with the numbers cast into the body. Most domestically manufactured shackles have the cast, raised numbers.

Ground Anchor for Winching

A ground anchor, such as the Pull-Pal, allows winching where no other winch line attachment points are available. If you have nothing to pull against with a winch, the winch is useless. The Pull-Pal provides an anchor point when no trees, large rocks, or other rigs are available. And this happens more often than you might expect. If you drive in snow, sand or desert areas, there are often no trees or rocks to anchor to. If you're on a narrow trail with a steep climb, even with other rigs, they may not be in a position to provide an anchor. And many times, finding a suitable anchor that lines up adequately with your winch so the pull angle is within an acceptable range can be impossible. The one thing that is always available is ground, and it is rare to find solid rock trails with no rock outcropping to anchor to. We have used the Pull-Pal in snow, ice, sand, dirt, loose dirt from mine tailings, gravel, and loose, small rocks. It has always dug in enough to easily pull from, and it is easy to use. How-

The Pull-Pal ground anchor is a two-piece unit that folds compactly to the size of an ordinary bumper jack for easy storage. You insert the plow point into the soil and attach the winch line to get your rig unstuck. As the winch line tensions, the point embeds itself deeply and firmly into the ground. The two-piece assembly includes the plow head and the articulation anchor arms. The plow attaches to the arm via slots in the plow head and a slide locking mechanism on the arm and head. No tools are required.

The point of the plow head inserts into the ground with the arm assembly pointing toward the winch. The winch line hook inserts into the hole in the arm end. By tensioning the winch line, the geometry of the plow head and arm pulls it into the surface at an angle. More force on the winch secures the plow head more firmly in the ground. The plow movement slows and the winched rig begins to move forward. The head takes a set and you now have a secure winching anchoring point.

To release the Pull-Pal, simply remove the winch line and lift up on the arm assembly until it breaks free of the surface. We have had situations where the plow head set so firmly, even in snow, that we could not pull it free by hand. We then placed the winch directly over the top of the arm end so that the winch pulled straight up on the arm. This easily released the plow head from the surface.

ever, it is, by necessity, somewhat bulky.

Extraction Boards, Sand Ladders, and Bridging Ladders

Extraction boards are used to get a JK unstuck from soft surfaces, such as snow, mud, and sand. The lugs on the board are designed to engage with the tire tread. When the tires begin to rotate, the tire tread pulls on the lugs on the board. The boards then elevate the Jeep as it moves forward (or backward) and provides a solid surface to get out of the hole in the surface. They are easy to use

MaxTrax extraction boards are made from injection molded nylon. This manufacturing method allows for a strong but flexible board. Extraction boards allow quick and easy vehicle recovery from soft surfaces, such as snow, sand, and mud. Lugs on the bottom grip the surface; the topside lugs engage the tire tread. By angling the boards between the tire and surface, then driving onto the boards, the lugs pull the boards under the tire tread and raise the vehicle out of the surface. The ends of the board can be used as a shovel for proper positioning of the board under the tire. Straps attached to the board handles allow easy retrieval of the boards when the tires have cleared the end of the board.

and often the quickest way to get unstuck. They do not work on hard surfaces or rocks.

Sand ladders, also called bridging ladders, can be used to keep tires on the surface of sand and snow, but they are not as effective in mud. These can also bridge small ruts and depression in which a tire could become wedged. The OKoffroad aluminum sand ladders are 60 inches long by 16 inches wide.

The Australian company Maxtrax created the first extraction boards. These are injection-molded from the highest-quality UV-stabilized engineering-grade "super tough" reinforced nylon. We have used the Maxtrax since they became available in the United States and they have helped us out of some tough situations. When we had a synthetic winch line freeze solid in a snowstorm, we used the Maxtrax to get unstuck. They are not designed as

bridging ladders, but they are strong enough to help get over deep but narrow ruts.

Bridging, or sand ladders, as the name implies, are used to cross over ruts or gaps that cause a tire to get stuck. A 40-inch-wide rut that is 3 feet deep sucks in a 37-inch or smaller tire and it is difficult to get out. A bridging ladder can bridge the gap.

Some bridging ladders are made of aluminum. They are also made from fiberglass composites and are often called "waffle boards." They are typically 4 to 5 feet long and 12 inches wide. Sand ladders provide traction in spots where a soft surface can allow tires to dig in and lose traction. They are usually about 5 feet long and up to 16 inches wide. They can also be used for bridging ruts and other obstacles.

Trail Tools and Spare Parts

Getting stuck on the trail is inevitable and breakdowns are also possible. Being prepared is the key to a successful and safe adventure in the backcountry. Always be prepared and have recovery tools as well as some key spare parts.

Max Ax Tool

The Max Ax tool kit is extremely versatile for a wide variety of trail needs, from digging out of sand, snow, and mud to chopping large fallen trees for easier removal from a trail. The ax head is permanently mounted to a stout fiberglass handle that has a spud for mounting the other accessories, including a shovel, rake, and a variety of pick heads. This recovery tool is not needed often, but when it is necessary, it's worth its weight in gold.

The Handle-All tool kit from Hi-Lift Jacks features four attachments and a two-piece aluminum handle. The Handle-All can be used as an ax, shovel, pick, or sledge hammer. All items fit in a storage bag.

The jerry can is the old standby for fuel storage. These metal fuel containers are sturdy, and newer versions meet EPA and CARB storage requirements. The latest JK models hold 22.5 gallons for the Unlimited and 18.6 gallons for the standard model. When driving off road, depending on modifications and terrain, most JKs use between 1 and 1.5 gallons of fuel per hour. If you need much larger fuel capacity, GenRight makes a 20-gallon auxiliary tank.

The Max Ax is a multi-purpose tool. The ax head is permanently attached to the ax handle; the other accessories attach to the ax head. The Max Ax can also be used as a shovel, rake, hoe, and pick.

The ax handle is 36 inches long and made from polyglass composite. Accessories attach to a bracket on the head of the jack with a clip.

Hi-Lift Handle-All

The Hi-Lift Handle-All is a multi-functional tool with telescoping handle and four full-sized implements, including a full-sized shovelhead, sledgehammer head, ax head, and pick-ax head. The kit is compact and rugged, while maintaining full-size utility.

Fluid Storage

Fluids are the lifeblood of your JK and your well-being. If you travel long distances, water and fuel storage is important. If your backcountry adventures are short, the onboard fuel supply and bottled drinking water are adequate. Several options are available to carry water and non-flammable fluids, but choices are limited for carrying gasoline due to strict Environmental Protection Agency (EPA) and California Air Resources Board (CARB) regulations on leakage and vapors. The Daystar Cam Can system offers several options for non-flammable fluid storage outside the passenger compartment.

RotopaX manufactures several sizes of gasoline containers, which comply with EPA and CARB regulations. The Daystar and RotopaX products include mounting systems in the kits. Metal jerry cans are another option; they can be mounted using a variety of options.

Tire Repair Kit

Although flat tires do occur off road, they are unusual with off-road tires with a "D" or "E" ply rating when the tires have been aired down. If a tire goes down, two options are possible: change the tire or plug the puncture using a tire puncture repair kit. Extreme Outback and Safety Seal make comprehensive tire repair kits. Simple kits are available from auto parts stores. A flat tire in a convenient location is contrary to Murphy's Law. It is extremely unusual. JKs equipped with larger tires face a difficult situation when changing a flat. Even a 35-inch-diameter M/T or A/T tire mounted on the spare tire carrier weighs more than 100 pounds. Even on flat, stable ground, that weight creates a difficult task. Imagine changing that tire on a loose dirt hill with an off-camber slope. Just jacking the vehicle to remove the flat becomes dangerous. A tire repair kit can be used to plug a tire without jacking or removing the tire, and it can be done in any location as long as the puncture is exposed. Plugging the tire is easier, usually quicker, and much safer than trying to change the tire.

Occasionally, a flat is caused when a rock or a shrub branch damages the valve stem. A new product is available to replace the valve stem from the outside of the rim. The

Extra fuel capacity allows for longer adventures without the need to return to civilization. The AEV fuel caddy adds 10.2 gallons of fuel stored in a polyethylene tank. The tank mounts to the AEV tire carrier. A shaker siphon hose allows easy fuel transfer to the main JK fuel tank.

Colby Valve uses a unique design that secures the valve stem to the rim from the outside without removing the tire from the rim.

Spare Parts

Simple tools and spare parts can save the day if you encounter problems on the trail. Here are some of the items to carry in your JK. A metric tool kit is a must. You should also have a lug wrench or breaker bar and socket, and the key if your wheels have anti-theft lug nuts. Also carry a multi-tool and knife, electrical test light, spare fuses, and gloves.

Radiator repair sealant, duct tape, electrical tape, tire valve cores, and lug nuts should also be included. Simple electrical repairs can save an adventure. Fuses are easily replaced. Carry spare fuses, a fuse puller, wire, side cutters, wire connectors, wire strippers, and electrical tape.

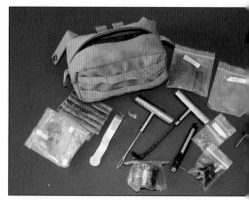

Flat tires are not as common as they once where. But flats do occur. Changing a tire on the trail can be difficult, even dangerous. Unless the flat occurs on relatively flat terrain, it can be risky to use a jack. And if you have a lifted JK with larger tires, the extra height needed to lift the tire off the ground combined with the increased weight makes tire changing daunting at best. Tire plug kits make the job much easier and safer. Extreme Outback's Ultimate Puncture Repair Kit has the materials to fix just about any tire.

The makers of FiberFix claim it's 100 times stronger than steel. This repair tape is soaked in water, applied to the repair area, and allowed to set for 10 minutes. We are not sure if it works on a tie-rod, drag link, or suspension control arm, but it sure is worth a try if you find yourself stranded in the backcountry.

Rocks, shrubs, or tree branches tearing valve stems off rims cause many flat tires. Changing the tire has been the only solution to this problem unless the tire can be dismounted from the rim. The Colby Valve has changed that. This unique design allows the valve stem to be inserted from the outside of the rim with the wheel in place. It takes only a couple of minutes to install and the tire can be inflated.

Some products are worth carrying even though you may never need them. WD-40 is an old standby that can be used to lube many items, such as the standard on a Hi-Lift jack, or to help loosen rusted fasteners. Silicone adhesive sealant can be handy for minor leaks. Bar's Leak can plug that rock puncture in a radiator. JB Weld can be used to fix all kinds of damage. We have plugged cracked transfer cases, engine oil pans, and other metal items on the trail.

GPS Systems

A good GPS makes navigation in the backcountry a breeze. Many types of GPS units are available. Screen detail is an important feature when using a GPS in the backcountry, but the map detail is more important. If you are planning a route in a new location (to you), check your GPS to see if the map files contain the route you wish to drive. If not, you may be able to find route information, such as latitude and longitude coordinates, that you can use to create waypoints on your GPS. Some GPS units have computer-mapping software available so that you can create detailed maps of your planned route.

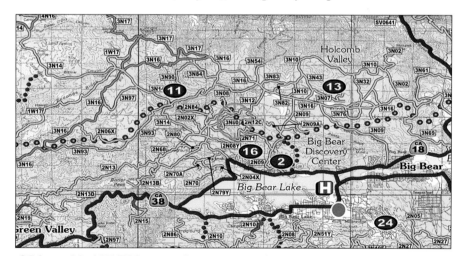

GPS-enabled PDF Maps work on a smartphone or tablet. After the app is downloaded along with the desired maps, an Internet or cellular connection is necessary. Avenza maps uses the latest technology to create geospatial PDF map files from existing digital maps. You can record routes for future reference and even add geo-tagged photos to the file.

Once you have driven a route and recorded the waypoint and track data, it's fairly easy to store the data for future use and to create detailed maps. We have been using GPS systems for several years. The Magellan eXplorist TRX7 GPS unit has recently proven to be extremely effective for off-road use. With hundreds of routes and trails available in the Magellan database, it is likely you can find the roads and trails you seek. In addition, it is easy to create your own routes with the online Magellan soft-ware. With a WiFi connection for the eXplorist TRX7 and your computer, the GPS unit automatically downloads your route when saved to your wishlist. The TRX7 is easily removed from its mount for use outside your JK for planning or geocaching purposes. Another good off-road onboard GPS unit is the Lowrance Global Map Baja 540C.

Handheld GPS

The market offers dozens of good handheld GPS units. We have used the DeLorme Earthmate PN-60 GPS. Handhelds are great for geocaching or to find specific locations away from motorized vehicle routes. Handheld units are small and lightweight, but the screen can be difficult to see while driving. New technology allows the creation of digital maps in PDF form that are GPS-enabled. GPS-enabled maps, such as the PDF maps app from Avenza, read geospatial PDF, GeoPDF, and GeoTiff files. Thousands of PDF maps are available for use with apps using this technology.

JEEP JK PROFILE

Don Alexander's Jeep 4x4 School 2013 JKU *Grizzlycon*

Don's JK was one of the first 2013 models sold in Southern California in late summer 2012. Running 35-inch tires was the original goal, to enable the JK to tackle any trail in the Big Bear Lake, California, area. This included some of the notable black diamond runs, such as Holcomb Creek Jeep Trail and the John Bull Trail. At the time, 35-inch tires were the norm with some 37-inch tires beginning to appear.

The first upgrade was a Daystar 1.75-inch lift with Mickey Thompson Baja MTZ 35-inch tires. This caused some tire rub during extreme articulation. To eliminate the rub, GenRight steel flat fenders were installed. Hanson and Pure Jeep products were added around the same time. The Hanson front winch bumper and rear bumper were installed. Pure Jeep skidplates were added for the gas tank, transfer case, and evap relocation. The *Grizzlycon* was now prepared to tackle any local trail and some of the challenging rock crawling trails in the nearby desert. A Power Tank carbon dioxide air system was added for quick airing up after a day of wheeling. SpiderWebShade provided a cool green sunshade for topless wheeling.

In 2014, Ray Currie asked Don to test the new Currie RockJock 44 front and rear axle assemblies. The Currie RockJock 4-inch-lift suspension was installed with Bilstein shocks, Antirock sway bars, and Currie suspension arms with Johnny Joint rod ends. The bolt-in replacement RockJock 44 axle assemblies were added. Gearing was changed to Motive Gear 4.88 ring and pinion gear sets and ARB air lockers. Falken WildPeak All Terrain tires (37-inch) mounted on Raceline Monster Beadlock wheels completed this round of upgrades. Most of the modifications and all the maintenance was done at All J Products in Big Bear Lake, California.

The next round of upgrades started a few months later. The Hanson rear bumper was modified at All J Products by adding an AEV tire carrier with Hi-Lift jack and Pull-Pal mounts. A sPOD was added to allow more electrical components without risk to the onboard computer. Rock-Slide Engineering Slider steps were added along with a Rock-Slide front shorty bumper and a Warn Zeon 10-S winch with synthetic winch line and wireless remote. Factor 55 ProLink winch line ends completed a closed winching system. After being sideswiped in a parking lot where the fenders were damaged, Rock-Slide Engineering formed flat fenders were installed. A Flex-a-Lite Trans Cooler was installed to help preserve the JK stock transmission.

The 2013 Jeep 4x4 School Grizzlycon belongs to Don Alexander. The Grizzlycon name refers to the trails in Big Bear where grizzlies roamed until the early 1900s. After four years of upgrading, the Grizzlycon is still unfinished. With new products for the JK appearing every week, modifications that are currently unknown will certainly become important. The Grizzlycon features a wide range of parts from Currie including RockJock 44 axle housing front and rear, the RockJock 4-inch lift and suspension, Currie Currectlync steering, and Antirock sway bars.

The *Grizzlycon* has been used for considerable product testing since the upgrades. In 2015, Mickey Thompson ATZ P3 All Terrain tires mounted on Mickey Thompson MM-366 black alloy wheels were tested extensively on the most challenging local trails. The next year, the new Falken mud-terrain tires were put to the test. Don tested these tires in just about every challenging off-road scenario possible. Both of Falken's new off-road tires, the MT and the AT3W all-terrain tire, were also tested.

Upgrading to the Currie RockJock 44 axle assemblies enhanced performance and reliability. At the same time, the RockJock 4-inch JK lift with Johnny Joint control arms, Synergy ball joints, and Currie sway bar end links were installed.

The Currie RockJock 44 is a direct bolt-in replacement for the stock Rubicon Dana 44 axle assembly. Motive Gear 4.88 ratio gears were installed along with ARB air lockers and heavy-duty chrome-moly axles. Later, the front axles were upgraded to the RCV constant velocity joint axles.

The Warn Zeon 10-S winch allowed the Grizzlycon JK to perform vehicle recoveries and recovery classes. This durable and powerful 10,000-pound winch features a Spydura synthetic winch line. A wireless remote was added for safety and convenience. An ARB recovery kit is carried with a selection of straps, including a winch line extension, a long tree saver strap, and a kinetic tow/ extraction strap. A large snatch block, shackle, winch line dampener, and gloves round out the kit.

Currie Currectlync steering adds durability and improves feel. Antirock sway bars help control body roll while offering maximum articulation without the need to disconnect the bars. Falken 37-inch MT tires are mounted on Raceline Monster Beadlock wheels.

In late 2015, All J added an ARB oil pan and transmission skidplate. The driveshafts were also upgraded to bulletproof shafts from JE Reel. Every upgrade was intended to improve reliability and performance. So far, all changes have had a positive effect. Fabtech Stealth monotube shocks were tested. Don later upgraded the shocks to Fabtech Dirt Logic reservoir shocks. To enhance cooling, a Daystar hood cowl and vents help evacuate hot air from under the hood. The 2-way air system allows easier airing down and up.

In late summer of 2016, the stock steering hydraulic components were showing wear. When the steering box failed, it was time to upgrade the whole system and add a power assist ram. A new heavy-duty steering box with a stronger sector shaft, a high-output power steering pump, and a ram assist from PSC were installed at All J Products. This system enhanced steering effort, especially in the big rocks with aired down tires. A Borla Climber exhaust and a K&N cold-air intake were added for improved performance.

With more testing and many other events on the calendar for 2017, some reliability upgrades were called for. The RCV constant velocity

To improve cooling, the Daystar hood cowl and vents were added to the hood and color matched to the Gecko green paint. Rock-Slide Engineering slider steps, stubby winch bumper with bull bar, and formed metal flat fenders altered the look and function of the Grizzlycon. KC HiLiTES are mounted to the A-pillars and a 20-inch light bar is mounted to the bull bar.

front axles are as strong as you can get. Although a broken axle isn't the end of the world, it's nice to know that one less item can break in the backcountry.

One of the biggest issues when upgrading to 37-inch tires is braking performance. This is apparent the first time the brakes are applied for a normal stop. Pedal pressure increases dramatically. When Don conducted a braking test comparing stopping distances from 45 mph with 33-inch tires compared to 37-inch tires, the difference was shocking. At maximum braking on asphalt with the anti-lock brakes engaging, the 37-inch tires took nearly 40 percent longer to come to a complete stop. That stunning outcome led to the next upgrade. Black Magic Big Brakes were installed. The bigger front calipers and rotors allowed stopping distances with 37-inch tires to match the distance with 33-inch tires. The bigger brakes made a big difference in safety and in rock crawling. Before the Black Magic kit, it took massive pedal pressure to control speeds dropping down big rocks and off drop-offs. Now the pedal pressure is much lighter, even to lock the front brakes momentarily. Next, DynaTrac big rear brakes were added to the brake system.

A Rock Hard 4x4 sport cage has been added to increase safety and add a little rigidity to the body and chassis. Baja Designs XL Pro LED lights have been installed on the front bumper. A Magellan eXplorist TRX7 GPS helps find new trails and offers many other features. A Rubicam 4 camera spotting system from Red Peak Off Road helps with spotting. This system works great and allows recording of adventures as well. A Superchips Trail Dash 2 provides a wealth of performance information, allows performance tuning, and even has an inclinometer so you know how scared you should be on slide slopes and steep inclines. An aluminum C&R Racing radiator replaced the stock radiator and a GC Cooling fan was added to increase airflow through the radiator. All J also added a set of Fox Shox hydraulic bumpstops to soften the impact over severe bumps and ruts.

It appears that the *Grizzlycon* is complete. Reality dictates otherwise. There are so many new JK products coming out that a JK project is never truly finished. But for now, testing, trail runs, and 4x4 training can continue with a high-quality JK ready to tackle the most difficult terrain. And have some fun!

Don Alexander's 2013 JKU *Grizzlycon*

Year/Model: 2013 Unlimited Rubicon
Engine & Transmission: Stock
Transfer case: Rock-Trac NV241 4.0:1
Tires: Falken WildPeak MT01 37x12.50R17LT
Wheels: Raceline RT232 ST Monster Beadlocks
Front & Rear axle housing: Currie RockJock 44/Currie RockJock 44 high pinion
Front & Rear ring/pinion: Motive ring and pinion 4.88
Front & Rear axles: RCV CV joint 30-spline/Currie 35-spline
Front & Rear locker: ARB air locker
Front & Rear suspension: Currie RockJock 4-inch lift
Front & Rear shock absorbers: Fabtech Dirt Logic remote reservoir
Front & Rear bumpstops: Fox hydraulic
Front & Rear control arms: Currie RockJock with Johnny Joint rod ends
Front track bar: Currie RockJock with Johnny Joint rod ends
Steering tie-rod & drag link: Currie Currectlync with Johnny Joint rod ends
Ball joints: Dynatrac heavy-duty
Steering knuckles: Reid Racing
Steering dampener: PSC
Power steering box, pump & cooler: PSC
Power steering reservoir: Howe
Steering dampener bracket: Currie
Rear brakes: Dynatrac
Front brakes: Black Magic Big Brake
Cold-air intake: K&N Filters
Cat-back exhaust: Borla Climber
Auxiliary switch system: sPOD
Onboard compressor: ARB CKSA12
Radiator: C&R Racing
Transmission cooler: PSC
Exterior cooling: Daystar hood cowl and vents
Rear bumper: Hanson
Front bumper: Rock-Slide Engineering rigid shorty with bull bar
Auxiliary fluid storage: Daystar Cam Can (2)
Engine/transmission skidplate: ARB
Gas tank skidplate: Hanson
Transfer case skidplate: Hanson
Evap relocation: Hanson
Fenders: Rock-Slide Engineering crawler style
Rock sliders: Rock-Slide Engineering electric slider steps
Auxiliary lighting: Baja Designs
Roll cage: Rock Hard 4x4 Ultimate Sport Cage with Overhead Center Bars
Performance tuner: Superchips TrailDash TD2

Advance Adapters
PO Box 247
Paso Robles, CA 93447
800-350-2223
advanceadapters.com

American Expedition Vehicles
51960 W 12 Mile Rd.
Wixom, MI 48393
248-926-0256
aev-conversions.com

AFe Power
951-493-7155
afepower.com

All J Products
41610 Brownie Ln.
Big Bear Lake, CA 92315
909-866-4800
boulderbars.com

American Eagle Wheels
5780 Soestern Ct.
Chino, CA 91710
800-242-4302
americaneaglewheel.com

ARB USA
4810 D St. NW
Suite 103
Auburn, WA 9800
866-293-9078
arbusa.com

Artec Industries
585 N. 700 W. Ste. C
North Salt Lake, UT 84054
855-278-3299
artecindustries.com

Baja Designs
185 Bosstick Blvd.
San Marcos, CA 92069
866-335-7050
bajadesigns.com

B&M Racing
100 Stony Point Rd. Ste. 125
Santa Rosa, CA 95401
707-544-4761
bmracing.com

Gale Banks Engineering
546 S Duggan Ave.
Azusa, CA 91702
800-601-8072
Bankspower.com

Bestop Inc
333 Centennial Pkwy.
Louisville, CO 80027
800-845-3567
bestop.com

BFGoodrich Tires
877-788-8899
bfgoodrichtires.com

Bilstein of America
Thyssenkrupp
4440 Muhlhauser Rd.
Hamilton, OH 45011
513-682-4850
bilstein.com

Black Magic Brakes
23360 La Bertha Ln.
Quail Valley, CA 92587
951-246-0313
blackmagicbrakes.com

BLM
blm.gov

Body Armor
258 Mariah Ct.
Corona, CA 92879
951-808-0750
bodyarmor4x4.com

Borla Exhaust
701 Arcturus Ave.
Oxnard, CA 93033
877.GO.BORLA
borla.com

California 4 Wheel Drive Assn.
8120 36th Ave.
Sacramento, CA 95824
800-4x4-FUNN
cal4wheel.com

California Off-Road Vehicle
Association
1500 W El Camino 352
Sacramento, CA 95833
916-710-1950
corva.org

Centerforce Clutches
2266 Crosswind Dr.
Prescott, AZ 86301
928-771-8422
centerforce.com

Crown Automotive
750 Greg St.
Sparks, NV 89431
800-453-8220
crownautomotive.net

Currie Enterprises
382 North Smith St.
Corona, CA 92880
888-338-7502
currieenterprises.com

Dana Corp
dana.com

Daystar Products Intl
800-595-7659
Daystarweb.com

Dynatrac Products Co.
392 Count Cir.
Huntington Beach, CA 92647
714-421-4314
dynatrac.com

Eaton
eaton.com

Edelbrock
2700 California St.
Torrance, CA 90503
310-781-2222
edelbrock.com

Eibach Springs
264 Mariah Cir.
Corona, CA 92879
800-507-2338
eibach.com

Enersys
2366 Bernville Rd.
Reading, PA 19605
610-208-1991
enersys.com

Extreme Outback
1051 Aldridge Rd.
Vacaville, CA 95688
866-447-7711
extremeoutback.com

Extreme Terrain
844-887-6500
extremeterrain.com

Fabtech
4331 Eucalyptus Ave.
Chino, CA 91710
877-432-2832

Falken Tire
8656 Haven Ave.
Rancho Cucamonga, CA
91730
800-723-2553
Falkentire.com

Factor 55
107 E. 46th St. #108
Garden City, ID 83714
208-639-1674
Factor55.com

FireStik Antenna
2614 E. Adams St.
Phoenix, AZ 85034
602-273-7151
firestik.com

Four Wheeler Magazine
fourwheeler.com

4 Wheel Parts
4wheelparts.com

Fourtreks
3625 Anita Dr.
Bell, CA 90201
818-517-6145
fourtreks.com

Fox Racing Shox
915 Disc Dr.
Scotts Valley, CA 95066
1.800.FOX.SHOX
ridefox.com

FunTreks
PO Box 3127
Monument, CO 80132
877-222-7623
funtreks.com

Garvin Industries
316 Millar Ave.
El Cajon, CA 92020
619-440-7415
wildernessracks.com

GenRight Off Road
4535 Runway St.
Simi Valley, CA 93063
805-584-8635
genright.com

Gobi Racks
14509 E. 33rd Pl., Unit E
Aurora, CO 80011
720-479-9372
gobiracks.com

Great Outdoor Products
2083 S. Thunderbird Dr.
Woods Cross, UT 84087
801-299-1885
rotopax.com

Hankook Tires
hankooktire.com

Hanson Off-Road
4775 E. Vine St.
Fresno, CA 93725
877-757-9779
hansonoffroad.com

Howe Performance
12476 Julian Ave.
Lakeside, CA 92040
619-561-7764
howeperformance.com

Jasper Engines
1477 E. Cedar St., Unit D
Ontario, CA 91761
800-827-7465
jasperengines.com

JE Reel Drive Shaft Specialists
448 S. Reservoir St.
Pomona, CA 91766
909-629-9002
Reeldriveline.com

Jeep 4x4 School
Big Bear Lake, CA 92315
jeep4x4school.com

Jeep Jamboree USA
2776 Sourdough Flat
Georgetown, CA 95634
530-333-4777
jeepjamboreeusa.com

JKS Manufacturing
491 W. Garfield Ave.
Coldwater, MI 49036
517-278-1226
jksmfg.com

JP Magazine
fourwheeler.com

KC HiLiTES
2843 W. Avenida De Luces
Williams, AZ 86046
888-689-5955
kchilites.com

K&N Filters
1455 Citrus St.
Riverside, CA 92507
800-858-3333
knfilters.com

Macs Custom Tie Downs
PO Box 1452
Chehalis, WA 98532
800-666-1586
macscustomtiedowns.com

Magellan GPS
800-707-9971
magellangps.com

MasterCraft
7991 W. 21st St.
Indianapolis, IN 46214
800-565-4042
mastercraftsafety.com

MaxTrax
us.maxtrax.com.au

Maxxis Tires
maxxis.com

MCE Fenders
12937 SE. 186th St.
Renton, WA 98058
206-859-9020
Mcefenders.com

MetalCloak
3290 Monier Cir.
Rancho Cordova, CA 95742
916-631-8071
metalcloak.com

Mickey Thompson Tires &
  Wheels
4600 Prosper Dr.
Stow, OH 44224
330-928–9092
mickeythompsontires.com

Mountain Off-Road
685 Hwy 92
Delta, CO 81416
877-JEEP-A2Z
mountainoffroad.com

Morris 4x4 Center
2031 SW. 2nd St.
Pompano Beach, FL 33069
877-533-5337
morris4x4center.com

Motive Gear
1001 W. Exchange Ave.
Chicago, IL 60609
800-934-2727
motivegear.com

National Products
8410 Dallas Avenue S.
Seattle, WA 98108
800-497-7479
rammount.com

NEXEN Tire
21073 Pathfinder Rd., Ste.
  100
Diamond Bar, CA 91765
909-923-4011
nexentireusa.com

Nitto Tire
5665 Plaza Dr., Ste. 250
Cypress, CA 90630
888-529-8200
nittotire.com

Off Road Evolution
1829 W. Commonwealth
  Ave.
Fullerton, CA 92833
714-870-5515
offroadevolution.com

Off Road Only
1971 Seneca Rd., Unit E
Eagan, MN 55122
651-644-2323
Offroadonly.com

Off Road Warehouse
Offroadwarehouse.com

OKoffroad
7422 E 63rd Pl.
Tulsa, OK 74133
800-622-5110
okoffroad.com

Olympic 4x4 Products
2645 S. Yates Ave.
Commerce, CA 90040
800-777-0878
olympic4x4products.com

Omix-Ada/Rugged Ridge
770-614-6101
ruggedridge.com

Petersen's 4 Wheel & Off
  Road
fourwheeler.com

Pit Bull Tires
1815 Locust St.
St. Louis, MO 63103
800-645-2006
pitbulltires.com

Poison Spyder Customs
1177 W. Lincoln St., #100A
Banning, CA 92220
951-849-5911
shop.poisonspyder.com

Poly Performance
870 Industrial Way
San Luis Obispo, CA 93401
805-783-2060
polyperformance.com

Power Tank
43 Commerce St., Ste. 103
Lodi, CA 95240
209-366-2163
powertank.com

Precision Drivetrain
16441 Berwyn Rd.
Cerritos, CA 90703
562-921-5656
revolutiongear.com

Pro Comp USA
400 W. Artesia Blvd.
Compton, CA 90220
800-776-0767
procompusa.com

Prodigy Performance
3200 Fairlane Farms Rd.
Wellington, FL 33414
561-790-3540
Prodigyperformance.com

Quadratec
1028 Saunders Ln.
West Chester, PA 19380
800-745-2348
quadratec.com

Raceline Wheels
12300 Edison Way
Garden Grove, CA 92841
800-529-4335
racelinewheels.com

RCV Performance Products
611 Beacon St.
Loves Park, IL 61111
815-877-7473
rcvperformance.com

Red Peak Off Road
redpeakoffroad.com

Rock-Slide Engineering
2561 N. 200 W. St.
North Logan, UT 84341
435-752-4580
rockslideengineering.com

Rock Hard 4x4
1005 Twin Forks Ln.
St. Paul, NE 68873
844-762-5427
rockhard4x4.com

Rubicon Express
1900 El Camino Ave.
Sacramento, CA 95815
877-367-7824
rubiconexpress.com

Rugged Radios
951 E. Grand Ave.
Arroyo Grande, CA 93420
888-541-7223
ruggedradios.com

Savvy Off Road
1680 Railroad St.
Corona, CA 92880
949-870-8106
savvyoffroad.com

Smittybilt
400 W. Artesia Blvd.
Compton, CA 90220
888-717-5797
smittybilt.com

SpiderWebShade
4605 L B McLeod Rd., #400
Orlando, FL 32811
spiderwebshade.com

SPod
28920 Ave. Penn, Unit 104
Valencia, CA 92315
661-775-7799

SPOT
300 Holiday Square Blvd.
Covington, LA 70433
866-OK1-SPOT
findmespot.com

Star Fabricating
1452 Lantern Ln.
Draper, UT 84020
801-244-5859
Starfabricating.com

Strattec Bolt Locks
3333 W. Good Hope Rd.
Milwaukee, WI 53209
844-972-7547
boltlock.com

Super Swamper Tires Interco
2412 Abbeville Hwy.
Rayne, LA 70578
800-299-8000
intercotire.com

Superwinch
superwinch.com

Trail Gear
5356 E. Pine Ave.
Fresno, CA 93727
877-4x4-TOYS

Tactical Recovery Equipment
4679 Valley View Blvd.
Las Vegas, NV 89103
800-933-7114
tacticalrecoveryequipment.
   com

Toyo Tires
800-442-8696
toyotires.com

Tuffy Security Products
25733 Rd. H
Cortez, CO 91321
800-348-8339
tuffyproducts.com

US Forest Service
fs.fed.us

Ultimate Trail Products
418 Valley Ave. NW.
   Ste. B-115
Puyallup, WA 98371
253-445-1111
ultimatetrailproducts.com

ViAir Corp
15 Edelman St.
Irvine, CA 92618
949-585-0011
viaircorp.com

Vision X USA
1601 Boundary Blvd.
Auburn, WA 98001
800-994-4460
visionxusa.com

Wilwood Engineering
4700 Calle Bolero
Camarillo, CA 93012
805-338-1188
wilwood.com

Walker Evans Racing
2304 Fleetwood Dr.
Riverside CA 92509
951-784-7223
walkerevansracing.com

Warn Industries
12900 SE. Capps Rd.
Clackamas, OR 97015
800-543-9276
warn.com

Wild Boar Off-Road
5312 Production Dr.
Huntington Beach, CA
   92649
714-891-8222

Yakima Racks
888-925-4621
explore.yakima.com